ENABLING ACTS

ENABLING ACTS

THE HIDDEN STORY OF HOW THE AMERICANS WITH DISABILITIES ACT GAVE THE LARGEST US MINORITY ITS RIGHTS

LENNARD J. DAVIS

BEACON PRESS
BOSTON

BEACON PRESS
Boston, Massachusetts
www.beacon.org

Beacon Press books
are published under the auspices of
the Unitarian Universalist Association of Congregations.

18 17 16 15   8 7 6 5 4 3 2 1

This book is printed on acid-free paper that meets the uncoated paper
ANSI/NISO specifications for permanence as revised in 1992.

Text design and composition by Kim Arney

Beacon Press gratefully acknowledges the Kessler Foundation
for its generous support of this book.

Some of the dialogue in this book was reconstructed with
information from interviews and archival materials.

Library of Congress Cataloging-in-Publication Data
Davis, Lennard J.
Enabling acts : the hidden story of how the Americans with Disabilities
Act gave the largest US minority its rights / Lennard Davis.
        pages   cm
Includes bibliographical references and index.
ISBN 978-0-8070-7156-4 (hardback) — ISBN 978-0-8070-7157-1 (ebook)
1. People with disabilities—Legal status, laws, etc.—United States.
2. Discrimination against people with disabilities—Law and legislation—United
States. 3. People with disabilities—United States—Social conditions.
4. People with disabilities—Services for—United States. 5. United States.
Americans with Disabilities Act of 1990. I. Title.
KF480.D38 2015
342.7308'7—dc23
2014046510

To all the people who gave much of their time and the best of their efforts to pass the Americans with Disabilities Act—from the politicians to the staffers to the activists. Without them, life would be that much harder for all disabled people in the United States.

CONTENTS

AUTHOR'S NOTE

MY INTEREST IN writing about the Americans with Disabilities Act (ADA) comes from my having grown up in a Deaf family in which both my parents had zero hearing and were sign language users as well as lip readers trained in speaking aloud.[1] My upbringing showed me firsthand how bad an impact discrimination against people with disabilities could be. As a child, I witnessed countless instances of hearing people treating my intelligent, talented, athletic Deaf parents as if they were lesser beings not much different from troglodytes or the lumbering clay people from Flash Gordon. From cringing when someone called my mother and father "deaf and dumb" to watching them being excluded from conversations at family holiday gatherings, I felt their isolation from and denigration by hearing people.

My parents' lives, before any major legislation relating to disability was passed, were difficult. There were no telecommunication devices that allowed their friends or family to call them and arrange to meet up. Every visit required that a postcard be sent and another one returned with place, date, and time arranged. They couldn't call a doctor to make an appointment or a travel agent to book a flight. No one ever just dropped by, and if someone did, the visitor couldn't get into our New York apartment, since the primitive electrical relay that made the lights flash when the doorbell rang often malfunctioned. There were no sign language interpreters available for doctor visits, hospital stays, or court dates. My parents couldn't go to religious services, because there was no way they could follow what was going on. Conversations in all settings had to be painstakingly written out on scraps of paper. Movies had no captions, so my parents ended up going exclusively to a foreign film theater on Forty-Second Street, where they could understand the subtitles but couldn't understand the existential plots and situations of Antonioni and Resnais avant-garde films.

My parents were routinely excluded from places of public accommodation. We lived in a Bronx slum, and when my parents applied to a more upscale housing development called Parkchester, their application was turned down. No Deaf people were allowed in. My father was a world-class athlete, but he was denied admittance to the New York Athletic Club for being deaf (as well as Jewish). If either of my parents had wanted to drive a car, they would have needed an elaborate set of mirrors in the car. But even this accommodation wasn't possible, since insurance companies charged exorbitant rates for Deaf people (even though they had lower rates of accidents than the hearing).

In other words, although my parents were American citizens, they had few if any civil rights. Life was a series of insults, denigrations, and exclusions that they had to accept because there was no other choice. It was only within the Deaf community that they thrived and were fully appreciated.

The same was true not only for Deaf people, but also for people with any disabilities well into the twentieth century. Before civil rights legislation for people with disabilities, there was a huge catalog of abuses and barriers. As the largest minority, people with disabilities are among the poorest, least employed, and least educated of all minorities. People who have disabilities are nearly twice as likely as people without disabilities to have an annual household income of $15,000 or less.[2] Moreover, some 58 percent of people over sixty-five have some type of disability.[3] If you had a severe disability that prevented you from taking care of yourself and getting around, you had only two choices: be taken care of by your family or go to an institution.

If you had a mobility impairment, you could not use local public transportation, railroads, or long-haul buses like Greyhound, and, of course, you couldn't drive, since automobiles weren't yet easily equipped with hand controls. You were essentially confined to your house. You might try to go around your neighborhood, but you could do so only if you could self-propel a wheelchair, since power chairs weren't yet widely used. With no curb cuts or ramps, most streets were impossible to navigate and most buildings were inaccessible. You were left in the unenviable position of only being able to go around the block. You couldn't go to restaurants, movies, or most stores.

If you went to school, you were segregated with other children with disabilities. You were discriminated against in college and university interviews, and if you got into a college or university, you couldn't stay in the dorms, since they weren't accessible. If you were deaf or hard of hearing, attending classes in any university was difficult to impossible, since sign language interpretation or real-time transcription services were not provided. And if you were a very skilled lip reader, you'd only get around 50 percent of what was being said. Very little material was published in braille or recorded for the blind.

If you were a person with Down syndrome, autism, or other cognitive disabilities, unless you had a lot of family money, you would be shipped off to a nightmarish institution like the now-deservedly shuttered Willowbrook. In places like this, the chances were good that you'd be sitting in your own feces or rocking back and forth to comfort yourself in the midst of stultifying ennui and neglect.

I could go on, but I think you get the picture. Life as a person with a disability was a much reduced if not reprehensively deprived life. Living like anyone else was a right denied to you, and keeping up with the Joneses was beyond imagination. Concomitant with the economic and political realities was the social view that developed along with those problems. Disabled people were treated like children—dependent, helpless, and, unlike children, pitiable. Most disabled people were not allowed the dignities of work, a love life, friends, children, advanced education, and a profession. And worse than all of this, being a person with a disability was tantamount to being an invisible person. No one cared about your plight; society ignored you. You essentially did not exist.

This invisibility is all the more ironic since close to 20 percent of the population are people with disabilities. One out of five people have disabilities—but the disabilities are hiding in plain sight. Some disabilities, like diabetes, muscular sclerosis, and depression, can be invisible. Others, like deafness or vision loss, are not immediately noticeable. Some chronic illnesses, like hepatitis C or HIV, aren't apparent to other people. Many people with disabilities were kept out of sight in special schools and institutions. It's kind of a magic act—how do you disappear a fifth of the population?

The history of the treatment of people with disabilities was intimately related to charity. All the major religions encouraged the giving of alms to the poor and disabled. And, of course, given the preceding discussion, most of the disabled were in fact poor—unable to work because of their lack of mobility, training, education, and access to accommodations. Rather than being gainfully employed and living independently, people with disabilities were therefore slotted to be the recipients of charity from church and later by the state—money doled out with the proper combination of condescension and pity.

The height of this paternalism was the television marathons, or as they were called, telethons, of the 1950s. In these spectacles, disabled children—of course children, because they were the most childlike and pitiable—were trotted out on the television stage to help raise money for organizations like the March of Dimes for polio "victims" or the Muscular Dystrophy Association. Jerry Lewis pranced and prattled around children with leg braces, extolling the kids' potential futures, while in fact lowering their self-esteem and those of their peers. Past poster children have spoken out about their humiliating experiences. But culturally and socially, such large-scale media events further diminished the civil rights of people with disabilities by indicating that "they" were a group that needed charity from "us." How could "they" ever be a group that would share something as basic as civil rights with "us"?

Those dark days of disability were only the recent version of even darker days. In the deeper past, disabled children were killed at birth; disabled adults were mocked, humiliated, exiled, sexually abused, or even burned at the stake. There was no golden age of disability that we can point to. In fact, the modern era I've just described was probably the golden age of disability until legislation made it against the law to discriminate against people with disability and granted rights to this formerly oppressed group.

Rather than recall the entire history of disability in the United States, this book will recount the complex and sometimes secret history of the Americans with Disabilities Act of 1990—the historic legislation that ended, at least legally, the kind of discrimination I've been describing while adding aid for those with disabilities. It wasn't a paternalistic law but rather one that people with disabilities themselves helped to create and to enact. We can see this act simply as a link in a long line of legislation for rights, justice, and redress, but this law also profoundly changed history forever. The ADA became the template for legislation around the world and eventually the UN Convention on the Rights of Persons with Disabilities.

After the ADA, never could anyone see disability as deserving charity. No longer could anyone see disability as a purely medical condition or a rehabilitation opportunity. Instead, disability would be seen now and forever as a civil rights issue in which aid and redress would not be focused on physical therapy or monetary benefits. Rather, it would be about the right of individuals to have access to the world that everyone else is part of. No longer would a significant portion of our fellow beings be considered different by virtue of being invisible or pitiable. Instead, they would be citizens of this country and entitled to the rights and privileges of all people. Instead of hiding in plain sight, people with disabilities are now visible, political, and in possession of their rights.

July 28, 1989

IN AN UPSTAIRS room at the Capitol, Senator Ted Kennedy slammed his hand down on the table with a force that shook the room. His hefty body, now raised from his seat, angled across the solid wooden surface as he glared at President George H. W. Bush's chief of staff, John Sununu, their heads inches apart. Kennedy screamed at Sununu, "You want to fight? Fight with me. You want to yell? Yell at me." Kennedy's face was red with anger, the tendons bulging from his neck. Sununu suddenly became pale and quiet and backed down.

Around the gleaming walnut table were a group of senior and seasoned legislators—Senators Orrin Hatch, Tom Harkin, David Durenberger, and Bob Dole, as well as Attorney General Richard (Dick) Thornburgh, Secretary of Transportation Samuel Skinner, and Senate and White House staff members. The date was July 28, 1989, and all of them were there to negotiate the details of the massive and significant legislation known as the Americans with Disabilities Act.

The meeting had been called because after ten weeks of staff-level negotiations between the White House and Congress, progress had been made but a deadlock was now apparent. The heavyweights had gotten together to see what could be done. Dole, the minority leader, offered his spacious conference room with its marble fireplace and large table. One by one, the members of the Senate and the White House filed into the air-conditioned room from outside, where the ninety-degree summer day was broiling the city. Harkin had brought along his staff member Bobby Silverstein, who used a luggage trolley to wheel in a stack of massive black binders—the legislation as it had been crafted thus far. After some brief chitchat, the principals began their own discussion. Sununu served as the point person for the White House, although Thornburgh, as attorney general, was part of the executive branch.

Hatch leaned over and whispered into the ear of his staffer Mark Disler: "You watch! In fifteen minutes you'll see how impassioned Kennedy is about this bill."

A majority of the Republicans in the room were of the conservative stripe, but Sununu's role in the White House was to serve as watchdog for archconservative values. He thought that some crucial mandates, including the very touchy idea of forcing businesses to retrofit their establishments to make them accessible, were too liberal in the bill. Wouldn't that measure cost ordinary small businesses a fortune? As an uncompromising conservative, Sununu had many objections to what he saw as wording that was not business-friendly. What if the business couldn't afford to make these changes? What if, for example, there was a barbershop on the second floor of an existing building in New Hampshire? Would you expect the poor barber to have to install an elevator to accommodate some wheelchair-using customer in need of a haircut?

Silverstein, small eyes peering through large glasses into the mysterious abyss of the pages upon pages of legislation, had been silently noting and mentally rebutting Sununu's objections. Kennedy cautioned Sununu: "You're flyspecking the bill." But Sununu continued picking away. Silverstein, having done his conscientious homework in advance, finally raised a defense to one of Sununu's objections about the bill. Sununu's features began to twitch with irritation. He started speaking to Silverstein in a controlled voice but worked his way up to more impassioned tones: "Every time I say something, you always bring something up. I don't want to hear from you anymore."[1]

Harkin, sitting between Silverstein and Kennedy, was just shuffling his papers, trying to think how to defend his own aide, when Kennedy jumped to his feet, his bulky frame creating seismic jolts as it crashed against the table. The hours of negotiations—indeed the years of maneuvering—to get this bill through Congress were taking their toll. Harkin remembers: "I thought [Kennedy] was going to grab [Sununu] by the collar." Kennedy pointed his finger at Sununu's face and bellowed, "If you want to yell at anybody, you yell at *me*, or you yell at Senator Harkin. You don't go after the staff! You go after the big boys. You got something to say, you say it to *me*. You want to *yell* at me? You go right ahead and *yell at me*!"

In a moment of disgust with Silverstein and his ilk, Sununu then suggested that the room be cleared of all staff and that only the elected members of Congress should stay. Kennedy's response: "I said, fine, then Sununu should leave because he was staff." That seemed to quiet things down.

Kennedy sat back down as an awkward silence filled the room. Sununu's usually robust frame seemed to sink down in his chair, and his face was drained of color. An hour and a half later, agreement had been reached. As they left the room, Kennedy said to Hatch, "Jack [Kennedy] wouldn't have done that. He wouldn't have sent his chief of staff; he'd have sent the attorney general or the chief counsel."

That is the story many of the major players tell.[2] It is compelling because of the high stakes in play and the success of the outcome. What raised the stakes was that the men and women gathered in that room all shared one thing in common—disability. Almost everyone in the room, aside from Sununu, had experienced firsthand the discrimination and inequity that can face a person with a disability. Each participant at the meeting was determined to end the kind of abuse and segregation that had held sway in the laws of the land. Not since the seismic upheavals around civil rights during the 1960s had a piece of legislation aimed at such a massive transformation of society and culture. Up until 1990, none of the members of the disabled minority group had the full range of civil rights that nondisabled US citizens had. One by one, other minority groups—notably African Americans, other people of color and various nationalities, and women—had all fought for and achieved those rights. Now it was the turn of essentially the largest minority group in the United States to claim its rights.

The only one in the room with a visible disability was Bob Dole. The senator was straight out of high school when his platoon shipped off to Europe in World War II. He had just arrived at his post in Italy, somewhat frightened but determined to do his part in the war. On his first foray, he was listening to his commanding officer, who was telling him what position to take, when he suddenly felt his shoulder torn out from his side. A sniper had chosen him for death. Dole narrowly escaped that fate, but his military career was over before it had even started. He was shipped back to his parents' modest farmhouse in Kansas. There he spent two years lying on a bed in the living room, never thinking he could walk or otherwise function in any way again. Dole's one arm did not work, his back was in shreds, and his hand was clenched into a fist. After many surgeries and years of rehabilitation, he was able to stand up by himself and walk unassisted. Eventually he went back to school and then into public service. His iconic pen in his clenched fist was almost as much a signature of his public identity as was his sartorial sense of style.

Ted Kennedy always had in mind his older sister Rosemary. She was an attractive young woman with a Kennedy smile and glint in her eye. Rosemary was diagnosed with an intellectual disability when she was an infant, never developing more than an IQ of an eight- to ten-year-old when she became an adult. Nevertheless, she could read *Winnie the Pooh* on her own and kept a simple diary. As she matured, behavioral problems led Joseph Kennedy to the disastrous decision to lobotomize her at the age of twenty-two. The operation left her much worse off than she had been. Now she had an IQ of a two-year-old and was unable to speak, walk, or control her bladder or colon. She was institutionalized. Ted Kennedy himself had various physical ailments, as did his brother John, but his family life was especially marked by his son Teddy's bone cancer at the age of twelve. Senator Kennedy spent much time with his son during his diagnosis, treatment, and rehabilitation. The younger Kennedy's leg was amputated above the knee, and then arduous chemotherapy followed, with the senator learning how to inject anticancer agents into his son's body. In spending all that time in various hospitals, Senator Kennedy came to appreciate both the realities of people with disabilities and the difficulties their families face in terms of the costs and care.

Tom Harkin grew up on a farm in Iowa. His older brother Frank was born deaf, and Harkin spent his childhood with his sibling, learning sign language in the process. The senator also had a nephew,

Kelly McQuaid, who became paraplegic in an accident when he was in the US Army. Harkin ended up a passionate champion of the rights of the Deaf and the disabled, making the first-ever speech in sign language on the floor of the Senate when the ADA was passed.

Dick Thornburgh was a young lawyer sitting at home when he received the phone call no one ever wants to get. His young wife had taken their three boys out in the family car to go shopping. An accident killed her and injured two of the children, one of whom suffered traumatic brain damage.

Steny Hoyer's wife was epileptic. Early on, he had met with lobbyists and staffers from whom he had learned much about other disabilities and the idea that disability was a civil rights issue. He was a tireless advocate for the ADA in the House, and most of the organizing meetings for that phase of the bill were held in his office.

Orrin Hatch recalls his own brother-in-law's challenges: "Ramon Hansen contracted both types of polio when he was a college student, but not only finished his degree but also a master's degree in electrical engineering. He worked until the day he died, even though he had to be in an iron lung every night just to survive." As a Mormon, Hatch would follow his church's teaching that holds people with disabilities in high regard and sees disability not as punishment resulting from sin, but as an opportunity, a benefit, and a learning experience. In 1989, before the ADA, the church explained that it was "seeking more creative ways of providing religious training for those with physical, mental, and emotional impairments. But there is an even greater need to reduce the barriers imposed by a lack of understanding and acceptance of those who have disabilities."[3]

President Bush, who was not present at the meeting, had an uncle, John M. Walker, who had had polio. One of Bush's brothers had been born with only one eye, Bush's son Neil had severe learning disabilities, and another son, Marvin, had had a colostomy. The president had also lost a daughter, Robin, to leukemia when she was almost four years old.

It could not have been a coincidence that all of these legislators shared the experience of disability. If one out of five Americans has a disability, then surely many other people would be relations. Far from being an odd and unlikely thing, disability is more the rule than the exception. Many of the other senators and congressional representatives who backed the bill had family members with disabilities. Perhaps the ideological—rather than personal—nature of Sununu's objections led him to see that Kennedy's anger was a force greater than his own conservative proclivities. Sununu's backing down that day might have been tactical, but he also might have recognized that the others gathered in the room had a lot more at stake than he did.

ONE

Forty-Six Words That Changed History

YOU COULD SAY the movement toward the Americans with Disabilities Act (ADA) started with four undergrads at the University of Illinois in Urbana-Champaign in 1962, when they rejected living in an isolated facility and moved near the campus to an accessible house. But you could also say it began with a determined undergraduate polio survivor named Ed Roberts, who, also in 1962, managed to persuade the University of California at Berkeley to admit him and others and to provide housing as well. Or did it begin with the civil rights movement and the landmark Civil Rights Act of 1964? You could look to 1970, when Judy Heumann founded Disabled in Action after she, a polio survivor using a wheelchair, sued New York City for denying her a teaching license on the assumption that a disabled person like her couldn't be a schoolteacher. The *Daily News* headline read: "You Can Be President, Not Teacher, with Polio." Or did it begin with the many other minor and major actions, pieces of legislation, protests, and accommodations that slowly accumulated to form a critical mass?

Trying to find a moment when the ADA began is like trying to find the source of the Nile or the Amazon. So many tributaries flow into the making of the ADA that you cannot say if any single stream is the true source. But you can say that at some point, like a mighty river, the movement toward the ADA surged powerfully and in a sense became inevitable.

But as inevitable as the act now seems in retrospect, Congress might very well have failed to act sufficiently to create a meaningful bill rather than a document simply expressing general platitudes. Certainly, an ADA could not pass Congress today. In fact, ratification of the UN Convention on the Rights of Persons with Disabilities was defeated in the Senate in 2012. Bob Dole, who was instrumental in getting the ADA through Congress, arrived on the Senate floor in 2013 to argue emotionally that the convention should be ratified. At eighty-nine, he'd been in and out of Walter Reed Army Medical Center for two years and appeared drawn and fragile. Despite his dramatic appearance, the convention ratification was defeated. Dole, Harkin, and Hoyer all have asserted that if the ADA came up for a vote in 2015, it would be defeated.

The ADA is an excellent example of a bipartisanship no longer extant but made possible when a Republican president, George H. W. Bush, worked together with a Democratic House and Senate. The cooperation of Republicans Dole and Hatch together with Democrats Kennedy and Harkin in the Senate, along with Republican Steve Bartlett and Democrat Steny Hoyer in the House, was essential. All these political leaders believed that disability was an issue both parties could agree on. In fact Justin Dart, a conservative Republican, said, "The Americans with Disabilities Act is an authentic issue for conservatives."[1] And that perennial conservative, bespectacled George Will, whose eldest son has Down syndrome, supportively called the ADA "that last great inclusion in American life."[2] Today, it is almost impossible to imagine such crossing of party lines for the common good. And the day-to-day workings of the principals and their staffs in passing the ADA should be an object lesson to those presently in the halls of power.

The 1960s legislation that guaranteed rights and gave benefits to poor people, Vietnam veterans, people of color, and, among others, the disabled, began to open the door to the concept that being disabled was not simply a medical fact or a social stigma. Disability, like ethnicity, was an identity, and as such, it needed to be protected from human rights abuses and civil rights abuses.

We use the term *civil rights* a lot, but what exactly are these rights, and why weren't they just inherently part of citizenship in a country with a bill of rights? Civil rights in general protect citizens' freedom from governmental or other intrusion into their lives and guarantee that citizens can participate fully in civil and political life. If those rights are applied unequally to citizens or are on paper only but not robustly part of citizens' lives, then specific legislation detailing how those rights should be protected and enforced is enacted.

Looking back, you can see the slow accumulation of civil rights legislation that produced precedents for the ADA. Acts passed by Congress piecemeal were deposited on the American shore like pebbles and sediment that would eventually transform the bedrock of the laws of the land. You could take the Civil Rights Act of 1964 as it combined with the establishment of Medicare and Medicaid in 1965. Add to that the Fair Housing Act that was passed in 1968 and prohibited discrimination in the sale or rental of property. The same year, the Architecture Barriers Act announced that all federal buildings or buildings built with federal funds had to be accessible. Then, in 1972, Title IX of the Education Amendments Act moved to add protections against discrimination based on gender in the realm of education. So in a mere eight years, a trend toward expanding protections for people based on their civil rights had developed.

Of course, it was a particular era in American politics when an expansion of the role of government provided help and services to a wide group of Americans. Lyndon Johnson's Great Society aimed to eliminate or reduce poverty and spread the postwar wealth to the general population.

In 1972, Hubert Humphrey, one of the architects of the 1964 Civil Rights Act, made a bold move to amend the act to include disability. On the Senate floor, Humphrey said: "No longer dare we live with the hypocrisy that the promise of America should have one major exception: Millions of children, youth, and adults with mental or physical handicaps. We must now firmly establish their right to share that promise, so well described by Thomas Wolfe [the novelist, in his *You Can't Go Home Again*]: 'To every man his chance; to every man, regardless of his birth, his shining golden opportunity. . . . [T]his . . . is the promise of America.'"[3] As the grandfather of a child with Down syndrome, Humphrey was keenly aware of the issues facing people with disabilities. But the idea had absolutely no traction. Despite Humphrey's efforts, no legislation was passed. It was all right to take a piecemeal approach to protecting various aspects of disability, but when the idea to simply include disability as an identity along with race was proposed, there was no strong force behind it.

Interestingly, many politicians, including African American politicians and leaders, were wary of "diluting" the signature civil rights established in 1964 by letting in other categories like disability. They also feared bringing the landmark legislation back on the floor. Once there, the legislation might be changed in nonproductive ways. In that way, the rights of people with disabilities were seen as a problem rather than a solution.

Party leadership proposed to Humphrey that his language from the failed attempt be added instead to the Rehabilitation Act in 1972. This act was itself designed to update the original 1920 act that provided services to World War I veterans who were disabled during the Great War. Now, as disabled soldiers returned from the apocalypse of the Vietnam War, rehabilitation became a national issue again. Although Congress passed the new act after much wrangling, President Richard Nixon twice vetoed it. He did not like the provision of federal funds to the states to pay for independent living for people with severe disabilities. Independent-living centers at this time were in need of funds, all of which were going to vocational rehabilitation centers. These rehab centers focused on a medical model of disability rather than a more humane viewpoint that involved the lived experience of people who were so much more than patients. Independent-living centers were run by people with disabilities themselves and stressed a noninstitutional model—people living at home with personal assistants and working at jobs in a way equal to able-bodied people. After the first veto, Congress proposed an ameliorating change in the bill, but Nixon vetoed it again. Finally, the bill was passed in 1973, this time without the guarantee of federal funds for independent living (although those were restored in a 1978 amendment known as the Title VII program).

On September 26, 1973, President Nixon signed into law the Rehabilitation Act. The spirit of the act was to shift federal assistance away from mere vocational rehabilitation and toward a more encompassing idea of improving not just job training but the overall lives of people with disabilities. Yet its lasting impact inhered in just four lines of the voluminous act. Like a magic phrase inserted into an incantation, those four lines changed the history of disability rights. In Section 504, the very last section of the last major category, a staffer inserted the following words trying to tie the act to previous civil rights legislation:

> No otherwise qualified handicapped individual in the United States, as defined in Section 7(6), shall, solely by reason of his handicap, be excluded from the participation in, be denied the benefits of, or be subjected to discrimination under any program or activity receiving Federal financial assistance.

In all the arguing on the Senate and the House floors, all the contention and rewriting of this bill, and all of Nixon's objections to the bill as a Great Society remnant, barely anyone noticed or commented on this squib. Yet Section 504 became the first brick in the groundwork laid for the ADA. It was the first federal language that clearly and uncompromisingly guaranteed the civil rights of people with disabilities; it was modeled on Title VI of the Civil Rights Act and Title IX of the Education Amendments Act—both of which never mentioned people with disabilities. Section 504 was only forty-four words, yet its tweet-like length belied the volumes of language it would generate in the coming years.

In 1969, John Wodatch, a green-around-the-gills Georgetown Law School graduate sporting a Kennedy-style haircut, had narrowly escaped being drafted for the Vietnam War. He had beaten the losing lottery numbers that would have sent him to the napalm-engulfed jungles of Vietnam. Instead of the war in Indochina, he set his sights on the war at home—working on civil rights and school desegregation. Wodatch applied to an honors program for recently graduated law students in the general counsel's office of the Department of Health, Education, and Welfare, was accepted, and found himself shuttling through all the departments, including the Civil Rights Division, where he ended up. There he started out working on school desegregation, exactly what he had wanted to do.

"Literally, I started in the office on Monday and on Tuesday had my first case," Wodatch says. "I look back on it, I was a good law student, but had absolutely no training for the real world. The night before my first case, I kept my wife up all night cross-examining her as the superintendent of schools. . . . A trained seal could have won that case." But almost by a fluke, he moved from desegregation in schools to desegregation in mental facilities. "All I was trying to do was get the white people caged in cages in white wards mixed with black people caged in black wards." He went to these snake-pit facilities and "literally saw naked people chained to walls. A room with four hundred beds, people chained in it, with three attendants, and basically white people were being treated better than black people, and so we were integrating them." He recalls having nightmares for years afterward, but as a result, he began working on disability-related issues for the Justice Department.

This is where he enters our story. That small paragraph called Section 504, as would all parts of any act, had to have written regulations in order for the law to be enforced. Wodatch spent many long and arduous hours writing these regulations for 504. He recalls: "I was able to hire a staff and basically went around the country asking people with disabilities, 'What is discrimination on the basis of disability?'"

On June 17, 1972, some intruders broke into the Democratic National Headquarters in a then-obscure housing complex called Watergate. The repercussions of that episode would lead to Richard Nixon's resignation in 1974. But in terms of civil rights, the September 1973 signing of the Rehabilitation Act created the circumstances in which Section 504 had broken and entered into the legal consciousness of the country, permitting the concept of civil rights to be applied to people with disabilities.

The years went by, and Wodatch and his staff continued writing the 504 regulations as part of his assignment to the Office of Civil Rights in the Department of Health, Education, and Welfare (HEW). The regulations were nearing completion when Gerald Ford took over from Nixon. With the change of administration, Wodatch had a new boss, and further delays ensued as the new director, George Matthews, decided to go slow on the regulations. In 1977, Jimmy

Carter became president. Even under this Democrat president, no regulations were implemented. James Califano, Carter's secretary of HEW, wanted clarity and decided to review and revise the regulations. He later claimed that his concerns were that the regulations should be properly written to avoid pitfalls, but at the time, few believed this statement, since the process had gone on for so long.[4]

What followed was a groundswell activist movement that in effect launched a nationally oriented disability movement. The movement had started a bit earlier in 1974, when the first cross-disability organization, the American Coalition of Citizens with Disabilities (ACCD), started as the first group that wasn't lobbying for a specific disability. This group, started by Eunice Fiorito, a blind New York City administrator, and headed by Frank Bowe, a Deaf educational psychologist from New York University, became crucial in rallying the troops to agitate for the issuing of the 504 regulations. By February 1977, there were protests around the country at regional HEW offices. The following month, the protests converged on Washington, DC, where hundreds of people with disabilities demonstrated at the Capitol steps. There were also demonstrations in Atlanta, Boston, Chicago, Dallas, Denver, Philadelphia, New York, Seattle, and San Francisco. Bowe sent a letter to President Carter, with a copy to Califano, saying that if regulations were not issued by April 4 (three weeks from the writing of the letter), a sit-in would be held at every HEW office in the United States: "Vast numbers of us endorsed your candidacy and worked vigorously for your election. . . . We are dismayed by this apparent breach of faith."[5] Jack Anderson described the situation: "Thousands of handicapped Americans may risk being wheelchaired off to jail in a militant attempt to shut down government offices in ten cities. The disabled are furious over what they see as a retreat by President Carter on his promise to help the nation's 28 million handicapped."[6] Carter's inattention was particularly galling, because he had blasted the Ford administration's dallying with the 504 regulations.

A meeting was held with Califano on April 4, but still no action ensued. Strangely, Califano attempted to get out in front of the demonstrations by announcing at a press conference that he "endorsed" the demonstration and "required all HEW personnel to cooperate fully with the protestors in the exercise of their constitutionally protected free speech."[7]

Of all the 504 demonstrations, the one that resonates most powerfully in the disability movement's imagination was the takeover of the San Francisco office of HEW. In a city associated with political protest and across the bay from Berkeley, birthplace and home of the independent-living movement, it wasn't hard to gather a lively group of protesters who were so devoted to their cause that they were willing to occupy a government building for twenty-five days. The protesters, looking visibly 1960s in appearance, with long hair, tie-dyed clothing, and fists held aloft in Black Power defiance (and actually including at least one disabled member of the Black Panthers), refused to leave the HEW building until the regulations were enforced. The media reverberated with images of people in wheelchairs, using canes, signing in American Sign Language (ASL), and camping out in the building from April 5 until April 30, the longest occupation of a federal building in US history. On April 28, Califano relented and signed the regulations as they had been written by Wodatch and company; the secretary changed none of the regulations. Finally, 504 came into effect almost four long years after Nixon had originally signed the legislation. People with disabilities now had civil rights—if only in the case of federal institutions and institutions that received federal funds.

While we like to think that political events are inevitable and that social movements sprout up like mushrooms in the wet spring of change, careful planning by devoted, although perhaps unacknowledged, leaders and staffers is what probably shapes the forces of history. Many people point to the role of activism in the passage of the ADA, and the force of that activism is undoubtedly true. The striking images of wheelchair users and others with mobility impairments crawling slowly and painfully up the steps of the Capitol Building are some of the most enduring and powerful icons of the disability rights movement. But those demonstrations had to be planned, and the planning for bringing people with disabilities to Washington was even more daunting and costly than for a protest involving nondisabled people, given the inaccessibility of buses, trains, and planes as well as the hotels and meeting spaces.

Furthermore, unlike the civil rights movement in the 1960s, with its spontaneous local demonstrations and riots and the ricochet of state police and militia violence, the disability movement did not arise quite so spontaneously. In the pre-1964 South, massive demonstrations and brutal reactions—including murder, mass assaults, police dogs, high-pressure water hoses, and tear gas—flooded into the national consciousness and made civil rights legislation a national necessity. Martin Luther King Jr. wrote in 1964: "The bill now pending in Congress is the child of a storm, the product of the most turbulent motion the nation has ever known in peacetime."[8] The ADA was born not in a storm, but rather in a metaphorical weather inversion in which the long-developing pressures were about to be unleashed.

However, there was no Selma or Birmingham in the disability movement. The national demonstrations that we saw and remember concerning disability rights were, and perhaps had to be, coordinated and orchestrated. Although they used grassroots sentiment, these demonstrations were more likely top-down affairs—in which organizers and planners in places like Washington, DC, could call upon networks of people with disabilities throughout the states. Further, there were not masses of disabled people protesting on the street and being beaten back by police and the army. This may have well been because many disabled people were dependent on caretakers and even institutions and thus could not spontaneously take to the streets. In addition, many people with impairments did not think of themselves as part of a larger political movement and merely saw themselves as individuals with medical problems. It took the movement to make many people see themselves as disabled in a political sense. And before the ADA and other legislation, as we need to recall, the streets were largely inaccessible to wheelchair users, because curb cuts were a consequence of those very laws.

This isn't to say that activism did not play a major role in pushing the juggernaut of the disability rights movement. For example, this hidden army contributed greatly to the protests against municipal transportation systems. The best known of these protests were organized in Denver by the Atlantis independent-living community and were spearheaded by a feisty, longhaired minister named Wade Blank. Though he himself had no disability, Blank worked with severely disabled youth who came to see themselves over time as a powerful political force. Chaining themselves together to block buses, using in-your-face political tactics, and counting on the reluctance of politicians to abuse people with disabilities, members of the Atlantis community (later becoming a nation-wide organization of affiliate groups called ADAPT—Americans Disabled for Accessible Public Transport) succeeded in opening up transportation systems. The initial success in Denver spread to many cities in the United States.

Another example of local action for public transportation took place in New York City in 1972, after Nixon's first veto of the Rehabilitation Act. Judy Heumann, a leader in the disability rights movement, and about sixty other people protested in the streets of New York. According to Heumann, no one paid attention to the protesters, who were performing a symbolic funeral of people with disabilities at the Federal Building in Lower Manhattan. Frustrated with the lack of attention, the demonstrators moved uptown to Nixon's election headquarters on Madison Avenue, where they blocked traffic. In the documentary *We Won't Go Away*, Ralf Hotchkiss recounts that after the traffic blocking, the demonstrators moved down to Washington, DC, "and basically stormed the capital, visited all their congressmen and all the congressmen who had voted against it and built up enough support so that I believe that was the strongest congressional override in history, override of a presidential veto." Hotchkiss and the narrator of the documentary imply that the passage of the final bill was the result of this activism.

But in reality, the bill was never overridden, as we have seen. The legislation had to go through three incarnations, of which the first two were vetoed. Congress never did have the votes to override any of those vetoes.

Yet, as the popular story goes, activism led to dramatic legislative results. This version of the story is the same one that Hotchkiss had in mind, and we see repeatedly: legislative reluctance, administration resistance, disability activism, and then success. It is an inspiring story, but there is so much more than such a story tells. These narratives are useful for group pride and to rally support, but it took a village—the efforts of many forces and people—to arrive at success. Judy Heumann's demonstrations in New York and Washington had valuable media-savvy coverage and perhaps some influence with the passage of the bill. But the efforts would have been ineffective if Democrats in the House and Senate didn't have majorities. As important as the street activism was, the work of unheralded staffers and lobbyists laboring in the corridors of Washington was equally if not more important. We perhaps should think of the complex thing we call politics as the work of three groups in coordination or in conflict—the high-profile politicians who are the superstars, the staffers who do the tedious and arduous work of writing the legislation and organizing the hearings, and the activists who provide the momentum when the other two groups encounter a slowdown. All three groups are important, and in each instance, the mix of these three groups will vary.

The aim of this book isn't to debunk the power and importance of activism. But as a scholar and a writer, I can't change history to create a needed or wanted outcome. Activism is revered in any political movement, and the story we tell about that movement serves many functions. One function is to create heroes and leaders; the other is to show the force of the many who put their bodies and lives on the line. Perhaps another is to create a knowable and easy-to-follow narrative of the march to triumph. But the devil is in the details. For everyone who crawled up the steps of the Capitol, there is an unsung person in an unknown meeting writing a forgettable memo or placing a telephone call lost to documentation. Especially in Washington, DC, so much goes on behind doors with a smile, a handshake, or an arm twisted into compliance.

We need to remember that there is no bright line between activist and behind-the-scenes lobbyists. Some of the most influential people in the disability rights movement were and remained activists in the sense that they attended rallies and organized them, all the while working the corridors of power. In fact, we might do better to think of some of the heroes of this story as activist staffers or activist lobbyists. We like to keep people's roles separate, but in reality, all lives intersect, and so one person's activism involving being arrested or chained to a bus could be another person's act of writing a letter or placing a strategic phone call.

The disability rights movement was undoubtedly modeled after the civil rights movement, which had immediately preceded the disability movement. In the latter movement, every video and rousing speech made in front of government buildings was draped by the shadows, echoes, and cadences of Martin Luther King Jr. and other civil rights leaders. Disability activists sang the songs of the civil rights movement. "We Shall Overcome," "Keep Your Eyes on the Prize," and "Ain't Gonna Let Nobody Turn Me Around" inspired those who wanted Section 504 implemented and those who wanted the ADA passed. In telling the disability activist story, those civil rights forebears were invoked—and rightly so.

But it was Marx who said that history repeats itself—first as tragedy, then as farce. The disability rights movement managed to avoid both outcomes, but the commonly accepted tale shaves corners and adds color to create the ideal narrative. While the model narrative of the African American struggle adds highlights to the disability struggle, it also adds contrasts. Ed Roberts, Judy Heumann, and Justin Dart were no King, Jesse Jackson, or Rosa Parks. The various marches on Washington were not equivalent to those during the civil rights era. The protests about the absence of transportation options do not easily map onto segregation on the buses of the old South, although there are, of course, telling parallels. The level of violence and the threat of death and imprisonment were not shared in the same way by the civil rights movement and the disability rights movement.

Again, this isn't to say that the de facto segregation of some people with certain disabilities wasn't dramatic and significant. If buses are built so that wheelchair users and the elderly cannot get aboard, the vehicles might as well have signs saying "No cripples allowed on board." If drinking fountains are mounted too high for some people to use, they might as well have signs saying "For normal people only." If meetings and conferences are held without sign language being available, they might as well put up a notice saying "No Deaf people need enter here." History is a house of mirrors, and sometimes where you stand and how distorted the glass is creates your vision of what happened.

TWO

DC Outsiders Turn
Washington Insiders

IN 1980, A TRICKLE of disability activists flew from various cities, mostly from Berkeley, California, and descended on the nation's capital. Not all of them knew each other. They didn't have computers or cell phones. They slept on floors of friends' apartments and begged and borrowed office space. If you were making a film about the ADA, you wouldn't have a dramatic moment to focus on. The movement began with a whimper, not a bang.

Four of those people who filtered into Washington in the very cold winter of 1980 were Patrisha "Pat" Wright, Bob Funk, Arlene Mayerson, and Mary Lou Breslin. All had been working in a small storefront office on Telegraph Avenue in Berkeley. That year launched the first twenty-four-hour news station, CNN. Politics was in the air and now in the airwaves. Wright jokes that one day, they were sitting in the back of the storefront and she passed a note to Mayerson saying, "Do you want to come with me to Washington, DC?" It was a long way from the health-food stores and head shops of the hippie highlands to the august avenues and marble halls of Washington, but all it took was an airplane ride to get there.

Wright, who came to be called "The General" for her organizing and persuasive abilities, was a round-faced woman with big glasses and blond, shoulder-length hair, parted in the middle. Her wry smile was punctuated with assertive front teeth. Born in Fairfield, Connecticut, to a Republican family, she suffered a serious head wound as a teenager and was unconscious for six weeks. When she woke up, she had amnesia, and later, she began to notice some problems with her eyes. Wright developed chronic, permanent double vision, and although she had a career in medicine in mind, when her disability became obvious, "it was suggested to me by rehab that, as a legally blind person I could make screen doors for a living."[1] She dropped out of school and headed to San Francisco in the 1960s—then the refuge of many confused but idealistic people. By her own admission, she "basically did hot tubs and wine for a couple of years till my money ran out."

Then she became involved with an alternative hospital that housed a group of about forty people with severe disabilities. Wright tried to create an independent-living situation for them, but she was fired. As she says, "One morning, I walked in, and they called me into their office and told me that one of the residents was found in bed with another one of the residents. My explanation was, 'Far fucking out!'—and that the program was a success. At that point, they fired me."

After this experience, Wright was called on to help develop a master's program about disability for the countercultural Antioch College. In doing so, she came into contact and worked with Berkeley's Center for Independent Living, which was cofounded by Ed Roberts. She worked closely with the center, and when the 504 takeover of the San Francisco federal building happened, Wright was there. She occupied the building with Judy Heumann and others and began taking the role of Heumann's personal assistant. Although this wasn't a paid position, Wright accompanied Heumann when she traveled to demonstrations and meetings. Without formal training in lobbying, Wright gathered contacts and ideas to become a formidable and persuasive player in Washington.

Bob Funk grew up poor in northwestern Ohio "in the middle of nowhere," he says. Kicking around the severe flat landscape of towns like Defiance and Napoleon, he lived in the echoes of black-and-white images of Walker Evans, moving from place to place like Ohio's hometown hero Johnny Appleseed. "We were poor white trash, as

I see it," Funk says. "We moved from farmhouse to farmhouse. My dad was a clown in the Ringling Brothers circus. He preferred drinking beer and playing cards over anything else." Funk went into the Peace Corps at nineteen, which made him the youngest volunteer in that organization at the time. "When I was in Nigeria, I caught an infection in my leg and ended up in the hospital. I had two amputations and various surgeries on that leg over the next three years." In fact, he had caught a leprosy-like disease called buruli. Returning from the Peace Corps with one leg, the curly-headed, longhaired Funk went to law school at the University of California at Davis. But then instead of practicing law, he reenacted his father's homelessness, this time with his son. He drove around from town to town. In British Columbia, he ran into a woman he knew in the Peace Corps, and she mentioned that there was a job at the Center for Independent Living in Berkeley. It seems as if, in this ADA story, all roads lead to Berkeley.

Knowing about poverty firsthand, Funk had been interested in poverty law, and the job in Berkeley seemed like a perfect fit. He began working at the center in 1976. "I worked there, doing attendant care, SSI [supplemental security income], whatever legal kind of stuff," Funk says. "I slowly got together with some other people there, and we started a group—the Disabled Paralegal Advocacy Program." Funk remembers a case of some people with disabilities who were thrown out of a restaurant because the owner found them "too disturbing" to look at. Previously, people with disabilities would have had little recourse but to feel humiliated and angry about such an event. But with the aid of a legal team funded by various sources, those lucky enough to live in Berkeley could go to court, as did this group of people, who won their case with the assistance of Funk and his colleagues.

Funk, along with Mary Lou Breslin, Arlene Mayerson, and others, founded the Disability Rights Education and Defense Fund (DREDF) as an offshoot of the Center for Independent Living (CIL). Originally, Heumann helped found the Disability Law Resource Center as part of the CIL, but when its funding ran out, DREDF sprang from the ashes of the expiring program. The declaration of independence of the new organization from the old CIL produced tensions with people like Heumann and Ed Roberts, but DREDF had momentum.

Funk directed the new organization from his office, which irreverently displayed on a bookcase his prosthetic leg and coworker Gary Gill's glass eyeball.

"As time went on," recalls Funk, "it became apparent that DREDF, whose name had been changed from the Disabled Paralegal Advocates Program, was too big for a community-based group. We were getting involved with issues on a national basis." Raising money through grants, Funk secured the funds to go to Washington along with his colleagues Wright, Mayerson, and Breslin. As they divided up their roles, they saw Funk as the architect, Breslin as the visionary, Wright as the political strategist, and Mayerson as the brains.

Mary Lou Breslin, the program's visionary, was born in 1944 and grew up in Louisville, Kentucky, in a wealthy family whose money came from tobacco. Her maternal grandfather was executive director of the Lorillard tobacco company, which made Newport, Kent, and Old Gold cigarettes—names that evoke the idealized America of the past in which she came of age. In her large home, the young Breslin was surrounded by African American servants. While she personally felt close to her nannies Catherine Holloway and Violet Holt, she witnessed her grandfather preside over the dinner table wearing a three-piece suit while making racist comments about the servants who "don't know any better."

Breslin lived the life of a Dixie belle in the warm breezes of Southern comfort until she contracted polio at the age of eleven. Suddenly she was plucked from her luxurious home and placed in various medical institutions for children with polio. Her parents' wealth allowed her, though, to avoid the warehousing and harsh life of such institutions that the less-advantaged children of the time experienced. Breslin was quickly brought back home to all the servants, now with hired medical help and physical therapy filling her young life. Her doctors insisted that she walk, so her father had a ramp built. She was forced to walk on it back and forth each day, which, Breslin remembers, took about one arduous hour to do a single lap.

Breslin's most positive experiences seem to have happened at Warm Springs, Georgia, toward the end of the summer of 1957. The Warm Springs Institute was the place made famous by Franklin Delano Roosevelt, who went there, eventually bought the place, and set up the institute. Its warm, humid temperatures during the day and night, combined with the natural spring that fed the pools with eighty-eight-degree mineral water, provided whatever benefits hydrotherapy can offer. That August, it had been particularly hot, reaching ninety-eight degrees when Breslin's family brought her to Warm Springs. Like any child, she was unwilling to leave home. "I screamed and fought and cried and went through all sorts of trauma over it." But her family said, "Too bad. You're going. It's settled."

Yet, within a few hours of arriving, Breslin realized that this was where she needed to be. It was languid with lovely rural scents and the drone of bumblebees and late summer crickets. She describes the place: "It was like a little resort as only the South can do it, with the smells and the quiet and the cicadas in the pine trees at night. It was a wonderful, beautiful place, and isolated and away from the main throngs and absolutely not near any big city except Atlanta, which was seventy miles away."

Being with children her own age was exciting, but the dreamy, benevolent quality of the place was darkened by her dawning awareness that some few black children with polio were kept in the windowless basement, whereas the white children were in the airy upstairs floors. Breslin doesn't remember even seeing black children around the grounds or in the pool. In fact, there were segregated dining facilities, bathrooms, and therapy rooms. The only African Americans who mixed with whites were the staff. But they were all called by their first names, while the white staff members were addressed more formally as Miss or Mr. This segregation was the legacy of a racist myth that African Americans didn't get polio (even the *Washington Post* reported this "fact" as late as 1951).[2] And so institutions like Warm Springs were essentially white until the late 1940s, when a few emergency beds were set up in the basement for black children—the basement, ironically or perhaps not, being the black servants' quarters in earlier times.

In the neoclassical buildings of the institute, which echoed the plantations of the South, Breslin learned all of her major skills and "could get around anywhere" after her stay. Bathing in the large, warm pool, which the black children were not allowed to use, she socialized with many other children who had disabilities. During this very positive time, more somber things were going on at home. Breslin's mother died of uterine cancer, leaving her father distraught and overwhelmed. Breslin remained at Warm Springs for a year, returning there often.

The University of Illinois was her next stop. The campus was relatively accessible and had begun a special program for people with disabilities, for returning World War II veterans. There she only half-attended classes, preferring to spend most of her energies being a wheelchair cheerleader for the disabled basketball team and other more amusing activities. After knocking around after college and having a very quick marriage and divorce, Breslin ended up in the Bay Area, where she became involved with the Center for Independent Living and met Wright, Mayerson, and Funk.

Arlene Mayerson, "the brains" of the group, was born in 1949 in Cincinnati as part of an extended Jewish family. A determined-looking woman with a mane of black hair, soulful eyes, and a bemused look playing around her lips, she recalls her parents—a father who was a real estate agent and her stay-at-home mother who did the books for the business. Her father developed melanoma when Mayerson was two years old, and some disfiguring surgery on his arm and body left him badly scarred. The family lied about the origin of those scars, even to the children, fearing the stigma that the diagnosis of cancer could carry, and this situation perhaps taught Mayerson an early lesson about disability and how it was perceived. She attended Boston University, where she became "a hippie and a radical," taking courses with the likes of leftist scholar Howard Zinn. Living in a typical 1960s commune, she waitressed and worked with community groups in Boston. She then decided to go to law school to do public-interest work and ended up at Boalt Law School in Berkeley. Her education led her to clerk in Washington, DC, and eventually return to Berkeley to find a job at the organization that became DREDF, where she met Breslin, Funk, and Wright.

All this is prelude to those days in 1980 when the foursome arrived in Washington, DC, as part of the startup of DREDF. Wright points out: "When DREDF was created in 1979, . . . we said . . . that we were not going to reinvent the wheel in a legal defense fund. We went to Washington, DC, and asked for meetings with all of the civil rights leaders that we had ever read about and heard about who we didn't know and said basically, 'We're going to start a legal defense fund, and we want to learn from you and figure out what the mistakes were, what you would do differently.'"

The DREDF crew had a genius idea. While meeting with people in Washington, they decided to invite a large group of significant movers and shakers in civil rights to Berkeley. In December 1981, they did so. The group included James Nabrit III of the National Association for the Advancement of Colored People (NAACP) Legal Defense Fund; Judy Lichtman, founder and president of Women's Legal Defense Fund; and Suzan Harjo, who a few years later was executive director of the National Congress of American Indians. Another significant person they invited to Berkeley was Ralph Neas, the director of the Leadership Conference on Civil Rights, a coalition of all the major civil rights organizations. Neas later played a large role in the ADA.

There were several days of talks and breakout sessions held at the San Francisco Holiday Inn, then the only reasonably priced, accessible hotel in the Bay Area. Each person was handed a hefty sheaf of information on disability. By the end of the conference, DREDF pretty much had convinced all concerned that disability was a civil rights issue.

The plan was clever because, first of all, it got the disability folks up to speed on civil rights and the civil rights people on disability. It also created strong ties between those two groups. Everyone realized that if you wanted effective legislation around disability, it could no longer follow the model it had in the past—rehabilitation for war veterans, assistance for disabled people, and jobs programs. Instead, legislation had to be focused on civil rights—a much more inclusive category that would open many more doors. Rehab programs might help some people, but if people had no access to places of public accommodation, courtrooms, bathrooms, and buildings in general, the rehabilitation wouldn't do very much. Only by thinking of the nation as a place where disabled people had rights to use transportation, watch television, use telephones, live independently, walk or roll on the streets, patronize businesses, and attend accessible colleges and religious institutions would the world ever change enough. No single governmental program would do that—only changing the way the world thought about civil rights would.

The DREDF folks commuted back and forth between Berkeley and Washington, but realized they needed an office and an apartment to live in. Funk had become friends with a man in his forties named Evan J. Kemp Jr. The friend ran a Ralph Nader–sponsored organization called the Disability Rights Center, which had a small office on Dupont Circle. Kemp invited Funk and company to move their operation into a back room of the center.

Kemp was another scion of a wealthy family. A six feet four gentle, blond, square-faced man with a Will Rogers shock of hair over his forehead, he had a gap-toothed smile, horn-rimmed glasses, and a preference for three-piece suits. Kemp was born in New York in 1937 and grew up in Ohio. His parents were Democrats, as was his uncle Drew Pearson, the muckraking news columnist who attacked Senator Joseph McCarthy in print and in return had the dubious distinction of having been physically attacked by McCarthy. According to Pearson, McCarthy had "grabbed [him] by the neck, and kicked [him] in the groin."[3]

At the age of twelve, Kemp was diagnosed with an incurable degenerative disease involving spinal muscular atrophy. The diagnosing doctor told him he wouldn't live past fourteen. When Kemp disproved the diagnosis and survived past that age, he was rediagnosed. This time Kemp was told he wouldn't live till twenty. Again, he beat those odds. Eventually he was diagnosed with Kugelberg-Welander disease, a genetic, muscular-dystrophy-like condition that leads to paralysis of the lower limbs.

Kemp attended the University of Virginia law school, where he graduated in the top tenth of his class. Like many fellow graduates, he sent out applications to law firms. After thirty-seven turndowns of thirty-seven applications, he began to see that his disability had become a major obstacle to employment. Systematically thwarted from going into private practice, Kemp found a position with the Internal Revenue Service in 1964 and then later moved to the Securities and Exchange Commission (SEC).

Working at the SEC, Kemp asked for permission to have handicapped parking in the garage of the agency's building because walking to the main entrance from the outdoor parking lot was too difficult. In the pre-ADA world, an organization could deny such a request, and the SEC did just that. However, he was permitted the dubious honor of entering the building on foot through the garage door. This partial and humiliating accommodation went seriously wrong one day in 1971, when the automatic overhead garage door suddenly crashed down on Kemp, crushing him and further injuring his already weakened spine. His previous limited ability to walk was now destroyed, and he began using a wheelchair. In a Kafkaesque turn, now that he used a wheelchair, the SEC denied him promotion to a supervisory position because they deemed him "too disabled." Kemp sued the SEC and won. With the history of prejudice inscribed on his body, Kemp was now more than willing to take up the cause of disability discrimination.

While the DREDF people were checking out Washington and trying to locate and meet with key civil rights people, Kemp wrote a *New York Times* op-ed titled "Aiding the Disabled: No Pity, Please." The article attacked the Jerry Lewis Muscular Dystrophy Telethon, a somewhat ironic attack since Kemp's own parents had helped in 1959 to start the first regional telethon in Cleveland.

Lewis's national annual Labor Day broadcast lasted for twenty-four hours. It showcased the gangly comedian entertaining, cajoling, and even mocking his audience while presenting a series of disabled poster children known as Jerry's Kids. Lewis emphasized their disadvantage and his own heroic marathon endurance efforts as he remained awake, active, and decreasingly coherent for the entire real-time event. An illustrative moment: In the 1973 telethon, Lewis holds up a child with muscular dystrophy and says, "God goofed, and it's up to us to correct His mistakes."[4] In a later essay, Lewis wrote that someone with muscular dystrophy was "only half a man." The emphasis on the show was to feature Jerry's Kids and beg for money for a cure, despite the fact that two-thirds of the people aided by the Muscular Dystrophy Association were adults and there is no cure for the disease itself.

Kemp wrote that Lewis did harm to disabled people because the entertainer only showed them as children and dependent. The article emphasized that evoking pity to get money was problematic.

Rather, he urged Lewis to focus his energies on changing the climate for employment and increasing access and rights for people with disabilities. Jerry Lewis's response to his critics grew increasingly shrill. An oedipal war broke out between Lewis and his own poster children. Even today, the Academy Awards are often accompanied by protesters in wheelchairs denouncing Lewis. Kemp's article in the *New York Times* helped put his name and organization on the map.

Kemp's apartment, which was actually two apartments combined, became the crash pad for various disability advocates and a hangout as well. Kemp's first wife, Jane, was no longer living there, being so disabled herself with a slow-growing brain tumor that she was now institutionalized in a semi-unconscious state in North Carolina.

The stream of disability activists who camped in his apartment, slept on his couch, and used his kitchen as a communal space began to influence the way Kemp saw things. One of the first things that the patrician Kemp learned from a number of his new Berkeley friends was that his manner of locomotion was unacceptable. Kemp had a nonmotorized wheelchair and employed an elderly African American man as a personal assistant who pushed him from place to place. As the California hippies and the civil rights folks told him, this arrangement wouldn't work very well in fostering his image as a civil rights reformer. Kemp was encouraged to buy a motorized wheelchair and did so. A second contribution of the Berkeley hippies to Kemp's image was a gift, according to Pat Wright—they purchased for him his first pair of blue jeans.

Wright and Kemp cooked up yet another, more profound change. Kemp was not a Republican. In fact, he came from a Democratic family and was interested in liberal causes. Wright, who was born into a Republican family but had reimagined herself as a Democrat, recognized that Kemp would have more influence and access as a Republican. Rebranded as a Republican, he and Wright would be able to cover all the bases in lobbying for disability rights and eventually the ADA. Kemp's second wife, Janine Bertram, recalls: "The first year he actually voted Republican was in the presidential election for Ronald Reagan. Our polling place was four blocks from our condo, and Evan told me it took him about two and a half hours to get there because he kept hesitating—going toward the polls and then retreating. It was just so hard for him, as a lifelong Democrat, to cast that first vote for the Republicans."

But, of all of Kemp's abilities and insights into disability, and with his new image as a Republican, the one talent that contributed in a major way to getting the ADA passed was his ability to play a ferocious game of bridge. Kemp had played bridge since college with a group of friends. He also taught bridge to the movers and shakers of Washington, which cleverly gave him insider access. One of those players who met every Thursday night around a card table was the Republican C. Boyden Gray, the chief White House counsel for Reagan and then for George H. W. Bush. Gray also was Bush's close friend and tennis partner just as their fathers had been golf partners. On any given Thursday night, you'd see two tall men, Kemp and Gray, towering over the bridge table, one a wheelchair user and the other not. As a Republican and an increasingly close friend of Gray, Kemp now had direct lines of access to the White House.

During this time, as Kemp capitalized on his newfound Republican identity, he began to create alliances and make horse trades. He began going to conservative think-tank Federalist Society meetings with Gray. William Bradford Reynolds, then assistant attorney general for civil rights, had just been nominated associate attorney general under Reagan and was facing Senate confirmation. Reynolds's confirmation would meet with resistance because of his extreme beliefs, including his anti-affirmative-action views. Reynolds told the *Washington Post* that affirmative action was "at war with the American ideal of equal opportunity for each person to achieve whatever his or her industry and talents warrant."[5]

The Department of Justice under Reagan was trying a series of frontal attacks on civil rights, and Reynolds's nomination would be a testing ground by which Congress, in rejecting him, would send a message to the president—don't attack civil rights. To deal with this problem, Gray dropped over to Kemp's house for a bridge game and said, "Evan, I think you should come out in support of Brad Reynolds for this position."[6] According to Kemp's wife Janine, he did just that and supported Reynolds: "We ended up meeting with Brad Reynolds and having lunches and dinners with him. We learned that a few years before, he had done one of those sensitivity exercises where he spent a day using a wheelchair. It made him support disability rights, despite his opposition to quotas." Reynolds turned out to be crucial in encouraging subsequent disability rights legislation, although he created problems as well. Such is the ebb and flow of Washington alliances.

The goal of Kemp and the other DREDF folks all along was to change Washington's thinking about disability as a disease in need of remediation to a political position in need of civil rights. Earlier, when Ronald Reagan became president, he made it clear that he would be cutting many government mandates—included in those would be costly disability legislation. The civil rights agenda of DREDF would have to wait a bit. Reagan, carrying out his supply-side economic agenda, zeroed in on those perennial conservative bugaboos—government spending and regulations. His plan was to starve the social and welfare state by encouraging massive military spending paired with huge tax cuts. One key element of this strong action was "an ambitious reform of regulations that will reduce the government-imposed barriers to investment, production, and employment."[7]

Reagan announced the formation of a task force on regulatory reform, to be headed by the newly minted vice president, George H. W. Bush, and composed of Reagan appointees handpicked to hack away at anything that looked like an excrescence of governmental largesse. Over 150 pieces of already-enacted legislation came into the crosshairs of the regulatory gun. The Great Society of Lyndon Johnson had to be pared down to a Not-So-Great Society envisioned by conservative economists and sympathetic leaders like Prime Minister Margaret Thatcher in the United Kingdom. Paradoxically, Bush himself had attacked these conservative policies in the primary when he was running against Reagan, calling them "voodoo economics." Now, in a turnaround, as Reagan's veep, Bush was drafted to be the one to poke those voodoo pins into the overgrown body politic. Three areas that received a particularly large jab were the Education for All Handicapped Children Act, the Architectural and Transportation Barriers Compliance Board, and, of course, Section 504—all disability-related laws that Reagan wanted eviscerated.

Fortunately for the DREDF folks and Kemp, one of the significant people on the taskforce was the White House chief counsel, Boyden Gray. Of course, Gray knew Kemp socially mainly by playing bridge, but they really had gotten to know each other more intimately when each represented opposite sides in a famous antitrust case that went to the Supreme Court in 1977. Gray was representing the business interests of Illinois Brick, while Kemp was on the government side. Gray notes that he and Kemp were "adversaries" and that although Kemp beat him regularly at bridge, in regard to Illinois Brick, "I won and that impressed him."

Like Kemp and Breslin, Clayland Boyden Gray grew up in wealth, and like the Breslins, the Gray family acquired its money from tobacco. The source of both families' wealth was ironic, considering that tobacco use is one of the serious risk factors that contributed to many citizens' disabilities. Gray's grandfather was president of the R. J. Reynolds Tobacco Company and founded Wachovia Bank. His ambitions were not small, and to personify his social status, he built Graylin, a huge stone mansion with turrets and a manorial spiral staircase on an eighty-two-acre estate in Winston, North Carolina, just across the road from the equally posh R. J. Reynolds plantation house. Citizen Kane would have been right at home in this monumental place. Gray's father was the president of the University of North Carolina and had served as secretary of the army under Truman and as national security advisor to Eisenhower. From this distinguished line of Republicans sprang Boyden, born in 1943, and his brother Burton, who was a founder of the conservative Federalist Society, to which Boyden also belonged. After attending Harvard and the University of North Carolina, Boyden clerked for Chief Justice Earl Warren, went into private practice, and then became White House counsel.

Gray, at six feet six, is a gangly man with an elongated face, deep-set eyes, and dramatic, overhanging eyebrows. The first time Senator Tom Harkin met him, the senator thought Gray looked like Ichabod Crane, the lanky schoolmaster in Washington Irving's "The Legend of Sleepy Hollow." The progressive Iowan describes Gray's politics as "conservative as all get-out!" Perhaps conservative in his values, Gray did have his madcap side, known among the Washington elite for making the first floor of his federal-style Georgetown home the exclusive domain of a pot-bellied pig named Penelope. He was also branded a "clean-air nut" who drove a ten-year-old dented Chevy that was powered by alcohol.

There were many programs and regulations that Reagan had his eye on cutting, and the big ones were related to disability. The disability-related regulations were so attractive partly because they were based on Title VI of the Civil Rights Act of 1964 and Title IX of the Education Amendments Act. Many conservatives wanted to make inroads into those civil rights acts but felt that those were untouchable because no politician would dare play the race or gender card. But in going after people with disabilities, many conservatives thought that a largely silent and unnoticed minority could provide a wedge to ultimately erode the Civil Rights Act.

This thinking turned out to be a big mistake. When word leaked to the disability community, especially after the 504 debacle, that key elements of the legislation protecting them would be dismantled, the silent minority was silent no more. Former majority whip Tony Coelho said that far from being a hidden minority, people with disabilities were a "hidden army." DREDF was able to take advantage of the leaks and organize not only disability groups but also the key civil rights players whom they had brought to San Francisco when the group was formulating strategy for its move to Washington.

Because of Gray's connection with Kemp, there was information flowing in both directions as freely as the hearts and diamonds in their weekly bridge game flew back and forth at the card table. Gray says that he received "enormous help" from Kemp: "In the process of all this, I learned about the power of the movement, how big it was—what an ignored civil rights issue this had been."[8] Although Gray might deny it, others have hinted that when the draft of proposed changes from the Department of Justice came back to the task force in January 1982 specifying which 504 programs were on the chopping block, Gray seems to have communicated this information to the disability folks, who in turn shared it with the rank and file. In any case, there were "leaks" that got into the hands of DREDF. Arlene Mayerson describes DREDF's connections with Gray and Bradford Reynolds: "We were talking to the Darth Vaders of the civil rights movement." But those communications helped DREDF a great deal, Mayerson points out: "When Boyden Gray called a meeting, because he was so high up in the White House, people, of equal rank, in the Department of Justice had to come. . . . Our meetings would last hours. We had an opportunity to go through all the changes and explain why they were bad, and why they would affect people."[9]

When the Office of Management and Budget (OMB), headed by David Stockman, well-known proponent of trickle-down economics, proposed further changes that would be coming two months later, these were also leaked. They included a particularly odious provision that said you could weigh the necessity of providing an accommodation against "the social value" of a particular person. Bob Funk commented: "This was a cost-benefit analysis of how human you are."[10] By 1983, roughly forty thousand angry letters from the "hidden army" were sent to the task force as a deregulating cleaver was being raised to hack at Section 504's stipulations related to disability. Gray traveled around the country to hear from disability groups. Finally, Reynolds, perhaps in return for Kemp's support of his failed nomination, abandoned any attempt to eviscerate 504 and other major legislation affecting people with disabilities. Vice President Bush sent a personal letter to Kemp, saying, "Your commitment to equal opportunity for disabled citizens . . . is fully shared by this Administration."[11] It was perhaps Bush's first overt statement of support concerning disability. From that point on, Kemp began writing Bush's speeches about disability. The vital connection had been made.

While Kemp was forging ties with the White House, Wright set her mind to connect with the myriad civil rights groups throughout the country. To do this, she connected with the most important civil rights organization—the Leadership Conference on Civil Rights (LCCR). The organization, founded in the 1950s to push for civil rights legislation, was responsible for promoting the Civil Rights Acts of 1957, 1960, and 1964, as well as the Voting Rights Act of 1965 and the Fair Housing Act of 1968. By the time Wright decided that this organization was the best party in town to promote disability as a civil right, the group had representatives from organizations of Native Americans, women, and one hundred other identity interests.

Ralph Neas had just become the director of the LCCR in 1981. A gregarious and garrulous man, he has a reassuring voice and a winning smile. He was born in Brookline, Massachusetts, in 1946, but grew up in St. Charles, Illinois, with a conservative, Catholic, Republican family. A seemingly oxymoronic Benedictine military prep school in rural Illinois provided Neas's early education. He then attended the University of Notre Dame, where he continued with ROTC and became a lieutenant. In May 1968, he marched his troops around several hundred students who were staging a sit-in protest against the very ROTC he was commanding. That event was perhaps a prognostication for Neas. Although he was conservative, many of his liberal friends were protesting that day. Neas says, "I had to perform a high-wire act personally and every other way, but somehow being able to negotiate myself through it all, I hope consistent with my own moral values, but also openness both to those who were profoundly antiwar and those who thought our country was doing the right thing." As the director of LCCR, Neas had constantly to balance the interests of many conflicting groups that were part of the coalition.

Neas then received his law degree from the University of Chicago and, after working at several positions, served as chief counsel to two Republican senators—Edward W. Brooke of Massachusetts, the first African American popularly elected congressional representative in the nation and David Durenberger. Under Brooke, Neas got up to speed on civil rights and became the senior staffer in the Senate who dealt with those rights. He also worked on women's and disability issues with the LCCR.

Then suddenly Neas contracted Guillain-Barre syndrome in 1979, when he was thirty-two years old. The disease is a form of paralysis brought on by an autoimmune response. As Neas describes it: "I got it in February of '79. . . . Over a period of weeks I became totally paralyzed. I could not talk; machines breathed for me; machines fed me and took care of every other vital function. . . . I was in terrible pain and was given general absolution. I fought for life on the critical list for about three and one-half months. It was a long time. When you get totally paralyzed, and you're on a respirator, and you're inert, and everything is paralyzed, it takes a long time to learn how to walk again and crawl again and sit up."[12] Although Neas went back to work for Senator Durenberger, the energy level slowly returning, he decided to take a sabbatical to build up his stamina. So he went to Europe for two months, began walking ten miles a day, and eventually recovered.

In 1981, Neas started as director of the LCCR. His appointment was opposed by Vernon Jordan, president of the National Urban League, and Benjamin Hooks, executive director of the NAACP. After all, Neas was a young, white, Catholic, Republican male heading up a coalition representing mostly Democratic African Americans, women, and minorities of all kinds. But Neas proved his worth over time.

Around the same time, Neas met Wright in the spring of 1981. He recalls: "She invites all of these civil rights leaders, people from the Carter-Mondale administration, from the Senate, from the House, from civil rights. We all convene because who's going to refuse a trip to San Francisco that's paid for to do good things, right?"

At the meeting, Neas asked James Nabrit III, of the NAACP Legal Defense Fund and son of James Nabrit Jr., if he would do the presentation to the assembly: "I said, 'Jim, why don't you make the presentation? Our message is that disability rights are civil rights. If we're having the son of one of the people who worked on *Brown v. Board of Education* make that presentation, it will have immense symbolic value.'" Previously, disability had been confined to the health committee of the LCCR. With Neas and Wright's help, disability now became a central issue for the group when DREDF joined. Previously, as well, there had been no gay or lesbian groups in LCCR, and Wright suggested to Neas that there be some significant representation. For Wright, this was particularly important because she herself was a lesbian. But it took till the mid-1980s for LCCR to allow gay groups into its fold than it did for disability organizations.

Together Neas and Wright, along with the other DREDF people, went through the next few years advocating for various laws and beginning a rear-guard effort to influence the way the courts were interpreting 504.

THREE

THE TEXAS CONNECTION

THE STORY OF THE Disability Rights Education and Defense Fund (DREDF) people, the civil rights people, and the White House staff is one of the many streams converging on the rapids leading to the ADA. Another stream we might call the Texas connection developed somewhat earlier than the one described thus far.

In 1971, a college student in his early twenties and sporting long, blond hair and a wispy moustache had gotten wind of a federal rehabilitation act in the works. Wanting to influence the outcome, he sent his Oklahoma senator, Henry Bellmon, letters typed with one finger as he sat in his wheelchair at college. The young man expressed his opinions about the importance of independent living and nondiscrimination. Senator Bellmon replied with a polite note—the student, whose name was Lex Frieden, was just one of thousands who write to their representatives every day and who receive back nicely typed, respectful, but bland responses. But Frieden was determined to make a difference. If his letters didn't influence anyone, he would find a way to get his opinions across.

Lex Frieden was born in 1949 in the tiny town of Alva, Oklahoma, a place that evoked the world in *The Grapes of Wrath*. In Alva, there were still dirt roads in the 1930s, the only major hotel shut down in the 1950s, and the main street was dominated by a Piggly Wiggly grocery store amid the stretch of a few isolated stoplights.

The night Frieden became a quadriplegic was a wild one by college standards. After a weekend of nonstop drinking and partying, he and his friends were driving through their college town's main street in high hilarity. The raucous scene ended suddenly when their car crashed into an oncoming vehicle. Although the driver and the other passengers had only superficial wounds, Frieden broke his neck. He underwent several operations and spent a lot of time in rehab. As Frieden adapted to his quadriplegia, he realized that he very much wanted to return to university. But his original campus was completely inaccessible. He tried to get into the newly built Oral Roberts University, much of which was built around the time of the Architectural Barriers Act and was much easier to navigate in a wheelchair. Oral Roberts also had a distance learning facility. It seemed perfect for Frieden, but when he applied, he was again rejected because he was a wheelchair user. Of this Frieden says, "That really was a setback to me, I mean psychologically. Before that, having a broken neck didn't seem like such a big deal. We were sending men to the moon. It was just another one of those challenges in life that people have. Then, when I was told I couldn't do something—the only thing I thought I could do—that I wasn't able to do it because of my disability, then I felt guilty. I felt like, my God, I screwed my life up worse than I thought here. That was really traumatic."

Since the family was living in Tulsa, some former classmates suggested he try the University of Tulsa. He set up a meeting with the dean. "My father took me in the car, and we couldn't even meet the dean in his office, because it wasn't accessible. He came to the parking lot, and I met the dean in the parking lot—two deans actually, the dean of education and the dean of students."

According to Frieden, the dean of students said, "Look, we've seen your résumé. We saw that you were valedictorian in your high school class. You're in the top five percent on the college admission exams, and so on. I mean, you'd be the kind of student we'd love to have here at the university." But Frieden countered saying that because of the campus environment with steps everywhere and no ramps, he worried he would not be able to attend.

The dean said, "Look across the green there. See that building? There's some construction." He said, "That's the first new building we've built in many years, but it's being built according to current standards. So there will be a level entrance on the building and an elevator. You take this catalog of the classes for the fall semester home with you and look it over. Tell me which courses you want to take, and they will be held in that building this fall." This solution, based on what Frieden calls "Oklahoma ingenuity," made it possible for him to continue his academic career. It wasn't rocket science or putting a person on the moon, but later it would come to be called "reasonable accommodation."

Frieden was able to attend the University of Tulsa, from which he wrote his letters to Congress. The student didn't start out as an activist. He was content to attend his classes until one day when his father showed up and announced that he'd read in the paper that there was a local group of people with disabilities who were trying to organize. Frieden said he had no interest in going, but his father took hold of his wheelchair and forcibly transported him to the meeting against his wishes. Frieden was in tears of frustration and anger when he arrived at the meeting where he realized he was the youngest person in the room. After the meeting, he decided not to have any part of it and he scolded his father for taking advantage of the young man's inability to get around himself by compelling him to go to the meeting. That week, though, one of the members of the disability group, Mike Phillips, called on him. Frieden watched as the van Phillips had driven opened up and a wheelchair lift folded out and lowered first the activist and then his wife. Frieden had never seen anyone with a wheelchair so mobile and able to get around like that. His own family had a Volkswagen van and ramps that had to be set up by a non-wheelchair-user. It was amazing to see the independence that the right technology and access could provide. In a short time, the college student was an active participant working to have disability recognized as a civil right.

In 1974, another disability activist, Fred Fay, invited Frieden, who was now in graduate school researching rehabilitation, along with Judy Heumann, Eunice Fiorito, Ed Roberts, and about ten others to come to Boston and participate in a meeting whose aim was to form a cross-disability national organization. Diane Lattin, one of the people attending that meeting, was a member of the President's Committee on the Employment for the Disabled, whose chair was Harold Russell, the double amputee who had starred in and won an Academy Award for the film *The Best Years of Our Lives*. Lattin suggested that the group meet up again a few weeks later in Washington, DC, to attend a meeting of the committee. Frieden and the others didn't particularly like that group. Frieden recalls: "We all to a person said, 'Why in the world would we be interested in that organization when it just involves nondisabled CEOs of the company, and they basically just give each other awards?'" But the group used the occasion as a way to get funded, and they met again, this time creating an organization they called the American Coalition of Citizens with Disabilities (ACCD). It was the first national cross-disability organization ever formed.

The disability rights movement was becoming a melting pot of activists, legal experts, and legislative staff. But there needed to be leaders to stir that pot. One of the most visible and well known of these was Justin Dart Jr., a frail-looking man using a wheelchair and with a silver-tongued voice. His role merged activist, strategist, and ambassador. Sometimes called the "father of the disability movement" (although he demurred from the use of that honorific), Dart was certainly older than most of the others in the movement. Yet Dart was the kind of father who might well embarrass a teenage kid. He never went anywhere without his signature cowboy hat, which was sometimes covered in DISABILITY POWER buttons and at other times just adorned with an American flag pin. He sported his tall, ornately embossed cowboy boots along with a suit and tie. Just as Ed Roberts's wheelchair has a prized place in the Smithsonian Museum, so do Dart's hat and boots.

Dart was born in Chicago in 1930, the grandson of the founder of Walgreens. Dart's father, Justin Sr., a conservative businessman, was to become one of the most influential men in the United States by being part of Reagan's "kitchen cabinet" that promoted and advised the president. Dart's mother was a "brilliant . . . flaming liberal feminist" who published, after her divorce from Justin Sr., an avant-garde magazine called *The Tiger's Eye*.[1] Caught between the conservative business values of his father and the progressive, artistic ones of his mother, Dart may have developed both a sense of the range of human opinion and the conviction that progressive change could happen in the midst of conservative values.

Dart's life, while privileged, wasn't golden. He was an obstreperous student who attended the elite prep school Andover, where he was punished so much that his demerits exceeded only those of the previous worst student—Humphrey Bogart. As Dart said of himself, "I never met a person I couldn't insult. I never met a rule I couldn't break. . . . People didn't like me. I didn't like myself."[2] He ended up attending seven high schools and not graduating from a single one.

Dart contracted polio at the age of eighteen in 1948 (as did his brother). After rehab, Dart began using a wheelchair. He also married a woman he had met in the hospital. Attending the University of Houston, he majored in education, but was prevented from getting his degree because of the claim that it was not possible for a wheelchair user to function in his supervisory teaching practicum. Dart eventually earned a master's degree in a related area, tried to go to law school, but then opted to start a business because he couldn't get a job that would hire someone with his disability—not even in his family's Walgreens business because of the claim that there wasn't enough room behind the counters in the drugstores for his wheelchair. Borrowing a considerable sum of money, he went into the bowling alley business and sold his US business to buy into a Mexican bowling alley. He did make a profit on the sales, but also found himself divorced after having had three children.

Throughout this time and throughout his life, Dart was addicted to many things. At various points, he was a heavy drinker—a bottle of whiskey per night—a womanizer who frequented prostitutes, and an addict using various prescription medications. He wrestled with severe and chronic depression and, by his own admission, was addicted to power and prestige. The depression may have been inherited, since both his mother and his brother eventually committed suicide.

Dart Sr. was now running Tupperware and wanted to make inroads into Japan. He commissioned his son with that task. When there, the younger Dart remarried and had two more children. He also helped establish a Japanese wheelchair basketball team for the 1964 Paralympics. However, during that period he was, as he said, "being flamboyant and doing photo ops, making money by any means, drinking, and chasing women."[3]

One of the women he chased was Yoshiko Saji, an employee, which led to the dissolution of his second marriage and created a furor. Saji became Dart's comrade as well as wife—the two of them would become very important in the run-up to the ADA. Saji, whom everyone refers to as Yoshiko, came from a poor rural family in Japan—a life in stark contrast to Dart's privilege.

Dart resigned after an internal conflict with the international corporation (including with his father). He started up a greeting-card business but eventually left that and retreated to a remote place in the mountains of Japan to face his demons. Dart and Yoshiko lived in a previously abandoned farmer's house without insulation, central heat, or telephone. Dart recounted, "In winter Yoshiko had to hammer the ice off the pipes every day, and the snow would blow up your ass from the hole-in-the-floor country toilet."[4]

The typical story of a ne'er-do-well transformed should by rights conclude that the protagonist conquered his demons and emerged from the agon a transfigured hero. And that did happen to a degree with Dart, although he struggled his entire life with his addictions. But what he did come out with was a philosophy, which he promulgated every chance he could get. It is impossible to read anything that Dart wrote that does not include ideas about empowerment and love. Every letter he and Yoshiko signed ended with "Power" added to the name of the person addressed and followed by the exhortation "Lead On!" In effect, Dart's philosophy was that change comes from within, that each person is the solution to the problem. Universal empowerment is the goal achieved by love: "I'm not talking about 'have-a-nice-day' love or love that controls," he said in an interview. "I'm talking about the kind of love that empowers people to values. . . . [T]his is the kind of love that has empowered our greatest leaders and their movements, Abraham, Jesus, Buddha, Muhammad, Gandhi, Martin Luther King."[5] There is a bit of the preacher in this statement mixed with the activist and even the cult leader. Dart's notion of empowerment was both semireligious and very pro-business—he called for "a revolution that confronts and eliminates obsolete thoughts and systems, that focuses the full power of science and free-enterprise democracy on the systematic empowerment of every person to live his or her God-given potential."[6]

The Darts moved back to the States from Japan, first to Seattle and then, in 1978, to Austin, Texas, to spread his new philosophy. He thought the disability movement would be fertile soil for the seeds of his great revelation and perhaps saw himself as a bodhisattva returning from enlightenment to bring the word to others. As Yoshiko puts it: "He was really searching for a place where he could contribute his experience, knowledge, and vision. He could not quite communicate those to people in a way that people could communicate back to him. Then he found a little light by joining this disability rights movement, and he found his small community."

Dart became involved in local disability groups, including MIGHT (Mobility Impaired Grappling Huddled Together) and others.[7] He started an independent-living center with a small grant and used his previous energies devoted to business and power in the service of disability causes. One of the patterns for Dart is that when he started working on a project, he started traveling in his beat-up automobile to survey the field. When the going got tough, the Darts got into their car. With the founding of the independent-living center, he and Yoshiko visited over thirty other centers. Because of Dart's work, money, and connections, the governor appointed Dart to several disability-related task forces and committees. Dart was a member and eventually the chair of the Texas Governor's Task Force for Long Range Policy for People with Disabilities. Having contributed heavily to the governor's campaign, Dart enjoyed much influence and the phone privileges to call the State House directly.

It was in Texas that Frieden met Dart in 1978, when he and Yoshiko were traveling to various independent-living centers. Dart called Frieden, who was involved with such a center. Frieden recalls: "I spoke to someone on the telephone who sounded like an elderly, gruff gentleman. He said, 'My name is Justin Dart. I'm from Austin, Texas, and I'm on the board of directors of the Goodwill Industries here.' I mean, that's the last thing somebody could've said to me that would've made me attracted to them at that point, because I had written some articles about how the Goodwill Industries were not really employing people with disabilities."

Frieden tried to dodge the meeting and had someone else show them the center. Nevertheless, Dart and Yoshiko invited him to dinner. Frieden recalls: "I was just amazed in this house because there was art all over the place on the floors, none of it on the wall. Just a floor piled—and some names of artists that I recognized. I think there might have been a Picasso there." When they sat down to dinner, places were set for everyone but Dart. In fact, despite Dart's ubiquity in the movement, not a single activist or lobbyist ever saw him eat or drink. He would sit at the table, but neither liquid nor solid ever passed his lips. One of his eccentricities was that his diet was so controlled and unusual that he preferred to eat alone. This regimen stemmed from a conviction that diet could help him control his addictions, including food addiction. Before he went to Japan, Dart was "very obese" according to Yoshiko. In Japan, he developed a diet with his second wife and later with Yoshiko that involved eating only once a day—at night—and only nonfat, non-starch dishes with bean sprouts, lots of vegetables, and *konnyaku*, a potato-like tuber and also the rubbery jelly made from it. He would take no alcohol. To wean himself from pasta and rice, he instructed Yoshiko to feed him one less strand of spaghetti or one less grain of rice each day till he was down to one solitary strand of pasta and one lone grain of rice.

As the unusual character of Dart emerged, Frieden found his curiosity sparked. The two remained in touch, and Frieden came to consider Dart a "philosopher" and a "genius." Frieden was also well aware of Dart's political clout and connections. Dart on his side was a tireless activist and ambassador who, according to Frieden, was also a "vociferous letter writer. He would write these handwritten personal notes to people, and they had a profound influence and impact. Most of us don't have the stamina or the training to do what he did. Most of us are not systematic enough in our approach to these types of things." Representative Steve Bartlett says of Dart, "Justin Dart was not a man to hint. He would, you know, he could always speak in decibels of a hundred or more. Enthusiasm, I don't mean volume." At Dart's funeral, Bill Clinton recounted how Dart had come into the president's office and lectured him "like a Dutch uncle" about how Clinton had to make sure that the ADA, then passed, was properly enforced.

According to Clinton, Dart didn't take "Let me get back to you" as an answer. Pat Morrissey, a Bartlett aide who interacted with Dart on a biweekly basis, says of him, "I always thought he was a walking, talking angel put on earth to remind us all what we were doing and doing it in the right way. He was almost a holy man. He didn't get into the weeds, but he reminded you of the outcomes and made sure you did it. He seriously underwrote financially a lot of the grassroots activity. He was everyone's collective conscience, and we better on a regular basis check in with him that we were on the right track. He'd go anywhere, talk to anyone, and was very close to President Bush and could get a meeting with him at the drop of a hat."

Dart was not above using his money to influence politicians. Frieden recalls: "He did, one time, give me an envelope that he asked me to give to a certain member of Congress as a gift on his behalf, and he wanted me to deliver it. I don't know what was in the envelope, but I saw the congressman open it and put the money in a drawer. The congressman was very grateful to me for being the messenger and, obviously, very grateful to Mr. Dart for making a contribution to his campaign." Frieden adds that Dart taught him a trick when giving cash: "'If you're ever making a gift to a member of Congress,' he [Dart] said, 'You can roll up some dollars and then put a larger bill on the outside and it looks like a really, really big gift.'"

In 1984, a few years after Reagan was elected, the president did one thing he regarded as necessary. He looked at a small and relatively unknown and ineffective committee housed in the basement of the Switzer Building, home to the Department of Education, and decided the group had to be changed. Founded in 1978 by President Carter, the National Council on Disability (NCD) had one thing missing: Republicans. Reagan replaced all the members with people he could count on, mostly friends with some interest in disability—largely through having children or spouses with disabilities. Among the dismissed were Judy Heumann and Elizabeth Boggs, an expert on people with cognitive impairments. The new committee—reconstituted as it now was—seemed like the least likely place that radical proposals could be fomented, and perhaps if there were another push to cut 504, Reagan would have the backup to argue that such cuts were needed.

At the same time that he fired all the Democrats, Reagan hired Joseph Dusenbury, formerly South Carolina's commissioner of rehabilitation, to head the council. Dusenbury hired Dart as vice chair of the council, a position Dart held along with Sandra Parrino, a major Republican donor and the mother of a cognitively disabled son. Dusenbury had known Dart from previous disability work, but didn't know the rest of the NCD.

When he heard he had gotten the job, Dart, with his usual preference for simplicity, boarded his funky truck along with Yoshiko, and they drove the whole way from Austin. Yoshiko remembers: "We just put the rice cooker and the computer and the mattress and the file cabinet and those essential things in a pickup truck and then came to Washington, DC." They probably had their valuable art shipped, but in keeping with their unassuming lifestyle, they found a very small condo when they arrived in Washington and crammed it with all their art and possessions. Yoshiko still lives in the condo today.

The NCD at that point decided, with the input of Dart, to write an ambitious strategic plan for disability policy. Dart did what he did best—he took to the road and canvassed the fifty states using his own funds and gathering evidence and testimony from people with disabilities. In less than a year, Dusenbury and Dart produced a radical report pushing civil rights and the implementation of independent living, with the federal government providing monies and structure. Not all the conservative Reagan appointees were happy. One of the more conservative members, Hunt Hamill, president of the National Sugar Refining Corporation, objected to the radical proposals in the report: "Thank you, but it goes too far to the left."[8] Dusenbury replied, "This was written by the American people with disabilities. Anyone object?" No one did after that.

Even so, the report was too radical for the Reagan administration. Private funds had to be used to publish the document. It had little or no effect on legislation. Dusenbury further annoyed the White House by going against its plans to dismantle various disability-related programs that should have been protected under 504. The result was a palace coup in which Dusenbury was asked to leave his office and Parrino stepped into place.

Dart's involvement and the role of the NCD would have been insignificant if the council had remained as it had been—a largely ignored, slumbering committee. But it was to become supercharged by a confluence of actions beginning, perhaps, with a first-term congressman from Texas named Steve Bartlett, who took his baby steps in Washington in 1983, elected in a midterm election during Reagan's nascent presidency. Bartlett, who looks like he was hired by central casting for the role of a Texas politician, with the requisite drawl, easygoing manner, and well-behaved hair, was born in 1947. He had been a city councilman in Dallas before coming to Washington. Bartlett describes himself as a conservative Republican, but was the type described by George W. Bush as "compassionate conservatives" and was engaged in what George H. W. Bush had called a "kinder, gentler conservatism." Bartlett had neither an interest in nor a family connection to disability, but as he sat at a hearing in Dallas in 1978 listening to people talk about *paratransit* (special transportation for people with disabilities), he realized that there truly was a problem. From the government's point of view, everything worked fine, but from the paratransit users' point of view, things were not working at all. "The government would say, 'Well, we've got these buses, and if you call them, they'll come and pick you up and take you there.' The difficulty is, is that what disabled people needed, is they needed a reliable replacement for the bus system to get to and from work!"

When Bartlett got to Congress in 1983, he was assigned to the Banking Committee. Despite having the lowest seniority, he volunteered to be on the Education and Labor Committee, where he discovered "a tiny little subcommittee" called the Select Education Subcommittee. That body had jurisdiction over what was then called "special education" as well as vocational education and rehabilitation for adults and other disability-related areas.

While Bartlett had his paratransit experience from Texas as a background, his main motive was perhaps more practical. The subcommittee was the smallest committee of all the committees in Congress, and no one wanted to be on it. Bartlett recalls: "I was thirty-four days old in Congress, by seniority. In my caucus, when I volunteered for the subcommittee, the rest of the Republicans in the caucus were stunned." But what seemed a gasp-inducing choice was really a very calculated one. "I recognized that in Congress, the people who are ranking members (if they're in the minority) or chairmen (if they're in the majority) have a higher level of clout than people who are not. The ranking member, or the majority equivalent, is the guy who actually gets to write the bill and present it to his colleagues. So I, being no fool, I said, 'Well, I'm going to do that.' This was the smallest subcommittee in Congress."

Since there were no other Republicans on the committee, Bartlett became the ranking member. Since the Democrats had little interest in the workings of the subcommittee that dealt with "special" education, the subcommittee became Bartlett's to do with as he wished. "I recruited a couple others, and they were fine, but basically it was me!" Of course, he realized that there might be some problems: "I remember my Republican colleagues, when I volunteered for it, I remember, they basically said, 'Are you sure you know what you're getting into? Because the wheelchair brigade is going to demonstrate in your office, and you're going to have people yelling at you and shouting at you,' and I said, 'What the hell, I had that on city council!'"

The same year, with Bartlett basically running the smallest committee in Congress, there were hearings on amending the Rehabilitation Act. Just as no one really understood the impact of the very few words of Section 504, no one would fully understand the impact of a very minor detail added to the larger amendment's legislation. Bartlett attended those hearings, and in one hearing on independent living, Lex Frieden spoke. Bartlett had recruited Frieden, a fellow Texan whom he had heard about from his staffer Pat Morrissey, who herself had cerebral palsy. Morrissey had been working on the small subcommittee beforehand, and Bartlett was instructed that no matter what he did when hiring staff, he had to keep her on. She was part of what Bartlett referred to as "the wheelchair brigade" in Washington. The group included Pat Wright, Paul Marchand, and the DREDF crew (even though only some of them used wheelchairs). Although Bartlett was resistant to many aspects of the ADA, Morrissey had great respect for Bartlett and says, "He is a man who responds to facts, and he has a great bullshit detector. So when people told him things that made sense, he would expand his understanding of what was going on."

At the hearing, which had been proceeding for a few hours, it was Frieden's turn to speak. He was supposed to testify on the need for a fully developed independent-living program. But as the testimony proceeded, Frieden watched as someone else made an eloquent defense of independent living. Not wanting to repeat what the previous speaker had convincingly said, and because he could see that the remaining House members were looking down in their notebooks and writing or doodling, Frieden thought, "Let me just throw something else in here while I'm at it. It seems to me that now is the time to create a blue-ribbon committee of leaders with disabilities to define for the Congress" the primary issues.[9]

Bartlett agreed and, in fact, may well have orchestrated this suggestion. The plan was to take the dormant National Council on the Handicapped, which Reagan had just staffed with fellow travelers and donors, and give it a mission—as well as some power to provide recommendations concerning the improvement of the lives of people with disabilities in the United States. An amendment the committee would put in the Rehabilitation Amendments Act would establish such a panel under the jurisdiction of the House of Representatives.

However, the Senate version of the legislation made no mention of the new blue-ribbon panel. When the House and Senate met to reconcile their two versions of the bill, according to Frieden, Senator Lowell Weicker said, "Wait a minute now; the Senate is not going to have the House throwing in some blue-ribbon committee here. There's not a need for another advisory group." Weicker, a moderate Republican from Connecticut, was a strong supporter of legislation for the disabled, particularly because his boy Sonny had Down syndrome. While Weicker was disappointed with the existing council, he didn't want yet another one, and certainly not one under House control. At six feet six, Weicker was imposing, formidable, and politically savvy. He was also known for his temper.

Weicker opposed Bartlett and Frieden's idea for a blue-ribbon panel because, as a senator, he didn't want the House to control this issue. But his staffer and friend John Doyle, formerly executive director of Connecticut Easter Seals, suggested making the panel a presidentially appointed independent federal agency. According to Doyle, "I dreamed up the idea that what we'd do was sort of having a Brookings or a Heritage Foundation inside of the government, but it would be a disability think-tank. It would not be beholden to any particular disability group or interest, and it would inform the Congress on a neutral basis on where disability policy should progress."

Weicker finally relented. What was a threat in Weicker's view turned into an amazing opportunity. That obscure council would become a powerful and effective voice within Congress and the White House and would write the first draft of the ADA.

Doyle was asked to be the executive director of the council, which he agreed to do only for six months. The council moved from the back basement of the old Mary Switzer Building to the eighth floor of the handsome Department of Transportation building. These new offices were in a cutting-edge, international-style building facing the equally modern circular Hirshhorn Art Museum and Sculpture Garden. As Frieden says, Doyle "understood that in Washington, perception is reality." Now the council moved literally and figuratively from its gloomy and hidden subterranean space to light-flooded, upscale real estate and into the klieg lights of Washington's center stage. The perception was now that disability would no longer be relegated to the back rooms but was front and center.

The council had half a million dollars to work with. Because of his insider knowledge, Doyle wrote the accompanying regulations, which in Washington is how you give teeth to a law, and in so doing, he deliberately strengthened the power of the council.

Within six months, Frieden was hired as the first full-time executive director along with Robert Burgdorf Jr., a disability rights lawyer. Sandra Parrino was now head of the council, with Dart and Frieden working below her. The perceived problem with the committee was that most of its members were rich friends of Ronald Reagan, and the committee was stacked with Republicans, many of whom were donors to Reagan's presidential campaign.

It wasn't just insiders who were suspicious. One of the major goals Dart and Frieden had was to convince the rank and file with disabilities that they should throw in their lot with this panel of elites. Remember that the average person with a disability lives at or below poverty level and that people with disabilities are the poorest minority group in the United States and have the highest unemployment rate of any minority. Add to that the legions of activists who cut their teeth on the civil rights movement and resistance to the Vietnam and Cambodian wars—hippies and yippies who were blocking buses and chaining themselves to bus stop poles. These people would be the least likely to put one of their eggs, let alone all of them, in the council's velveteen basket.

As Frieden notes, "Well, when I took the job as the director of the National Council on Disability, all the people . . . appointed to be council members, with the exception of Justin, were regarded as being elitist in the disability movement. I kept telling people, 'Look. Don't discount these Republican members despite the fact that they have heavy-duty Republican credentials.'"

Frieden points out that although the appointees were wealthy, they were very interested in promoting civil rights for people with disabilities: "Take a person like Marian Koonce, who was a personal friend of President Reagan's. President Reagan's son lived in Mrs. Koonce's garage apartment. Mrs. Koonce was the first woman to be elected chairman of a bank in the state of California. If anybody could've been associated with the Reagan conservatism, it would've been Marian Koonce. Yet she was the parent of children of short stature. Despite her wealth, fame, and personal friendship with the president, she understood as well as any other parent of a child with a disability what the issues were." But, Frieden adds, "That's what the disability community—the ADAPT advocates and others—didn't really understand about these council members. They just saw them as people who wore nice jewelry and fine clothing to dinner, and they didn't really understand that they understood—knew about disability and faced these issues."

Wright herself was skeptical that these Republicans could come up with an acceptable bill. As Yoshiko recalls, most DREDF members were initially wary of Reagan's National Council of the Handicapped: "Most of our advocates were Democrats, so they were very suspicious of the intention of the National Council. Justin had to really convince a lot of people that there were no vicious ambitions. Justin sincerely believed that we had to get what we really needed, regardless of the government [or] administration at that time. Anyway, little by little, he started convincing our colleagues. They were on the verge of being convinced when Wright said, 'Well, Justin, if you promise to eat lunch with me or with us if we pass the ADA, then I would cooperate with you.'"

Dart hadn't eaten a meal with anyone since he came back from Japan. Nevertheless, Dart agreed to Wright's wager. And when the ADA was passed, Wright called him on his bet to eat in front of her. Yoshiko remembers: "He said, 'I will,' and he did."

FOUR

LET RIGHT BE DONE

WHEN DREDF CAME to Washington and Ralph Neas teamed up with Pat Wright, and when some activists took to the streets, no one was actively thinking about a civil rights act for people with disabilities. As Mary Lou Breslin says, the claim that the ADA started in the early 1980s is a bit of "revisionist history." The main reason that people came to Washington was to preserve the laws about disability already on the books. The courts were making decisions that would negatively affect the lives of people with disabilities. There was, in fact, a backlash against the Section 504 regulations as they rolled out across the nation. In particular, the transportation industry became a big opponent since its livelihood was being encroached on by the demand that all trains, local transport, and buses, including over-the-road vehicles run by Greyhound and other carriers, had to be accessible. Conceivably, if the legal backlash hadn't happened, then there might not have been a need for the ADA, since people's civil rights would have been covered by the wide interpretation of Section 504. But the courts were slowly narrowing the scope of 504.

The first major court decision following 504 was a favorable one. Hard on the heels of the signing of the regulations and the occupation of the HEW office in San Francisco, the Seventh Circuit Court of Appeals in Illinois ruled that three disabled people who were suing the Chicago transit system could sue that agency because it received federal funds.[1]

But also in 1979, a ruling virtually negated or weakened that right. Frances B. Davis had been a nurse for about ten years. She was also profoundly hard of hearing and relied on hearing aids and lip reading to communicate. Like many nurses, she had the desire to advance a step and become a registered nurse. She applied to an advanced certification program in Southeastern Community College located in the small, sleepy town of Whiteville, North Carolina. The college, founded in the 1960s, was a public institution that received federal funds. Davis was hopeful in her application, but she was denied entrance because of her disability. Using the opening phrase of Section 504 ("No otherwise qualified individual with a disability . . . [can] be excluded"), she argued that she was precisely such an "otherwise qualified" individual who just happened to have a hearing loss. After all, she had been in the profession for a decade. The college argued that her impairment would interfere with her ability to care safely for patients. It said that lip reading would not be possible in the operating room, intensive care, or neonatal settings, since wearing a surgical mask would be required and therefor no lips would be visible. According to the college, sign language interpreters and other accommodations would present an undue burden on the finances of the college.

A lower court ruled against Davis, but a circuit court overturned that ruling. The case then went to the Supreme Court, which ruled unanimously that "otherwise qualified" was a tricky term. Essentially, the court said that a person might be "otherwise qualified," but particular disabilities would disqualify him or her from taking a job. The court used the example of a blind person who was applying to be a bus driver. That person might be otherwise qualified, but limited vision would disqualify the person from safely driving a bus.

Further, the court ruled that if the modifications were too burdensome, they did not have to be implemented. Indeed, the 504 regulations included the phrases "reasonable accommodation" and "undue hardship," and the Supreme Court decided that these phrases would carry a lot of weight. Lex Frieden, who helped write the 504 regulations, claims that he came up with the idea of "reasonable accommodation" in light of his experience with the dean in the parking lot. The wiggle room of that concept was clearly appealing to the business-friendly sector, and there would be much contention in the courts over the meaning of that simple two-word term.

The legal decision of *Southeastern Community College v. Davis* knocked the foundation of 504 to the ground, and within a couple of weeks, a cascading effect resulted in a decision in *APTA v. Lewis*, in which the basic tenets about making public transportation accessible were undone. APTA (American Public Transportation Association) was the main lobbying group for the domestic transportation industry. These municipal transit systems were against the 504 regulations that required providers to retrofit older buses with wheelchair lifts and to buy only new buses that had such accommodations. The association argued that the regulations were illegal, capricious, and made without due consultation with stakeholders. Coincidentally, or perhaps not, in a move akin to the role Michael J. Fox would play in *The Good Wife*, APTA hired a lawyer with a disabled child to plead their case.

The lower court ruled against APTA, but the US Court of Appeals ruled unanimously in favor of the association. While the Reagan administration could have contested the ruling, it did not. In fact, the decision specifically mentioned Reagan's new Task Force on Regulatory Relief and implied that the 504 regulations could now be revised in the direction the administration had been hoping it would.[2] Immediately following the ruling, the administration requested that the Department of Transportation write a new set of 504 regulations in keeping with the themes of deregulation. Interim regulations were issued in 1981, although it would take until 1986 for the final regulations to take place.

The interim (and final) regulations included a duo of two-word phrases to add to earlier pairs of "reasonable accommodation" and "undue hardship." These new phrases were "local option" and "special efforts." "Local option" did away with the notion that public transportation would follow a national policy as specified in the previous 504 regulations. Rather, localities would come up with their own mix of options, which might include buses with lifts but could also include vans with lifts or simply door-to-door paratransit systems. "Special efforts" would highlight the use of "special"—as in special education—and would set aside specific solutions for "special" people, most particularly specifying that if transportation companies spent 3.5 percent of their budget on accommodations, that would suffice. Full accessibility, a hope of the disability community, was now no longer a possibility. The ability to travel now would all depend on which cities or towns you were in and what decisions each locality had taken. And when you traveled from city to city, it would be like going from one country to another.

Wade Blank, the founder of the Atlantis independent-living community and a devoted transportation advocate, weighed in on the decision: "'Local option' is nothing but a sophisticated states' rights argument. . . . Anyone who's been through the 60's recognizes and understands that 'states' rights' was a mechanism through which Governor Wallace and other racist governors intentionally blocked civil rights for black people. I think the Reagan policy of local option is simply another slap in the face to disabled people."[3]

Was there a connection between the segregation of the past for African Americans and the issue around transportation and other accommodations for people with disabilities? The disability activists certainly thought so, and there are analogies. On the other hand, the political issues were a little different in the 1970s and 1980s. In the segregation era, the aim of the Southern states was to maintain the status quo and prevent the mixing of black and white populations. The goal of judges and legislators who questioned the broad sweep of 504 was somewhat different. There was no conscious motivation, and certainly no stated aim, to keep disabled people at home and away from nondisabled populations. It seems clear that the motivations were ideological and economic. And those two motivations were interconnected like dovetailed boards. The administration of Reagan and subsequent Republican presidents (and to some extent the business-friendly policies of the Clinton administrations) sought to reduce the role of government, eliminate unfunded mandates, and limit the ability of citizens to bring legal suits against the government, corporations, and businesses. To the extent that 504 and other laws went against those tenets, they seemed undesirable. Republicans were not trying to ghettoize people with disabilities.

Nevertheless, it would be an oversimplification to deny any element of discrimination in the opposition to laws that sought to integrate people with disabilities into the mainstream.

The legal decisions of the 1970s and 1980s weren't driven by animus toward people with disabilities as much as by misinformation or political conviction. In fact, the final Reagan regulations were written for the Department of Transportation when it was under the directorship of Elizabeth Dole, who is married to Senator Bob Dole, himself disabled and a supporter of legislation for people with disabilities. Elizabeth Dole's approach to the regulations would be typical of the complexity being discussed. She obviously supported people with disabilities, but her ideology led her to the notion that nationwide programs pushing against business interests were not appropriate. In fact, in 1985 a federal court ruling criticized her "unimaginably leisurely pace" in coming up with the final accessible transportation regulations.[4] If someone like Secretary Dole was delaying, then the Republican stance—being both pro-disability and pro-business—was no doubt creating a cognitive dissonance not easily resolved.

In that era, as now, conservatives feared activist judges who strongly interpret laws and act more like administrators than judges. In that climate, the courts were often favoring the presidential role and leaving the administrative and conceptual work on regulations to the president's men and women. This happened with the Department of Transportation regulations that produced "local option" and "special efforts." In favoring Reagan's regulations, the courts provided an Occam's razor to the complex issue involved in the string of vague terms with subtle variations of meanings that cry out for explication: *reasonable accommodation* (or *modification*), *fundamental alteration, undue burden* (or *hardship*), *otherwise qualified, special efforts*, and so on.

In 1984 and for several years afterward, the courts continued to hand down case after case that limited the scope of 504. In response, disability advocates forged new legislation to overturn those decisions. This was a battle between the interpreters of the law and the makers of the law. It seemed obvious to disability advocates like Wright and Neas that the courts were fiddling about 504 while disability rights burned.

The goal of the "wheelchair brigade," as Steve Bartlett had called the disability activists, was now to draft new legislation that would uphold the spirit of 504 and countermand the effect of legal decisions as quickly as those decisions were being made. One of the subsequent legal decisions that affected this quickly crumbling foundation was *Grove City College v. Bell*. Grove City is a small town in Pennsylvania not far from Pittsburgh. The college with its clock tower, church steeple, spacious lawns, and red brick turn-of-the-century architecture seems idyllic and bucolic. Founded in 1876 with Sun Oil Company (the company that would become Sunoco) money and powered by the Pew family, the college is listed by *US News and World Report* as the second-most politically conservative institution of higher education in the United States.[5] The college prides itself on promoting the values of free enterprise and free markets, as did Joseph Pew and his children, one of whom called FDR's New Deal "a gigantic scheme to raze U.S. businesses to a dead level and debase the citizenry into a mass of ballot-casting serfs."[6] Perhaps not uncoincidentally, the school has also been on the American Association of University Professors list of violators of academic rights longer than any other institution in the United States. So it is not surprising that in the early 1970s, Grove City College took the dramatic step of refusing all federal funds so that it would not have to comply with US government regulations and laws concerning civil rights. At that point, these rules were only applicable to institutions of higher education receiving federal funds. The particular regulation Grove City was trying to avoid was Title IX of the Higher Education Amendments Act of 1972, which prohibited gender discrimination in colleges and universities (the 1964 civil rights legislation had only protected people in the case of race and ethnicity).

Grove City College thought it was safely out of the grip of the government control because in 1976, it had been asked by HEW to sign an "assurance of compliance" form and had refused, thus also refusing to comply with Title IX's anti-gender-bias provisions. But after that maneuver, the college was surprised to find that its students were being denied federal grants and student loans for which they had applied. The college, along with four students, brought a legal action against the director of HEW. The Supreme Court ruled that the college was indeed subject to Title IX regulations, but that the entire college was not culpable—only the specific program, in this case the financial aid office, was subject to those regulations.

The fact that the entire college was not subject to the government regulations had a devastating effect on civil rights law in general and 504 in particular. From this point on, civil rights could only be enforced in private university settings if the discriminating program was receiving federal funding. If that program were not, then gender, race, age, and disability discrimination could blithely continue without punishment or sanction. For example, if an athletic program that was not directly receiving federal funds discriminated against women, people of color, or people with disabilities but the financial aid office that was receiving federal funds did not discriminate, then there was no problem with the athletic program's continuing to discriminate, as far as the law was concerned.

The cumulative effect of the three legal rulings—*Davis*, *APTA*, and *Grove City*—was to further erode civil rights and disability rights enforcement. One might reasonably wonder why there was such a judicial attack on 504 and other legislation related to disability. Was it a full-on legal attack by the Reagan administration in an attempt to deregulate and shrink big government? That argument would only work if all the judges were lined up in their ideological perspectives. But the American judicial system has a strong time-lag mechanism in which previous administrations' appointments linger on to create a judicial *longue durée*. Undoubtedly, the power of a presidential administration is significant both in the legislature and in the courts, but by no means is the power absolute. Moreover, business interests also combined with a pro-business presidential administration to apply pressure to the courts. In this case, the costs of implementing 504 were extensive, even though the law mainly applied to entities receiving federal funding. Yet businesses might well balk at being told what to do and spend regarding people with disabilities.

However, the judicial backlash, as it has been called, against 504 should not be considered a vast conspiracy to rob people with disabilities of their new-won and tentatively held rights. A more nuanced approach might study how 504 got inserted into the Rehabilitation Act. It was slipped in like a drug into someone's drink. Its effects were profound, but there was not a lot of legislative history and debate behind the insertion.

Remarkably, after all these years, no one takes credit for having inserted the 504 language into the bill. Most histories simply refer to "a staff member" or "staff members" who did the deed. Some suggest that James K. Pedley, who was an intern to Representative Charles Vanik, a Democrat from Ohio, may have been responsible for the language. Vanik was an old-style liberal who took seriously his commitment to the poor and working classes. He made a point of never spending more than $2,000 or $3,000 on his own campaign when he ran for election—a figure that, in today's terms, seems like it wouldn't buy enough pizza for a politician's staff.

In the late 1960s, Vanik became aware of the difficulties that people with disabilities had in the areas of transportation and employment and helped his Ohio voters on a case-by-case basis. Pedley was his legislative aide, a mere twenty-one-year-old at the time. The young intern wrote up the nondiscrimination civil rights language that Vanik then introduced in 1971 as a bill to amend the 1964 Civil Rights Act. This was the amendment that Hubert Humphrey sponsored in the Senate to no avail.

But the civil rights language traveled by some legislative sleight of hand into the Rehabilitation Act of 1973. Throughout the hearings and the three rounds of legislation following two vetoes by Nixon, no one actually discussed this nondiscrimination language; nor did Nixon mention it in his veto. In the second round of hearings, only John F. Nagle, chief of the Washington office of the National Federation of the Blind, referred to it.[7] In the third round, Martin LaVor, a legislative associate who was present, said, "As the Conference on the 3rd bill concluded, a few items remained. The last of them was Section 504. Although members were tired, they all agreed there should be no discrimination against the handicapped. Because it seemed so simple and straightforward, Section 504 stayed in the final version and became law."[8]

So simple and straightforward indeed! Probably no stringing together of words had such a profound yet confusing effect on disability rights until the ADA itself. Yet, given its import, Section 504 had virtually no legislative history, so when judges came to parse it for meaning, they had some evident difficulty. One of the ways that judges determine a ruling on legislation is by looking into the intent of Congress in passing a bill. That legislative history can flesh out the mere skeleton of words that define the law. But there were no discussions, no speeches, nothing by which to determine what the lawmakers had in mind. Further, being written up by staffers, the 504 regulations had little to no input from Congress.

To even further complicate the impact of these judicial rulings, Assistant Attorney General Bradford Reynolds, who, under the influence of Boyden Gray and Evan Kemp, had backed off attacking the Section 504 regulations, told the *New York Times* after the *Grove* ruling that he would apply it across the board. Previously, the main groups organizing to overturn *Grove* and related legislation had been those associated with the civil rights of women, African Americans, and the elderly. Now that Reynolds announced that 504 would be limited by *Grove*, disability groups got involved.[9] As Arlene Mayerson summarized: "Everyone was going to be in bed together whether we liked it or not. . . . It was kind of a shotgun wedding. . . . People in the civil rights movement had to be interested in what happened with disability rights."[10]

If you wanted to create civil rights legislation in Washington, you had to involve the Leadership Conference on Civil Rights (LCCR), which was headed by Neas. Wright had been working with Neas on issues related to gay and lesbian issues and had become close to Neas, gaining a seat on the LCCR executive committee. When *Grove* was expanded to include people with disabilities, she was placed perfectly to work on the Civil Rights Restoration Act of 1987, which aimed to repair the damage done by *Grove* and *Davis*.

Mayerson was the lead lawyer with Wright, who served as the strategist. The idea was to get involved in all the Supreme Court decisions that related to disability. It was kind of a David-and-Goliath story in which a rube from Berkeley comes to Washington to fight the power brokers. Mayerson recalled: "When I look back on then, I'm amazed at having the confidence or courage or whatever it took to kind of do what I did for the next few years which was just kind of bully my way into all the cases that were in the Supreme Court."[11] Mayerson presented what are known as *Brandeis briefs*—documents that present the sociology and psychology of the issues before the court. In doing so, she had two aims. One was to educate the court that there was discrimination based on disability. Her other aim was to actually get involved with the lawyers representing the client. She did that with several cases and coached the lawyers on how to approach the Supreme Court by persuading the judges that there was a specific kind of discrimination against people with disabilities.

In 1987, the Supreme Court seemed to have gotten it, at least for the moment, concerning disability. This realization came from *School Board of Nassau County v. Arline*. Jean Arline was a public-school teacher who had contracted tuberculosis twenty years earlier. She was in remission since that time, but recently had several lapses in which she tested positive for TB. The school board first put her on leave and then fired her. They claimed that she was not "otherwise qualified" and that she was not a person with a disability and thus not covered under 504, because she had a contagious disease. Mayerson and other advocates realized immediately that this case would have huge implications if Arline lost. Such a loss would mean that anyone who was HIV positive or had AIDS would not be seen as a person with a disability and thus would not be protected under 504.

Reagan's Justice Department had already taken a stand on this issue. Charles "Chuck" Cooper, who headed the Office of Legal Counsel and was extremely conservative by his own admission, issued a memo that stated that AIDS was not covered under 504 because of "fear of contagion" rather than physical handicap. Since Wright had been working on gay and lesbian issues, she had contacts with that community. Along with the disability folks, the gay and lesbian community wanted to act in the strongest possible way to defeat the Justice Department, which had also gotten involved with the school district in this case.

In addition to filing Brandeis briefs, Mayerson wanted to work with Arline's lawyers to get them up to speed on disability issues. The lead lawyer was George Radhert, who had taken up the case once it appeared that the case was going before the Supreme Court. Radhert, a large man with a prepossessing air, was a Yale-educated lawyer specializing in constitutional law. He had edited the *Yale Law Review*, represented the *St. Petersburg (Fla.) Times* publisher, and published many articles and books. He obviously believed he knew this law and had the stature to face the Supreme Court.

But Mayerson felt he didn't know about disability. After many unsuccessful phone calls, she finally reached him, but he said he wasn't interested in her help. He didn't want the case tied to AIDS, which was widely misunderstood and stigmatized at the time. He wanted to keep his case purely about the issues concerning his client.

Mayerson hopped on the first plane to St. Petersburg and "just showed up at his office." Radhert was busy, but Stephen H. Malone, who was Arline's original lawyer, was actually writing the brief. Mayerson hunted him down and persuaded him to work closely with her. She even ended up sleeping in his apartment. Together they "basically forced George Radhert every time he walked in the office to sit down and talk with us and kind of progress along that way."[12] Mayerson researched the legislative history behind the issues in this case, particularly emphasizing the point that disability is not just the impairment or disease you have, but is how others regard you. If others are fearful of you because you have AIDS or TB, then you are part of the protected class of people with disabilities. This concept is not intuitive, and so the judges needed to be educated in depth to be able to make a sound decision. Mayerson and Nan Hunter, who worked at the American Civil Liberties Union (ACLU) along with Chai Feldblum on lesbian, gay, bisexual, and transgender (LGBT) issues and AIDS, also held a moot court where Radhert could be coached on his answers. They worked on him so hard that they pushed him "beyond the point he thought was necessary."[13] Remarkably, Mayerson, this upstart, hippie lawyer from Berkeley, was now structuring the cases before the highest court in the land and providing deep background for superstars like Radhert.

And Mayerson prevailed. The decision written by Justice Brennan "sounded like a civil rights opinion." Mayerson and crew had succeeded in making the court understand that no longer would disability be about "that poor woman," as it was in *Davis*. Rather, according to Mayerson, "this decision is just filled with underlying principles like 'It's not the disability itself that causes the inferior treatment but the barriers, and fears, and stereotypes that are just as disabling as a disability.' And all that kind of civil rightsy stuff."[14]

FIVE

BANGING THE DRUM LOUDLY

THE NATIONAL COUNCIL ON Disability had its work cut out for it. Senator Lowell Weicker had told the NCD that it had to produce recommendations and do so quickly; otherwise, the council would disappear. Under pressure, Lex Frieden, as director, saw that he had to move.

The committee was made up of a variety of people with no activist background and no agenda. Frieden remembers: "The parents of kids with disabilities wanted to focus on fixing the special-education programs or the process for ensuring that kids could be integrated into public schools. The parent of an older child who had difficulty finding housing and attendant care wanted to focus the council's efforts on that. Another one of the members wanted to focus on transportation." For Frieden, there was an element of making sure these Reagan appointees kept focused on the more radical agenda of creating proposals that the larger disability community could endorse.

To that end, Justin Dart did what he did very well—he and Yoshiko Dart took to the highway as he'd done in Texas. When he was in Texas, he had already written up a document that might serve as the basis of the report, but he needed to road test it throughout the country. He started taking his first trip around Texas in 1978, and then took his first trip around the United States in 1981. By the time he was done with all his travels, he had traversed the lower forty-eight states on the continent five times. And except for the last trip, which he took after the bill was passed, he paid for all the trips out of his own pocket.

The drill was that Dart and Yoshiko would get in their car and drive from place to place by themselves. Arriving in a location, Dart would meet with local disability groups and local business leaders and politicians. Sometimes the members of the NCD would be with him. He listened to thousands of people with disabilities talk about their issues, and he would modify his Texas document to address the concerns of each locality. At first he thought each state would just rubber-stamp his Texas disability proposals, but he was surprised to learn that in each of the forty-eight states, people had specific objections, additions, and experiences that made him have to rethink his proposals. Dart was constantly asking people in each meeting, "So what did you think? Is this going to be okay?" Each night, according to Yoshiko, he would return to the motel room and scribble on his original document various amendments. In addition to his fact gathering, he collected what he called "discrimination diaries," personal accounts of the kinds of discrimination people with disabilities had experienced and had then written up for him.

Dart's trips are well known in the disability community and beyond. But few people understand the role Yoshiko played in making these cross-country canvasses possible. Yoshiko is an attractive woman with large glasses, hair pulled back tightly, strong cheekbones, and a beautiful smile. On any given trip, she would remain in the hotel or motel room when Dart went out to meet people. Her role was quite arduous, and she didn't particularly like what was required of her. "I enjoyed meeting our people, but, as you might imagine, Justin was very, very perfectionist. He was at meetings all the time, and in them, people would give us communications and contacts. We were constantly updating our documents and collecting the discrimination diaries. I had to send them all back to Washington, DC. I'd have to carry these heavy packages to either Federal Express or the post office wherever I was. After that, I'd have to do grocery shopping and then cook in the motel room. Cooking in the motel room meant cooking in the bathroom. The bathroom was my kitchen."

Yoshiko brought along ice coolers that had to be constantly refilled so that the food wouldn't spoil. As described earlier, Dart was perennially on a very special diet of vegetables and roots cooked in a Japanese style. Yoshiko had to prepare that food since he could never eat out. "I had to bring along a hot plate, but because many hotels and motels didn't allow the use of a hotplate, I had to be very careful, which was hard because I had to cook the bean sprouts for three days in a row. I couldn't cook large amounts, because they would go bad. I didn't have enough space to store the cooked food. I only had the ice coolers, and those had to be constantly drained of water and refilled with ice."

The housekeeping chores involved in living out of a motel room were substantial. Yoshiko laughingly remembers: "The bathtub became my dishwasher. I had to wash dishes and dry the dishes on towels I put on the floor." Asked if she was ever fed up or angry, she responds: "I didn't get angry, but there was just so much pressure, you know? I'd be cooking, particularly boiling bean sprouts, and then the telephone would ring. I'd go back to my cooking, and then Justin calls and asks 'How's everything going?' Then back to cooking. It was endless, that kind of stuff."

Dart would sometimes fly from one city to another and return in the same day, so Yoshiko would have to drive him to the airport and then pick him up later while also shopping, cleaning, and cooking. "I am not praising myself by any means, but I was determined to do whatever it takes. I come from a very hardworking, modest, poor part of Japan when I was growing up. We lost the war, and we had to pick weeds to eat them and all that stuff. I am very good at surviving—tremendous fighting spirit and modest living. That way, I did not get angry by any means, but I was under a lot of pressure. As soon as we came back to Washington, DC, then Justin had meetings with all these people in Washington, DC. Then, ahhh, finally, I can catch up on my business and so forth and take a shower. Sleep a few more hours longer." Then she ruefully adds, "But then the following Monday, we would start all over again and go to more places."

Like Yoshiko, so many unsung people were essential to getting the ADA passed into law. Conceivably, the ADA might never have been passed had not Yoshiko boiled bean sprouts in motel rooms. The work of numerous people, many of them female, while not making it into history books, provided the means for many other people to act in historical and political ways. And this supportive activist, we might call such a person, was particularly necessary in the case of people with disabilities living independent lives. Independence can be a solitary triumph, but more than likely, it takes a village to make people independent. If not a village then perhaps simply a crew of home health-care workers, a contingent of assistants, and even, in some cases, support animals. Of course, Yoshiko Dart was much more than simply a support staff, but the many unrecognized, dedicated people who helped the more prominent players in the disability movement well deserve our attention.

John Lancaster, who accompanied the Darts on two of their five trips and who was himself a disabled Vietnam veteran, remembers an incident in the Seattle airport when they were awaiting a plane to Hawaii. As the plane pulled into the gate, Lancaster noticed with surprise that written on the side of the plane were the words *Justin Dart*. When he asked about it, he was told that Dart's father had been on the original board of directors of United Airlines. As Lancaster boarded with the Darts, the flight attendant said they would like to upgrade the party to first class. But Dart demurred. According to Lancaster, he didn't like to take advantage of his social status or wealth. He told the flight attendant, somewhat huffily, that he would prefer to sit in economy with "the people." But Lancaster and Yoshiko, tired of their cross-country trip, prevailed on Dart to move up to the front of the plane, which he did reluctantly and with displeasure. He of course refused all food and alcohol.

But Lancaster did recall a paradoxical moment in Hawaii. Dart announced that he would take Lancaster out for a drink at the Halekulani Hotel in Waikiki, a five-star hotel that Dart mentioned he'd been at several times. Dart said, "I want to take you to one of the grandest hotels in the world." Lancaster recalls: "We sat in this covered space that forms part of the open-air lobby of the spectacular hotel." The beautiful blue sweep of the ocean was in front of them, with the white sands of Waikiki beach running down to the shoreline. Warm caresses of tropical air breezed over them. What was called for was a drink after their long trip. Lancaster continues: "The server came up and asked us what we wanted to drink. Justin asked me what I wanted, and then the server turned to him and said,

'And you, sir?' And he ordered a glass of the best red wine in the house." Lancaster was surprised because, as everyone knew, Dart didn't drink alcohol at all. They sat there talking for two and a half hours. "He sat there with that glass of red wine in front of him the whole time and he never took a sip of it. He just wanted it in front of him. He picked it up a couple of times and sniffed it, swirled it to check the body of the wine, holding it up to look at it, and then he'd set it back down." Like Ulysses resisting the sirens, Dart managed to have his wine and sniff it. But this incident perhaps gives us an insight into the powerful restraint necessary for accomplishing the nationwide trotting (or wheeling) that was needed to move the ADA forward.

Dart wasn't the only NCD member who traveled. Lex Frieden did as well. In light of all the experiences of the members of the council, they began discussing what their report would look like. Of the major recommendations, one would be that "Congress should enact a comprehensive law requiring equal opportunity for individuals with disabilities, with broad coverage and setting clear, consistent, and enforceable standards prohibiting discrimination on the basis of handicap." The report further notes: "Such a statute should be packaged as a single comprehensive bill, perhaps under such a title as 'The Americans with Disabilities Act of 1986.'" It would take four more years before such a bill would be put into law, but the council was taking the first steps toward that idea.

It took a lot of arm-twisting to even get the council itself to agree on this report. Made up of major Republican donors and people of wealth and privilege, the NCD wasn't the most likely place from which this recommendation would come. For example, Jeremiah Milbank Jr., a member of the council, was a prominent Republican donor and philanthropist who contributed to major neoconservative and libertarian groups. He was a strong backer of Barry Goldwater and was the chairman of the Republican National Finance Committee during the terms of Richard Nixon and Gerald Ford. Milbank had his own business and sat on the board of Chase Manhattan Bank. His bona fides for NCD membership included his involvement with the International Center for the Disabled, founded by his father in 1917 to help World War I soldiers returning from battle. He was exactly the kind of Republican who might well object to the concepts that John Doyle, Justin Dart, Lex Frieden, and Robert Burgdorf had cooked up. According to Frieden, Milbank was dubious: "He said, 'Well, the implications here may be profound when you're talking about the economy. A lot of my friends run and own businesses. I'm not going to be part of a group that's fought to put them out of business.'"

Frieden was puzzled about how to stem the mutiny. "I took Mr. Milbank aside after the meeting and I said, 'What would make you feel like these are rational recommendations?'" Milbank said he'd give it some thought. The next day, he called Frieden and said in his patrician voice, "I've got a guy flying in tomorrow to meet you. I hope you can spend time with him. He's an economist." Like Dart and many of the wealthy people on the council, Milbank used his personal wealth to hire John Raisian, an economist from the conservative Hoover Institution at Stanford University.

Frieden says, "I was in shock. I was frightened to death, because I knew the Hoover Institution was the most conservative public policy think tank in America. I felt like I'd been set up, in a way. Here, Milbank is . . . paying the bill for an economist who's going to tell us that this cannot be afforded, and this is going to be the end of the ADA."[1] Frieden and Burgdorf met with Raisian, and all three stayed up until midnight in the council offices trying to crunch the numbers and come up with the economic impact of the council's recommendations. Frieden recalls that, initially, Raisian said, "Frankly, I don't understand how I'm going to evaluate these somewhat arbitrary and somewhat esoteric and somewhat general recommendations of the council. . . . I can surely tell you how much it costs to run public transit systems in the United States, but it's going to be difficult to say what the economic impact of making every bus accessible will be." Frieden notes, "We had to educate Raisian about every one of the recommendations that we made and what the intent would be and what the implications would be and so on." Raisian did an economic impact study that was presented to the council.

Raisian's conclusions formed the core of the public relations pitch that was used from this point on to convince conservative Republicans that the council's recommendations made economic sense. Raisian emphasized that if the recommendations were implemented, there would be a general improvement in society. By improving employment opportunities for people with disabilities, there would be larger societal benefit. Taking people with disabilities off the government payroll would save money. As employees, these same people who had been a drain on the tax rolls would now be contributing to the tax base and would become more involved consumers. Everyone benefits. Raisian, according to Frieden, said, "Regardless of how you add the dollars, the outcome will be a benefit to the nation." Frieden adds, "If we hadn't done that report, the council probably never would have agreed on a consistent set of recommendations and certainly not a civil rights recommendation." He also notes that Raisian's name and his imprimatur of the Hoover Institution carried much weight in the Congressional Budget Office and at public hearings, especially with conservative Republicans.

The council held only four meetings a year, so the work of writing the report had to be vetted in those quarterly meetings. But the bulk of the daily work went to Frieden, Burgdorf, Dart, and the staff members. Some of the meetings were held away from the home office, at various locations around the country. Thus, Dart's travels and the council meetings afforded the opportunity to talk with and get feedback from a variety of disability groups and other organizations. Dart said, "We didn't have a lot of hearings but had a lot of consultations with service providers and with disability rights people, and did a lot of research."[2] Frieden had a list of fifty grassroots people around the country with whom he would speak each month.[3]

The biggest sticking point was whether the council should recommend an entirely new piece of legislation or should try to amend either the Civil Rights Act or the Rehabilitation Act by expanding Title V. Burgdorf and Evan Kemp favored amending an earlier act. At first they favored changing the Civil Rights Act, but then began to realize that since Reagan and his administration weren't so keen on provisions of the act in the first place, the council shouldn't open this can of worms. Amending the Civil Rights Act would risk weakening the initial act with debilitating amendments. Also, African American groups were reluctant to tamper with the existing civil rights laws that they had fought so hard to get enacted. As Lisa Walker, who worked on early disability rights legislation, said, "Saying that people were concerned that amending the Civil Rights Act would open it all up for amendment was not an overreaction. The busing fights were a huge problem at that time. There were many school systems that were still fighting desegregation." Rochelle Dornatt, Representative Tony Coelho's senior aide, recalls that when she approached Representative Major Owens and his committee, she perceived little enthusiasm for the ADA. In dealing with Owens's largely African American staff, including his wife, Maria Cuprill Owens, Dornatt said she received little initial support. She speculated that they felt civil rights were the domain of people of color and did not apply to this newer cohort.

In opposition to the amending approach, Pat Wright, Dart, and Frieden moved to supporting the idea of an entirely new piece of legislation. Eventually the council went with the ADA proposal, with one of the council members, Alvis Waldris Jr., coming up with the name Americans with Disabilities Act. Dart described the implications of making a whole new act and not amending the earlier Civil Rights Act: "The discrimination [against people with disabilities] takes far different forms and the Act of 1964, by just including us without any further measures, would leave a lot of the solutions to the imagination. You don't just have to open the door; you have to rebuild the door."[4] The requirements of the Civil Rights Act didn't require a lot of money. You just had to let people of color into places they were forbidden to go. But as Dart said, with the ADA, you would have to physically and conceptually transform places with ramps, accessible bathrooms, elevators, and so forth.

Dart felt that it would be wise to vet the report with the White House before it was released. Concerned that the Reagan administration might consider the proposal too radical, Dart arranged a meeting with Bradford Reynolds. As described earlier, Reynolds was variously in and out of the camp of disability rights. Frieden was very dubious about this meeting, given Reynolds's ruling on Section 504, so he refused to attend.

But Dart brought along a persuasive entourage. At the meeting was Madeleine Will, the then wife of the conservative columnist George Will, whose oldest son, Jonathan, had Down syndrome. The Wills had been dinner hosts to the Reagans, and George was

Reagan's occasional debate coach. Madeleine Will was appointed assistant secretary of special education and rehabilitation in 1983 and was a persuasive disability advocate. Also present was Gordon Mansfield, a friend of both Dart and Reynolds, who worked at and later headed the Paralyzed Veterans of America and would be appointed in a few years to be assistant secretary for fair housing and equal opportunity in the George H. W. Bush administration.

Reynolds had to be sympathetic to this appeal. Dart waxed eloquent: "Bradford, all we are asking for is that the promises of the Declaration of Independence, the Constitution, and the Bill of Rights be kept for people with disabilities. And I don't think that President Reagan wants to go down in history as being the president that opposed keeping the promises of the Declaration of Independence to thirty-five million people with disabilities." Dart recalled that Reynolds thought about it for five or ten seconds and said, "Justin, I agree with you. Not only is the president *not going* to oppose this; he is going to support your proposal, and you are going to get it in writing." When the larger report was published, it contained an endorsement from Reagan using language that Dart had supplied.[5]

While much preparation went into hammering out the details of these major recommendations, an even bigger part of the work fell into the area of public relations. The council needed to bang the drum loudly. It was important to get Congress educated and on the side of people with disabilities, and it was important to include the disability community so they were on board with the report. Many legislators might have some notion of fairness combined with pity, but the idea of disability rights as civil rights had to be promoted. Although the NCD initially came up with a three-hundred-plus-page report with appendixes and supporting data, the members realized that such a weighty tome delivered to a senator's office would probably end up as a doorstop or a bookend. The first step was to find out how the report's essence could be distilled into a potent and digestible form that would reach key players and the larger disability community itself.

Frieden went outside the usual box. He says that instead of presenting a dry-as-dust report in the usual vanilla binding, "we hired a professional to help us with the report. We did a survey. I went to members of Congress and said, 'What would you like this report to look like?' and they started talking about the contents. I stopped them short and said, 'No! I mean physically, what do you want it to look like?' You know, 'You want it to be eight and a half by eleven?' They'd look at me and then think for a minute and they'd say, 'I'd like it to be nice so that I can put it on my coffee table in the waiting room so other people can see it' . . . 'Use graphics,' and 'Make the print big enough for me to see it without my glasses.'"[6] With that thought in mind, the council published, in addition to the full report, twenty thousand copies of a slim seventy-five-page booklet: *Toward Independence: An Assessment of Federal Laws and Programs Affecting Persons with Disabilities—With Legislative Recommendations.* The report had a deep-blue cover in 8½-by-11 format, and instead of the usual agency seal, there was emblazoned on the cover the bold silhouette of an eagle printed in brightly reflective silver. The eagle was gliding decisively, beak forward with its talons assertively flexed. It was an eagle you didn't want to mess with.

On the day before the press conference was to be held to release the report, Frieden received an abrupt call from Robert Sweet, who was in charge of domestic policy at the White House. Sweet called Frieden at 6:30 a.m. and said, "Be in my office by eight a.m." Sweet had been sent, as a courtesy, an advance copy of the report. But he wasn't happy. In fact, he was appalled and said he was going to block the report in its entirety. "What in the world are you people thinking about up there?" he asked when Frieden arrived. "The President isn't going to touch this with a ten-foot pole. This goes even farther than Kennedy. . . .You've got to fix this!"[7] Sweet added firmly, "You will not issue this report."

Frieden replied, "Well, we are. We're an independent federal agency."

Sweet countered, "Yes, but every one of those members is appointed by the president, and they'll be discharged. We can do that. The president can fire them."

Frieden tried to hold his ground. "I'm sorry," he said, "but we're not going to do that. We're going to publish our report, and if the president wants to discharge people at that point, all well and good, but you will not tell me not to publish the report."

Sweet called in his boss, William Roper, who arrived at Sweet's office and asked, "What's the problem here?"

Frieden responded, "Dr. Roper, you're a physician. You're trained. You worked at the University of Alabama at the medical center there, and you actually had patients who had disabilities. What we're trying to do here is to produce a report with recommendations that will make those people a part of our communities, a part of our societies."

Roper replied, "That's exactly what we should do. Now, what's the problem?"

Sweet responded, "Well, you know, they're going to propose an equal rights law here. They don't understand that Reagan is the president."

Roper said, "They're an independent federal agency, and I'd love for them to make that recommendation, and I think the president will too."

The report was released with fanfare on January 28, 1986. The council held a reception on the night of the release. Like a scene out of the *West Wing*, Frieden and Sandra Parrino were fitted with concealed earphones that whispered the names of all the dignitaries who attended and facts about their lives. Frieden wryly observed, "To me, now, this was kind of amusing. That's the way things are done. When the disability movement started in 1972 we were like kids playing around at a little game. Now . . . it was like we'd gone from the pony league baseball players to the pros."[8] Remarkably, with the exception of Dart and Kemp, all of the people involved in the creation of this major legislative initiative had no training in Washington or elsewhere. They hadn't been interns or aides before. They came from the cornfields, the heartland, or the crash pads of Berkeley, stumbled around the corridors of power, cut their teeth on things they'd never tried before, and now were about to push through the largest civil rights legislation of the twentieth century.

Attending the event was, among others, Senator Lowell Weicker, who had threatened to sunset the council if it didn't make recommendations. He was so delighted with the results that he took the booklet to a reception for the report, held it aloft, and proclaimed, "This is the Declaration of Independence for people with disabilities!" And then, according to Steve Bartlett, Weicker physically embraced the report and said, "With this report, we will stand up to Nancy Reagan!"

Unfortunately, the date of the report's release was also the day on which the Space Shuttle *Challenger* blew up. Media savvy can only get you so far, and the national disaster was covered in the twenty-four-hour news cycle while the release of a report by a minor committee dropped off the radar. The crisis that resulted from the *Challenger* explosion also canceled a subsequent meeting at the White House with President Reagan. Instead, Vice President George H. W. Bush took Reagan's place, and perhaps that bit of kismet helped in the end, because Bush would become in a few years the pro-ADA president who helped get the bill passed. Present were Justin Dart, Parrino, Frieden, and Milbank from the disability side, with Bush and Boyden Gray on the White House side.

The group was told that the meeting with the vice president was simply a photo op. The photographer would come in, and there would be a picture taken with the vice president. Frieden recalls: "We went in there, and the vice president invited us to have a seat. He sat down behind his desk. I thought, 'Who changed the plan?' Bush sat back and he said, 'You know, I was briefed on this report yesterday, and I had a chance to read it last night. I'm really interested in what you all have done here.'" Bush talked about his own personal experience of disability with his brother Prescott, who was born with the use of only one eye; his uncle John Walker, who had polio; his daughter, who died in infancy of leukemia; his son Neil, who was severely dyslexic; and his son Marvin, who had had a colostomy as a result of ulcerative colitis just a few months earlier at the age of twenty-nine. The five-minute photo op turned into a twenty-five-minute meeting. At the end of that meeting, Bush said, "You know, obviously, I'm just the vice president. I'll be glad to share my ideas with the president at our morning meeting tomorrow." He added, "If there's ever anything I can do more to help you with this, I'll do it."

Although federal agencies cannot use taxpayer money on self-promotion, the private funds of the wealthy members of the council could provide assistance. Milbank was friends with Lou Harris, of the famous Harris Poll. Using monies from his International Center for the Disabled (ICD), Milbank suggested and funded a poll to uncover the attitudes and experiences of people with disabilities to make a stronger case to the public that this legislation was needed. Milbank, afraid that Dart's survey of Americans with disabilities might be biased, said to Frieden, "If my buddy Lou Harris does a poll of people with disabilities, and he tells me that most of them aren't working, I'd believe it. You could publish that in *New York Times* or the *Wall Street Journal* and everybody else would believe it."[9]

Frieden worked on the questions for Harris with the assistance of Deaf advocate Frank Bowe, who was the head of ACCD, the national cross-disability organization. Frieden admits, "Frank and I sort of dictated the beginning of that poll. . . . Predictably, he [Humphrey Taylor, president of the Lou Harris Poll] came up with answers that we expected him to come up with. I say 'predictably' because we knew which questions to ask to get the right answers."[10] The results were published by Milbank's organization as *The ICD Survey of Disabled Americans: Bringing Disabled Americans into the Mainstream.* Some of the conclusions were shocking: half of the one thousand respondents said their incomes were less than $15,000 compared with a quarter of nondisabled citizens. Sixty-seven percent were unemployed. The number of disabled in the United States was determined to be thirty-six million. If those numbers were accurate, something had to be done. All eyes turned to Congress to see how well it would follow the council's recommendations.

SIX

FLAT EARTH, DEAF WORLD

ONE LONG YEAR passed after the report was issued, but no legislation was forthcoming. In those dark days of 1984, Richard Scotch,
professor at the University of Texas at Dallas, noted that "the effec-
tiveness of the disability rights movement appears to have peaked in
1978." Scotch attributed this decline of the disability rights movement to the absence of any "single charismatic figure who serves to
unify its various components and factions." He added, "Decline can
become self-reinforcing, for in the absence of political advances the
incentives for collective action diminish."[1] From his vantage point in
1984, there wasn't a great deal of hope. In fact, in reading Scotch's
words, one has a hard time imagining that anything like the ADA
was on the horizon. By 1988, it looked as if the majestic eagle on the
cover of the report was spiraling down for a sobering crash.

In addition to negative court rulings, corrected by some smaller
victories in the legislative realm, the 1980s saw a continual chipping
away at the larger civil rights claims of Section 504. The erosion of
universal transportation to the lesser "local option" was contentious
and disturbing. But one of the most notable of these erosions was the
increasing use of "carve-outs" to restrict 504 from applying to various groups—notably those with conditions that essentially offended
the sensibilities of conservative politicians and their constituencies.
This meant that people with AIDS or who were HIV positive, along
with sexual minorities in the LGBT community, people who were

drug or alcohol addicted, and the like, were made personae non gra-
tae when it came to civil rights.

According to Ruth Colker, this practice of carving out groups
for which portions of section 504 would not apply began in 1985
with one legal case and continued the following year with another.
In *Doe v. US Postal Service*, a Jane Doe had been offered a job with
the Postal Service. When she announced that she was having sexual reassignment surgery, the offer was rescinded. Doe sued and ran
into trouble because the court ruled that Section 504 was intended
to cover only "traditionally recognized handicaps." Sexual reassignment was not, therefore, in this parlance, a traditional handicap.

In the following year, another case brought forward was *Blackwell
v. United States Department of Treasury*. William Blackwell was up
for a job at the Treasury Department but was passed over in favor of
another candidate. Blackwell claimed bias because he wore feminine
clothing. This time the court found that transvestites could qualify
under 504. However, the Treasury Department claimed in trial that
it did not discriminate against Blackwell for being a transvestite (a
condition the court ruled was protected under 504 as a disability) but
for being a homosexual (a minority not protected under 504 since
homosexuality was not an impairment or medical condition). Homosexuality had been removed from the *Diagnostic and Statistical
Manual of Mental Disorders* (DSM) in 1973, so it was not a medical
disorder. Transgender identity was still in the DSM and would thus
fall under the category of impairment. The court found this rather
twisted and distasteful argument valid and made a decision in favor
of the Treasury Department.

These decisions made their way to the floor of the Senate when the
Civil Rights Restoration Act was under consideration. Senator Jesse
Helms, the well-known ultraconservative, used these court decisions
as a basis to tar the act, claiming that it sanctioned "transvestitism and
other compulsions or addictions, which churches or religious schools
might once have felt comfortable in regarding as moral problems, not
medical handicaps."[2] Although Helms lost on the veto override, he
obviously found grist for his Moral Majority mill and set a precedent
of criticizing disability rights laws by pointing to sexual minorities and
people with addictions as the main beneficiaries of such legislation. In

the Fair Housing Act Amendment in 1988, Helms succeeded in carving out transvestites from civil rights protection. Tellingly, only two senators had the courage to oppose this amendment.

Meanwhile, another factor that played out in the role of HIV/AIDS in disability legislation was spurred by the Reagan-appointed Commission on the Human Immunodeficiency Virus Epidemic. The commission's findings recommended civil rights legislation particularly for people with HIV/AIDS who were experiencing discrimination. Since this was the height of the AIDS panic, discrimination abounded. Disability proponents would be faced with a difficult choice—include AIDS in the ADA and face the wrath of Moral Majority conservatives, or drop AIDS from the ADA and face the distress of the LGBT community.

One of the people who worked on promoting HIV/AIDS-supportive legislation was Michael Iskowitz, a slim man with a corona of curly hair framing his face. He received his PhD in clinical psychology from Temple University and went to work as a therapist. But he realized he wanted to do more about the poor and underprivileged on a bigger scale than he could do one-on-one in his practice. To accomplish this goal, Iskowitz went to law school at Northeastern University. As a gay man, he was haunted and concerned about AIDS and felt that Washington was not doing enough. He traveled to DC during an internship period and relentlessly followed Senator Ted Kennedy around for ten weeks. Iskowitz recalls: "I just decided to start stalking him until I could get an opportunity to say to him that I thought he should hire someone to work specifically on AIDS, to kind of begin to put a framework of AIDS policy in place. Anyway, I finally got to have that conversation with him, and suggested he hire someone to deal with AIDS. He said, 'Well, that would be you!'"

In working on an AIDS agenda with Kennedy in 1987, Iskowitz inevitably came upon the disability rights advocates. At this point, according to Iskowitz, the AIDS community was new and fearful: "The most vocal folks, in an AIDS advocacy context, were rich gay men, whose life experience was very different from people who had lived their entire life with a disability. These men didn't see themselves as disabled. The disability community had lived with all of these assaults on it for all these years. Then, asking the disability community to take on AIDS and all of the baggage and fear that was connected to it at that point was a big thing. They were quite leery of it as well."

It wasn't a match made in heaven, initially. The AIDS community didn't see itself as disabled; nor did the disability community see itself as automatically aligned with the gay men who were at that point the main victims of AIDS. Iskowitz describes how this alliance was accomplished: "It was really Kennedy and Pat Wright, who were both the people, in a situation like that, to bring the communities together. It really requires people who have the trust of everybody."

A crucial concept in the disability-AIDS alliance was that there was not going to be a divide-and-conquer mentality. It would have been easy, given the Jesse Helmses of the world, to sign deals to get things passed in Congress by allowing carve-outs for LGBT people. As Iskowitz explains, legally speaking, disability had to include sexual orientation: "Particularly anything that went to the definition of who was covered under the bill, that was sacrosanct. For legislators who always want to make definitions more restrictive and less 'onerous,' there would be attempts to chip away at groups that are protected. The community really needed to hold together and push off any attempts to do that. Because, I mean, in the end, it was all about going with the facts and getting past the fear, and saying that no matter who you were or what piece of the community you were from, you would be protected."

Holding this coalition together was not that easy. Janine Bertram, Evan Kemp's wife, recalls: "There was a fight over HIV. . . . It was not a fight, really, but certainly a strong discussion between Pat Wright and Evan, because the civil rights groups were adamant that HIV be covered. And Evan called several disability groups all over the country, leaders of independent living centers, and nobody at that time—I mean this is certainly early on in the AIDS awareness campaign, too—but really, nobody cared. It was not a bottom-line issue for the disability community."[3] It would be the job of people like Wright to get disability activists to care.

Wright wasn't working on this alone. In fact, many of the people fighting for disability rights and later the ADA were gay and lesbian. Included in that group were Curt Decker and Congressman Steve

Gunderson, who was not out at that time, along with Allen Gins-more and Tom Sheridan.

One person concerned with the LGBT community in the disability rights struggle was Chai Feldblum. The small, thin, wiry woman with glasses speaks with a rapid-fire New York accent. Her animation, when she talks, bespeaks the Hebrew meaning of her first name—"life." Born in Washington Heights in Manhattan in 1959, she is the daughter of an Orthodox Jewish rabbi. Her mother died in a car accident when Feldblum was only fifteen. Feldblum graduated from Harvard Law School and clerked for two judges, one of whom was Justice Harry Blackmun of the Supreme Court. In 1986, she was fresh out of law school and clerking for Blackmun during the *Arline* case, in which Jean Arline was fired for having tuberculosis. That case, which ended up asserting that people with contagious diseases were covered under 504, was Feldblum's lesson in disability studies since she conducted the research for the case for Justice Blackmun. This was the same case that Arlene Mayerson had done so much preparation on. Feldblum recognized the significance of *Arline* for the LGBT community since the finding implied that AIDS was therefore protected under 504. Feldblum, herself lesbian and bisexual, was a natural fit with these insights. She recalls: "It was because of the AIDS—the ravaging of the community that was happening at that point in 1987—that I decided I would work for an AIDS advocacy group. I worked for six months for the AIDS Action Council and then, after that, moved to the AIDS Project of the American Civil Liberties Union."

In those years, Feldblum worked on fighting all attempts to exclude people with AIDS from Section 504. These attempts included the Justice Department memorandum of 1986, the Civil Rights Amendments Act of 1987, and the Fair Housing Act of 1988. Each of these efforts had conservatives like Helms trying to eliminate AIDS from legal protection. Feldblum worked with Senators Tom Harkin and Gordon Humphrey to come up with an amendment that would protect people with AIDS. However, the language of the amendment was somewhat confusing. It protected people who were HIV positive and who had AIDS, but it also said that anyone with a contagious disease would not be "otherwise qualified." The next day, National

Public Radio and the *New York Times* announced that people with AIDS were excluded from the Civil Rights Amendments Act. This was exactly the opposite effect that Feldblum had wanted. "I was already on edge from working on the AIDS Action Council, and that really put me over the edge," she says. Believing she had failed, she experienced her first panic attack, which eventually led to a diagnosis of anxiety disorder.

During her involvement with the Civil Rights Amendments Act, Feldblum met Pat Wright, and the two women became romantically involved. The relationship lasted a year, but it had an effect on the political situation. According to Feldblum, they met after her feelings of failure and panic: "It was shortly after that time in January 1988. Pat likes to go in when you're vulnerable. That was always her thing, so I was totally vulnerable in January 1988. I thought I had screwed things up for people with AIDS and HIV, and Pat sort of took me home. I have so much to be thankful, actually, for Pat in terms of my life. It was a fine relationship from about January 1988 to December 1988. . . . She's also the best nurturer ever when you're vulnerable."

Feldblum emphasizes that Wright's greatest strength is also her greatest challenge: she is "completely, completely manipulative. I mean, that's who she is. That's part of her brilliance. The disability community has benefited from her manipulation." On a personal level, that quality put a further strain on Feldblum, who had never been in a long-term relationship before. Now she was going out with Wright, who was not only ten years older but also a very dominant, "ballsy woman," as Wright herself put it.

Feldblum tried to end the relationship after six months, a period she notes was her normal neurotic maximum. "Pat, who hates to lose, she was like, 'I am gonna make it past the six-month mark,'" Feldblum remembers. "I literally once said to her in the fourth month that, 'Oh, we should split up.' She goes, 'Let me make you a counter offer.' She really said that—'Let me make you a counter offer!' I mean, the woman was fucking brilliant." Feldblum stayed on and became the official lawyer for the ADA negotiations. Normally that position would have fallen to Mayerson, who had done so much work for Wright and DREDF, but she had continued to live in Berkeley with her two small children. With the ADA, a full-time lawyer in Washington was a necessity, and Feldblum took the job. She says, "I'm sure that Wright would have never allowed me to do the work I did on the ADA if I had left her. I mean, she wouldn't have—no matter how much she needed a lawyer, she would have gotten rid of me. It's about control."[4]

The relationship began to break up at that point, with Wright returning to her former partner, Kelly, who had a young daughter, Nicole. Kelly had broken up with Wright but now wanted her back, and Wright, in turn, wanted the relationship with the child. As it turned out, Kelly's partner was killed in a car accident and Wright ended up coraising Nicole. Michael Iskowitz, who by now had been working with Wright and had become a friend, took on the role of father.

Wright made sure that Feldblum always checked everything with Mayerson. "She wasn't thrilled with, essentially, substituting me as the main lawyer, as opposed to Arlene, who actually worked for her," Feldblum says. "Arlene wasn't as available. What she made sure to do is to say, essentially, 'Chai, I'm anointing you to do this, but you must always check everything with Arlene.' Which was fine with me. Arlene was a brilliant lawyer and had been doing this for fifteen years."

Aside from trying to keep the LGBT community together with the disability community and trying to thwart legislation that would remove Section 504's protection of people with HIV/AIDS, the larger problem for the disability community was that the recommendation of the council was being ignored. The blue-covered, silver eagle inspired *Toward Independence* came out in 1986, and while various groups were working on reversing court decisions, Congress was not acting on the recommendations in that report. In fact, the report had basically sunk to the bottom of the dust heap of forgotten legislation. The National Council on Disability felt it had to act, despite discouragement in the disability community. Dart summed up the sentiment at that moment: "We can't even enforce 504. Why waste our time talking about more? The day of civil rights is gone; there will never be another civil rights law passed."[5]

It seemed quixotic to be championing civil rights when all around were despairing. Yet that's exactly when Dart decided to act on an idea that seemed so crazy it just might work. On January 29, 1988, the NCD published a follow-up report titled *On the Threshold of*

Independence. It was a wake-up call to legislators. As a kind of re-port card for disability rights legislation, the new report implied that Congress would receive a failing grade thus far. Like a good teacher, the report printed at the end a sample piece of legislation that could be used as the ADA, as if to say, "Look, class, this is how to do it." Dart and staffer Burgdorf wrote the sample legislation.

Burgdorf, a square-faced man with a moustache and a receding hairline, was the principal author. He was born in 1948 in Evans-ville, Indiana, and a case of polio when he was a year old atrophied his right arm. Growing up in a working-class family in which his father was an electrician, he was stung by various kinds of injustice. In particular, he was denied employment as an apprentice electrician because of his disability. To redress those wrongs, Burgdorf became a lawyer in order to work for the rights of others. He attended the University of Notre Dame, graduated with a law degree, and held positions in a variety of disability-related agencies while managing to write articles and books. Finally, on the NCD, he drafted the leg-islation he hoped would become the ADA.

Not everyone agreed that writing up this prototype of disabil-ity legislation was the right thing to do. Liz Savage, a lobbyist very involved with the ADA, noted that "the Council had no legislative expertise and came up with the proposal, and I don't think that's appropriate. You know, when you work in Washington you're aware of what's going on." Savage thought that Burgdorf and the council didn't know "what was going on." They were naive to write up leg-islation that clearly had no chance of passage. Savage did concede that Burgdorf's "act" was "introduced as a vehicle for discussion."[6] Frieden put it another way; the proposed bill "was pretty gutsy, in a way, because a federal advisory agency doesn't write legislation, Congress writes legislation."[7]

Senator Harkin aide Bobby Silverstein says that he and Wright had argued with Burgdorf and the NCD: "We had hour after hour of discussion with the council . . . to try to get them to do a bill that was very strong but still reflected some sense of what's possible. And we weren't successful . . . because the National Council was in fact going around the county talking to advocates and saying, 'We're going to include what we think is right, and the hell with politics.' And so the actual bill that was drafted had some . . . extreme provisions" like the provision that creates only one reason for a company not to comply with the law—bankruptcy. Anything short of bankruptcy, such as "undue hardship," would not apply in this version of the ADA. Such a draconian punishment obviously went down well with the grassroots disability folks, but would never work with Congress or with the powerful business community, which demanded a less stringent standard. Silverstein, an old hand at Congressional politics, adds, "We . . . recognize[d] that this was not the members' [of Congress] bill. It was the disability community's bill." And that meant it would not be "the strongest possible defensible bill."[8] Summing up, Silverstein says that "there was no way in hell . . . [it was] going to be adopted. It was just a bill that was not going to go anywhere."

The proposed ADA was an ambitious and overly idealistic piece of legislation. Many refer to it as the "Flat Earth ADA" or the "Flatten the Earth ADA." The idea was that the legislation would flatten the playing field for people with disabilities by eliminating all barriers and doing so immediately. In this view, all buildings, new and old, would be transformed. All transportation would become accessible. The proposed legislation was about as radical a piece of civil rights legislation as one could imagine, and it was coming from a largely conservative Republican council.

According to observers, Burgdorf always thought that he was right and that other people were always wrong. He thought his version of the ADA was the morally correct one, and he may well have felt that people sold out in later versions of the bill.

The council now went into lobbying mode and approached senators and congresspeople. One of the obstacles to overcome was the disability community itself. Cynthia Jones, a disability activist and journalist, said that Dart had met with her, trying to push this version of the ADA. She was fearful of the outcome if such a bill were to pass: "Oh, my God—trying to get a civil rights piece of legislation passed in a Republican administration. I said, 'The only concern we have is that we don't want to screw up what little rights we have under 504. We don't want to kill it, even though it's not where it needs to be.'"[9]

To get the bill passed, the NCD had to approach major politicians. Parrino, Dart, and Frieden regarded Senator Weicker as crucial.
Obviously, he would support the legislation. But what was needed
now was Democratic support. One of the major players was Representative Tony Coelho, Democratic majority whip.

Coelho might have been the perfect choice. He had epilepsy and
was very public about this disability. A thin man with striking dark
eyes and eyebrows, he resembled a cross between Rudolf Nureyev
and Don Knotts. Coelho was born in 1942 in Dos Palos, a small,
dry, flat town in the San Joaquin Valley in California. When he
was sixteen, he had an accident on his parents' farm. A farmhand
was recklessly driving a pickup truck with Coelho in the passenger
seat. The vehicle went out of control, flipping over in the process
and then landing in the water of a roadside canal. Coelho's forehead smashed against the windshield, but he managed to get out
from under the water through the truck's window. A year after that
trauma, he lost consciousness one afternoon in the dairy barn as he
was milking the cows. His family found him convulsing and staring
without seeing, spittle bubbling out of his mouth. They called a
doctor, who told his parents he was having seizures. Coelho recalls: "My parents didn't accept that diagnosis. They were taught
in their religious beliefs that if you had [seizures], it meant that you
were possessed by the devil. They believed that God would punish
a family if someone in it committed a major sin." In his Portuguese
peasant culture, "they believed that the cause of [seizures] was that
somebody had had sex with an animal. So it was a heavy burden
that they were carrying. Of course, they didn't tell me any of that;
I didn't know any of that. So they were reluctant for me to have
seizures in public."

His parents then took him to faith healers. "We would go to these
witch doctors who would turn the lights off, have candles lit, [and]
they would pour hot oil on my chest, on my head, on my forehead,
pray in many different languages, and so forth. That didn't work,
and I didn't believe. Finally, one witch doctor spoke to my mother
in Portuguese, which I understood, and said to her that there was no
way he could help me, because I didn't believe. My mother scolded
me for not believing, and I said I just didn't believe, and I couldn't

believe and I didn't want to go to another witch doctor." The family ceased its efforts.

Coelho didn't get the diagnosis of epilepsy until he tried to enter the priesthood in 1964, inspired to do some good in the world after the shock of the Kennedy assassination. His parents, frat brothers, and girlfriend of five months were all aghast. In his physical exam for the seminary, he was properly diagnosed. The physician, John Doyle, told him, "I have some good news and some bad news. The good news is that you're unfit for military duty. The bad news is that you will not be able to become a Catholic priest, because canon law, established in 400 AD, said that if you have epilepsy, you're possessed by the devil."

This began a personal downward spiral for Coelho, who applied for various jobs but was rejected every time because of his epilepsy. His driver's license was revoked because people with epilepsy are not permitted to drive, and for a twenty-one-year-old in California, the loss of a license is tantamount to taking away your right to freedom, justice, and the American way. Coelho drove anyway, breaking the law. He was so depressed that he took to drinking and was, by his own estimation, drunk by noon every day. He became suicidal and decided to take his life. One day, he got drunk and went to a precipice in Griffith Park, in Los Angeles, and planned to leap to his death. As he hesitated before jumping, he had a moment of revelation watching children below playing with that supercharged life-force ricocheting between them and amplified by screams and laughter. "Something clicked, and I said I was going to be just like those little kids, and that I was never going to let anything get me down again." Coelho says he never considered suicide after that moment.

Through a random connection, Coelho got the opportunity to live at Bob Hope's house and be a companion to Hope's son Kelly, who was two years younger than Coelho and in need of support. Hope suggested that if he couldn't go into the church, Coelho might consider politics. The movie star signed a loan that allowed the young man to make the transition to politics and become a staff person for Democratic representative Bernie Sisk. Coelho recalls: "Sisk became my father, my mentor, everything. I had seizures in front of him. He never let that bother him. He got very upset when his chief of staff tried to fire me, saying I was not capable of doing the job. Sisk ended up firing the complainer and promoting me to chief of staff."

On Sisk's retirement in 1978, Coelho ran for the same congressional seat and won. In that election, his Republican opponent used the epilepsy as a campaign issue. The opponent said at an event, "Tony's a very sick man. What would you think if he went to the White House arguing a very critical issue for us in California, such as water, and had a seizure?" A reporter called Coelho asking him to comment. "You know," the reporter said, "your opponent last night said you might go to the White House and have epileptic fits. What's your reaction to it?" Coelho's response: "Well, in the thirteen years I've been a staffer in Washington, I've known a lot of people who went to the White House and had all kinds of fits. At least I'd have an excuse for having one." Coelho notes that after that riposte, no one ever used his epilepsy against him again.

Coelho was not just public about his epilepsy; he also sponsored and supported bills related to disability. One day in 1988, Roxanne Vierra of the NCD approached him. Her husband, Fred Vierra, headed a cable company, was Portuguese, and was very close friends with Coelho. Roxanne brought along the cochair of the council, Sandy Parrino. They pitched Burgdorf's proposed legislation to a skeptical Coelho.

He had by then already met with and talked to Wright, who had expressed her opposition to the proposed legislation as it stood. She and other leftists were deeply suspicious of Burgdorf's proposal especially because it came out of the conservative council. One thing it lacked, and that many radicals wanted, was stronger language for employment opportunities. Without these, Wright and others felt, you could have all the legislation in the world, and still employers would not routinely hire people with disabilities. Since unemployment among people with disabilities was nearly 75 percent, this was a very big issue. Coelho recalls: "Pat and her group—the Judy Heumanns and so forth—they were talking down the NCD group. They were saying that it was too conservative. Roxanne's group was saying that what Pat's group was trying to get done would never get through Congress. So I started looking at both proposals. I was determined that I wanted to do something, and it corrected a lot of the discrimination that I had been through. I decided that . . . I would . . . put the NCD proposal before the House, and then listen to Pat and her crowd, and make modifications as we went through. So they were not happy with me, because I put in the so-called conservative Republican proposal, but I did."

As a Democrat, Coelho saw himself as naturally aligned with the DREDF people. He characterized himself and them in blunt terms: "You know, raving idiots: 'We want everything *now*.'"[10] Coelho supported the NCD proposal despite the warning from his staff assistant Heidi Hicks, who said, "You know the [disability] community is going to go bananas. They're going to think you're crazy to be part of this." Coelho responded, "Well, they may be wrong. You're never going to get through what they want, so maybe I start somewhere in the middle."[11]

A month or so after the NCD report was released and while these lobbying efforts were beginning, major shock waves began to rumble from a small college campus in the northeast corner of Washington, DC. Gallaudet University is one of only three federal institutions of higher education, along with West Point and Annapolis. While the latter two are devoted to the training of military elites, Gallaudet is dedicated to educating Deaf students. Gallaudet was founded in 1864 by an act of Congress signed by President Lincoln, and its master plan was designed by Calvert Vaux and Frederick Law Olmsted, who created Central Park and Prospect Park in New York City and the campuses of the University of California at Berkeley, Stanford University, and the University of Chicago. Gallaudet is a stately collection of High Victorian Gothic buildings thronged with Deaf students animatedly communicating in ASL as they go about their studies.

On March 6, the board of trustees of the university, all of whom were hearing, came up with a much-awaited recommendation for the new president of the university. The trustees nominated Elizabeth Zinser, the only hearing candidate of a pool of three finalists. Students and faculty had been hoping that after more than a century, a Deaf president would at last be selected. As disability rights and activism had grown over the past decades, Deaf rights and activism had too. Upon receiving the bad news, the Gallaudet students reached a breaking point in their frustration. On the following day, in the wee hours of the morning, students pulled fire alarms that set off blinking klieg lights to awake the nonhearing. They assembled in a mass meeting and then marched to the wrought-iron front gate of the university, where they chained the doors shut and pushed a bus to block the entrance. Mass demonstrations not only gripped the campus but also captured the interest of national and international media. Congressman David Bonier remembered: "Students, faculty, staff and friends of Gallaudet stood symbolically, peacefully, and uniformly chanting, 'Deaf President Now,' [and] the public saw those chants every day on TV, in the newspapers not just in Washington but around the country. . . . When hundreds marched from Gallaudet to Capitol Hill to demonstrate against decades of discrimination and to protest for civil rights, I was proud to meet them. I invited students, and teachers and alumni, all deaf, into my office and they communicated with such passion. Their determination was very, very strong. And I remember thinking to myself, 'This is the Deaf Selma; [t]here's no turning back.'"[12]

Given that Gallaudet was a federal institution, the attention of the government also turned to those tumultuous days on campus as students took over university buildings and held twenty-four-hour protests. Vice President Bush had written a letter to the board of trustees on March 1, urging them "to set an example and . . . appoint a president who is not only highly qualified, but who is also deaf."[13] By Friday, March 11, twenty-five hundred Gallaudet students and allies marched on Capitol Hill. Two days later, in response to the demonstration, the trustees relented and I. King Jordan, one of the Deaf candidates, was appointed president. Phil Bravin, also Deaf, was named chairperson of the board of trustees. A revolution had occurred.

It was impossible to be in Washington during this time and not be impressed by the persistence of the students and the power of this Deaf protest. While many Deaf people didn't consider themselves disabled (seeing themselves as a linguistic minority rather than being defined by a physical impairment), certainly the members of Congress had to be aware that there was powerful ferment for disability rights. Coelho later said in Congress, "It is time, I think, to stand up. I think Gallaudet proved that and sort of lit a spark not only with the hearing disability but with the disability community all over the country. We do not want to be patient anymore."[14] The dark days of disability rights might have been brightened by the success at Gallaudet. With the wind of change blowing at their backs and within weeks of the Gallaudet victory, Weicker and Coelho introduced the ADA legislation to the House and Senate on April 28 and 29, 1988.

At this point, the Democrats controlled the House but not the Senate. It was the end of the Reagan presidency, and elections were coming up in the fall. It was also the end of the 100th Congress, whose clock and energy were winding down. There were probably good and bad reasons for introducing the bill at this time. One would assume that with a Democratic House and Republican Senate, the bill might have a chance. But of course things are always more complicated than they appear. Most members of Congress had no idea that disability was a civil rights issue.

Even Democrats might well be suspicious of the breadth and impact of this bill. While they might not be beholden to big business, Democrats would be sensitive to the impact, for example, on metropolitan transit systems, light rail, heavy rail, and unions. They might feel pressure from universities that were reluctant to retrofit campuses. And of course, this version of the ADA would impose very difficult constraints on business with the requirement that compliance kick in immediately concerning the retrofitting of buildings, streets, buses, trains, places of employment, and public accommodations such at hotels, restaurants, and movie theaters. Also, the bill allowed people to sue anyone who didn't comply and to receive three kinds of relief from the court—injunctive, compensatory, and punitive. *Injunctive* means that the business, for example, would have to stop its bad behavior immediately. *Compensatory* means that the business would have to pay for the losses, pain, and suffering that the person incurred by being discriminated against. And *punitive damages* means that a given business would be punished with a fine for its discrimination.

Another concern was that the Civil Rights Restoration Act had had a difficult time getting through two Reagan vetoes. Less than a month earlier, on March 22, the vetoes had been overturned. The Leadership Conference on Civil Rights (LCCR), with Ralph Neas and Pat Wright, had been fighting for the passage of the restoration act, particularly to overturn *Grove City College v. Bell* as well as the Fair Housing Act. Neas, Wright, and the rest of the LCCR had little involvement with this disability bill and hadn't brought it to their own legislative committee. They saw the ADA more as a strategic and educational move. In fact, the LCCR did not become involved seriously until the following year, when the ADA was proposed in its revised form. Without the backing of the LCCR, however, a civil rights bill would have very little chance of being passed.

So why was this early ADA introduced at all? Jonathan Young theorized that "ADA sponsors and the disability community used 1988 as an opportunity to publicize the act, mobilize grass roots support, solicit the endorsement of presidential candidates in the upcoming election, enlist congressional cosponsors, and establish the act as a top priority for the next Congress."[15] Despite being involved in writing it, Dart in hindsight said that the act's insistence on immediate compliance was "an unreasonable demand." He implied that the actual reason the bill was introduced in its earliest form was to get endorsements for the concept of a disability rights bill during an election year.[16]

For Bush, the competition of the Republican primaries, which began in mid-January, was a motivating force in getting him to support the ADA. He was running in a tight pack, with Bob Dole and Pat Robertson breathing down his neck. Because Senator Dole had a disability, he didn't have to actively endorse any bill to get the votes of people with disabilities. Later polls would show that the disability vote might have actually made a significant difference in this election. Bush was in trouble in February with the key states of Iowa and New Hampshire. He had come in third in the Iowa caucuses, behind Dole, who led substantially, and was even trailing Robertson. This was a danger sign to Bush, who had easily won Iowa in the 1980 election. New Hampshire was looming, and Dole was leading in the polls there. If Dole won in the closely watched New Hampshire primary, he would certainly win the nomination. Robertson was faltering because of the revelation that he had lied about his military experience.

By Dole's own account, it was one of the few times in his own career that his disability came into play: "I won Iowa, and the next state was New Hampshire, and had I won New Hampshire, I'd have been the nominee. But we had a big snowstorm the weekend before the election. And Bush was out running these big machines removing snow, and I couldn't do any of that. It was one time my disability—I really could have used two good arms. So I ended up going into grocery stores and shaking hands, and he [Bush] was out there on the nightly news clearing out driveways. I think the snowstorm defeated me." Dole noted the irony that the last thing that patrician George H. W. Bush would have normally done was run a snow blower: "Yeah, I think he probably would've tipped the guy who did it."

It might have been coincidental, but on March 31, a few weeks before Weicker and Coelho proposed the bill, Bush came out with a three-page, single-spaced statement on official White House stationery singing the praises of disabled Americans. Perhaps Bush was hoping to consolidate his win on Super Tuesday in the Republican primaries. The statement came a few days after the Gallaudet Deaf president revolution, which he supported, and was pitched at disabled voters. In this broad affirmation of support for people with disabilities, Bush mentioned having personally met a wide range of people with disabilities, many of whom had been strategically invited to the White House by Dart and Kemp: "These handicapped individuals made it very clear that those in the disability rights movement have two critical goals: the right of people with disabilities to control their own lives and make meaningful choices; and the right to be integrated into all aspects of society."[17] The declaration, probably penned by Kemp or Dart, went on to summarize the major findings of the NCD Harris Poll and the NCD report.

Showing his disability credentials could well have helped Bush defeat Dole in the primaries by motivating disabled voters. At this point, Dole was not actively involved in the evolution of the ADA. He had spoken in support of the bill on the day of its introduction but with reservations: "I have reservations about many aspects of this bill . . . [but] despite my concerns . . . it is and always has been my belief and my commitment to eliminate barriers to the full participation of Americans with disabilities in this society and in this vein I want to extend my support for a bill which begins to address some of the remaining areas." His reservations would lead him to consider writing his own bill within a year.

Bush also was developing his campaign theme of a "kinder, gentler" conservatism. The campaign was in part a response to the perception that Reagan's administration (and Margaret Thatcher's in the United Kingdom) was a rough-edged, blunt, and unkind instrument. Milton Friedman's economics (what Bush referred to as "voodoo economics" in his primary run against Reagan) was in the air, resulting in factories downsizing and the "fat" being cut out of social programs. Bush wanted to convey the sense that being a Republican could also imply being compassionate (a term his son was to use in the beginning of his presidential term). What better way to show his kinder, gentler credentials than supporting a movement of people with disabilities claiming their rights? In the statement, Bush also strikes a conservative theme, noting that disability benefits cost the nation too much money. Taking disabled people off the welfare rolls and into the workforce would be a double benefit—it could reduce costs and fill the employment rolls.

On April 28, Weicker introduced S. 2345 in the Senate. He began with what now seems like a momentous statement: "I rise today to introduce, along with Senator Harkin and 12 other of my colleagues, the Americans with Disabilities Act of 1988." Calling it "this historic legislation," he echoed the major points put forth in the NCD report. He mentioned at the outset that the bill was the work of the council. But he didn't mention that the bill he was then proposing was missing a central area of concern to the council—insurance for people with disabilities. Not until the Affordable Care Act were people able to obtain low-cost health insurance if they were not employed and had previous conditions. Obviously, people with disabilities were for the most part poor, but many might not be poor enough to qualify for Medicaid. The NCD had included this insurance provision, but the provision was a nonstarter for Weicker, who represented Connecticut—the insurance capital of the United States. The provision was quickly dispatched, and Weicker made no mention of it in his historic introduction of the first ADA. In addition, Harkin represented Iowa, also a big insurance state. Des Moines is described by *Business Wire* as the top location for insurance companies in the United States and the third-largest center in the world. Given that involvement, it was unlikely that Harkin, as progressive as he was, would be pushing for an ADA that would retain an insurance measure.

Senator Harkin rose to the Senate floor and voiced his support for the bill. Senator Kennedy cited the upcoming Fair Housing Amendment and the Civil Rights Restoration Act that would overturn *Grove*: "The wheels of justice are once again turning." Eventually, this early iteration of the ADA would have twenty-seven cosponsors.

The next day, Coelho introduced the bill H.R. 4498 in the House with 33 cosponsors, a number that grew to 125 by the end of the legislative session. On the floor, he talked movingly and personally about himself and others: "I can tell you from my own experience with epilepsy, employment discrimination is one of the most pervasive problems affecting Americans with disabilities." He gave examples: "I know one woman with epilepsy who was employed for nearly 8 years as a secretary for a company. One day she had a seizure at work and was fired, simply because her employer felt that her coworkers should not have to work with someone like her."

Representative Major Owens of New York followed next. As an African American congressman, he used language that linked this civil rights act to previous ones: "The Americans with Disabilities Act will go a long way to stopping a problem that should have never started. We may have inherited a society that segregates and excludes people with disabilities, but we don't have to maintain it." Owens ended with a sweeping statement of inclusion. He noted that he had recently learned the term "temporarily able-bodied" could be applied to all "non-disabled" people. The phrase indicates that being "normal" is only a temporary state. He went on: "When you think about it, our entire country is made up of disabled people and temporarily able-bodied people. The people we are protecting are not a mysterious, distant 'them,' but rather ourselves."

The bill itself contained nine sections dealing with all aspects of disability discrimination, from employment to housing, and from public accommodations to transportation and telecommunication. It was a stronger bill than the second and final ADA that was proposed the following year. Notably, its strengths were that it required compliance to start immediately and that it had no carve-out for "undue hardship" to businesses (as did the 504 regulations). Regarding architectural barriers, the bill provided no exceptions for existing structures, so all structures—new, old, or rebuilt—had to comply. A wide variety of telecommunication devices, including visual alarms, decoders, relay communications, and the like, were required and were to be regulated by the Federal Communication Commission. And of course, legal suits brought by people discriminated against would include monetary damages (both compensatory and punitive) along with injunctive relief. As James Weisman, a lawyer who worked on the ADA, noted wryly, "Under this law, the space shuttle would have had to be accessible."

After the introduction of the bill, there were further debates in the House and Senate. Meanwhile, the presidential election was in full swing. Partisan politics, of course, intruded into these debates. On the one hand, if you were running for reelection, it wouldn't do to oppose legislation that empowered people with disabilities. On the other hand, Republicans didn't want to offend business interests or seem to be growing the "welfare" state. Democrats also had to placate wealthy donors who owned businesses so as not to look like "tax and spend" liberals. At the same time, the HIV/AIDS community linked to the disability community seemed to be another force you didn't want to provoke in delicate times.

In addition to sponsoring this bill, Owens, who chaired the Subcommittee on Select Education, created the Task Force on the Rights and Empowerment of Individuals with Disabilities on May 2 and chose Justin Dart to head it. Lex Frieden would be the coordinator of this group, which was composed of thirty-five other members from the disability community. As usual, when Dart took on a job, he and Yoshiko again hopped in their pickup truck and drove or flew to all fifty states, gathering five thousand discrimination diaries by people with disabilities.

The objections to the first ADA bill would guide the drafting of the second ADA for the following year. Among these were Dole's hesitation about leaving out the "undue hardship" language, the lack of clarity about public accommodations, and the scope of the transportation requirements. In the month following the introduction, further debate took place in the Senate. Senator Donald Reigle, a Democrat from Michigan, was also concerned about the "undue hardship" issue. He worried about the expense of the bill on businesses and local governments.

By the middle of the summer, the election was heating up. A false rumor, generated by a Lyndon LaRouche publication, said that Democratic presidential candidate Michael Dukakis had mental health problems. When President Reagan was asked about this at a press conference, he said, "Look, I'm not going to pick on an invalid." White House aides were shaken by Reagan's response, and within twenty minutes, the president retracted his statement, saying: "I attempted to make a joke in response to a question. I think I was kidding, but I don't think I should have said what I said."[18] In his own defense, Dukakis released his medical records to prove his sanity. That same week, George Bush released his own medical records emphasizing that his doctor described his health as "excellent and vigorous." According to the *New York Times*, Bush said he had never been treated for depression or other forms of mental illness.

Bush's kinder, gentler campaign was being run by Lee Atwater, known for his meaner, harsher campaign tactics like the mental health rumor. Atwater was best remembered for his Willie Horton ad, which is widely credited for beginning the modern era of negative campaigning. Horton, on a furlough weekend in then Governor Dukakis's Massachusetts, twice raped a woman, beat her boyfriend, and stole their car. Atwater reportedly said, "By the time we're finished, they're going to wonder whether Willie Horton is Dukakis's running mate." Atwater also attacked Dukakis for being a "liberal," saying that he was a "card-carrying member of the ACLU" and thus tarring him with this McCarthyesque epithet.

The flap over Dukakis's mental health headed straight to Capitol Hill. Coelho took to the House floor to comment: "Last week, President Reagan made a wisecrack about invalids. As a person with epilepsy, I resent the callous attitude exhibited by the Reagan-Bush administration toward those with disabilities of which this remark is symptomatic."[19] Within days, Bush tried to spin the damage. In a White House meeting with over one hundred people representing various disability groups, he pledged to promote a civil rights act for people with disabilities: "I am going to do whatever it takes to make sure the disabled are included in the mainstream. For too long, they have been left out, but they are not going to be left out anymore."[20]

While Bush, under the tutelage of Evan Kemp and Boyden Gray, pursued the disability vote, Dukakis was less energetic. The Massachusetts governor most likely didn't want to seem like a tax-and-spend liberal by supporting a bill like the ADA. Bob Funk, working with Kemp, remembers trying to get Dukakis to endorse the ADA: "We couldn't get Dukakis to say anything like that. He was more of 'I will work for Medicaid.' It was just [a] typical medical model [rather than a civil rights model of disability]." Cyndi Jones, the editor of the disability magazine *Mainstream*, echoed Funk's lament: "We couldn't get Dukakis to make that statement [supporting the ADA] to save his life."[21]

The Democratic Convention was held from July 18 to July 21 at the Omni Hotel in Atlanta. When disabled members of the delegation assembled to enter the hotel, they discovered that they could not get in. The only accessible entrance to the convention was through the hotel's loading dock. There, the delegates joined the garbage and crates of food being hoisted on the lift. It was a humiliating moment, according to Rochelle Dornatt, the senior aide to Coelho. Later, the delegates tried to persuade the Democratic Party to agree that all future conventions would be held in accessible venues. But the leadership was too busy to deal with what probably seemed a minor issue to them.

The disabled delegates were "hepped up," according to Dornatt, and decided to stage a protest the following night, when Senator Kennedy would be speaking and would be introduced by the young law student John F. Kennedy Jr. The wheelchair users were going to block the doors while other mobility-impaired people were going to lie on the floor and block the aisles. Coelho learned of this planned disruption and realized it would be particularly bad for the Democrats to be the object of scorn by the very people they were supposed to be upholding. He told Dornatt to "take care of it."

Dornatt had a meeting with the disabled delegates at a location of their choosing—the loading dock. Dornatt says, "It was where they all came into the building for the plenary sessions. They insisted on meeting there because they wanted to make sure someone could experience what they were experiencing in terms of being treated like packages or deliveries that come in and garbage that goes out. I clearly remember one bit of turnabout: they all had wheelchairs and got to sit down; I had no chair and nothing to sit on, so I had to sit on the dirty floor. Point taken." Dornatt spent the next twenty-four hours trying to get the attention of Paul Kirk, the head of the Democratic National Committee, and eventually managed to wake up Mike Mc-Curry, who handled public relations and later became Clinton's press secretary. She finally succeeded in getting a written commitment to make future conventions accessible. The delegates backed down, but Dornatt recalls that the lack of interest in the disabled delegates was a sign of the general lack of interest or excitement around disability issues in the Democratic Party.

Not so the Republicans. A week after his White House statement on August 18, Bush accepted his party's nomination at the Republican Convention, stressing the country's diversity and including the disabled: "This is America: the Knights of Columbus, the Grange, Hadassah, the Disabled American Veterans, the Order of Ahepa, the Business and Professional Women of America, the union hall, the Bible study group, LULAC, 'Holy Name'—a brilliant diversity spread like stars, like a thousand points of light in a broad and peaceful sky." And in the presidential debates, Bush took one sentence of his efficiently worded closing statement to touch on people with disabilities: "I want to help those with disabilities fit into the mainstream."[22] Dukakis in the debates said nothing. Tim Cook, Dukakis's disability advisor, couldn't motivate him.

It may seem odd that Bush would be devoting part of his electoral vision to including people with disabilities. There is no doubt he was influenced by his staff. Gray remembers his part: "Well, I think the most important thing that I did personally was to key it [disability] up as a campaign issue, help shape it as a campaign issue. All of us thought that it was an important thing to do." Gray recalls that Bush was prepared because he was comfortable with people with disabilities. It was a logical outgrowth of Bush's interest as vice president. "He'd been working on it for eight years and had understood the issues and had dealt with them firsthand, far more than Dukakis had."

Of course, there was the political reality. At the end of June, Bush and Dukakis were in a dead heat, according to an ABC poll, while Gallup put Dukakis ahead by 5 percent. A Harris poll conducted that same month had shown that disabled people constituted 10 percent of the voting public—a statistic showing that they were "a force to be reckoned with in the politics of the future" and that their vote could be a deciding factor in a close election.[23]

Boyden Gray thinks that the very close election may have been decided in Bush's favor by the disability vote: "I don't think he won the majority of the disability vote, which is huge—it's the largest minority group in the country—but he certainly split it. Lee Atwater said that it was a big, big part of the victory. He acknowledged that it was a very important part of the election outcome." Louis Genevie, a Harris pollster, communicated to the Bush campaign that two million out of four million voters with disabilities had come over to Bush's side because of his stance on disability.[24] In what became the worst election turnout since 1924, Bush won by about seven million votes, or about 7 percent of the popular vote, after coming from almost 17 percent behind. People with disabilities made up 10 percent of the voting population and amounted to about forty million people in the United States. It seems clear that Bush's position on the ADA might well have helped push him to victory in a year of low voter turnout. George Bush, thinking back now on why he was for the ADA, recalls that it was "the innate fairness of it all. Throughout the 1980s, I had worked with some remarkable people like Mike Deland, Justin Dart, and Boyden Gray who helped convince me that the time was right— in fact, it was past due—to help our fellow Americans with different abilities become fuller partners in society. I was already inclined to do something substantial to help, but they and so many others kept pushing the ball down the field."[25]

SEVEN

A NEW BAND OF REFORMERS

A SIGNIFICANT STEP toward recognition of the Americans with Disabilities Act was the joint House and Senate hearing held in September and October 1988. The inquiry was to be the first congressional hearing composed not of policy wonks and bean counters, but of people with disabilities or their relatives.

The hearings involved testimony by over ninety people. The room was packed with people with disabilities who had traveled from all over the United States to attend. At one point Senator Weicker had to address the space issue, saying, "Those who are in wheelchairs, I'd like to get as many as possible up here. This is a tremendous statement by the entire community. I think we have the entire community right in this hearing room." Applause broke out. Coelho spoke with emotion about his epilepsy and his suicide attempt, explaining his despair by saying that with his diagnosis, "the light had been turned off, the light of opportunity, the light of hope." Admiral James Watkins, the head of Reagan's AIDS task force, indicated strong support for the inclusion of people with HIV/AIDS in the ADA. He noted that because each state was making its own laws, this state's-rights approach was perpetuating "confusion." Watkins said, "It's time for federal action."

Numerous people testified about their difficulties with obtaining equal rights as a person with a disability. Jade Calegory, a twelve-year-old boy with spina bifida and who was in the film *Mac and Me*, testified along with Mary Ella Linden, a fifty-five-year-old woman with cerebral palsy trying to get a college education while living in an institution. Dan Piper, an eighteen-year-old with cognitive disabilities, was interviewed along with his mother, who described how keeping him home and using early intervention helped his life significantly. Lakisha Griffin, a fourteen-year-old blind girl from Alabama, expressed her concerns: "I worry that people will treat me differently because I am blind, black, and female. My parents worked hard in the textile mill. . . . I hope to be the first person in my family to go to college." That trifecta of prejudice and inequality—disability, race, and gender—seemed to embody the call for justice in the hearing room that day.

Although we now look back on the year 1988 as significant in disability history—with the introduction of the first ADA and all the election focus on disability—it was a sleeper year as far as the press and the national consciousness were concerned. According to Jonathan Young, "there was virtually no mainstream press coverage, either of the bill's introduction, or during the rest of 1988. Since the ADA's advocates were not pushing for immediate passage, the bill drew neither the press coverage nor the opposition it would" the following year.[1] Yet Bush's campaign was sending hidden, targeted messages to the disability electorate. The average American would not have noticed Bush's insertion of *disability* into the list of identities that made up the national idea of diversity. But people with disabilities would.

George Bush was elected president in November 1988, and at the same time, the Democrats took over the Senate—now controlling both houses of Congress. Lowell Weicker, on the other hand, lost his Senate seat by a mere seven thousand votes to then Connecticut attorney general, Joe Lieberman. The ADA followed Weicker's trajectory and never came to the floor. It moldered in committee like so many bills that fail to get widespread support. In fact, only about 4 to 6 percent of bills manage to make it through both houses of Congress.[2]

When Bush performed his first major task as president and addressed a joint session of Congress in February 1989, he lived up to his word about promoting the ADA. "To those 37 million Americans with some form of disability," the president said, "you belong in the economic mainstream. We need your talents in America's work force."

With Weicker defeated in the election, the responsibility in the Senate shifted to Harkin. Lex Frieden recalls that Weicker invited him, Dart, and Sandy Parrino to his office right after the election: "Weicker said, 'Look, I want to introduce you to the person who is going to carry this bill for us.' He brought Senator Harkin in with [his aide] Bobby Silverstein."

HARKIN IS A TALL, affable man with an Iowan accent and a lot of folksy expressions scattered like corn seed on the landscape of his speech. He was born in 1939 in Cumming, Iowa, a town that numbered 35 families in 1908 and boasted 351 citizens in 2014. It had one barbershop, two general stores, one hardware store, and, of course, one post office. Its major attraction was a grain elevator that was owned by a farmer's cooperative. Perhaps the sense of collective responsibility learned from farmers cooperating influenced Harkin's career as a senator who could be counted on to support legislation to help spread social and economic justice.

Harkin's father was a coal miner, and his mother, an immigrant from Slovenia, died when Harkin was ten. His older brother Frank was Deaf. Harkin looked up to him and thought Frank was rich compared to the impoverished lifestyle of his family: "I remember [in] the early days, he would live in Des Moines during the week. He was a baker at that time. Then he would come home on the weekend, and he always had a big duffle bag filled with all his dirty baker's clothes. My mother then would wash his clothes. He worked bakers' hours, started work at two a.m. or some damn thing like that. We kids would be excited and empty all the dirty clothes because we knew in the bottom were all the comic books, plus another bag of the most delicious rolls or pastries and crème horns and pecan rolls and things that he'd baked. We were very poor. We didn't have stuff. To me, my brother was like gold."

In addition to seeing his Deaf brother as a provider, he was aware of the discrimination and injustice Frank experienced. When his brother had saved up some money and wanted to buy a car, he faced prejudice. "They weren't going to let him drive," Harkin recalls, "so he took driving courses in the city and learned to drive. By gum, he got a driver's license and bought himself a car—a green 1949 Ford." But Harkin was also impressed with his brother's determination in the face of discrimination. "He was torn up by how, first of all, they told him he couldn't drive and then they told him you can't own a car because you're deaf and you can't be driving a car around. He just wouldn't accept that. He just kept on till he got what he wanted." In those pre-ADA days, it was very difficult for Deaf people to get a driver's license and even harder to get car insurance.

Frank had attended a school for the Deaf, but he didn't like it and was rebellious. Harkin recalls: "He always wanted to be independent. He talked about the Iowa School for the Deaf and Dumb, as it was called in those days. He didn't like that name and always said, 'I may be deaf, but I'm not dumb.'" Harkin continues: "I think he got punished a lot. They used to whack him and beat him. He didn't want to do what they wanted him to do." The school, like many Deaf schools at the time, had a very limited vocational training program. His choices were limited to a mere three professions—baker, cobbler, or printer. Harkin explains: "Frank said, 'I told them I didn't want to do any of that. So they told me I was going be a baker, and they made me a baker.'" Frank was miserable. He hated his job and felt that he was being taken advantage of.

Harkin continues the story: "This one guy would come in who knew some signs. Why, I don't know, but he knew some signs. He talked to Frank and he said, 'These are really good cakes. I really like these.' I guess Frank probably said, 'Okay, yeah, fine. I make those.' The guy asked if Frank liked his job, and he replied, 'No, I hate it. It's a terrible, terrible job.' It turned out this guy had a plant that employed about two hundred people maybe. It was an old World War II government plant that made nozzles for jet airplanes that was then privatized. The owner's name was Delavan. So Old Man Delavan said, 'Come down. Maybe I can find something for you.' Got Frank down there, and kind of took a liking to him. He taught him how to operate a drill press. The work was very precise. These had to be finely drilled with a micrometer. I used to see the machine he operated. You had to do this—be within—just perfectly precise."

Frank turned out to be the most productive worker at the factory. It occurred to Delavan that Frank's focus and precision might be exactly because of his deafness. Harkin hones in on this fact: "This was before OSHA [Occupational Safety and Health Administration] and all that kind stuff and noise. It was a noisy place. Things were hellishly noisy and banging, and all kinds of stuff was going on all the time. Didn't bother Frank a bit. He would just pay attention and drill those little holes and all that kind of stuff, and clean 'em out with his oil jet." Delavan realized that Frank's productivity was linked to his deafness. "He went out and hired more Deaf people. He had a bunch of Deaf people working there for him. They were unionized. They joined the union; the United Auto Workers Union. Frank now had pay, benefits, a good job."

Harkin takes the time to tell this story because it illustrates how an enlightened employer can benefit from skilled disabled workers. And that was the whole point of the ADA—the benefit to people with disabilities and employers as well.

Tom Harkin went on to Iowa State for college and then law school. Through an ROTC program, he joined the navy, where he served as an active-duty jet pilot from 1962 until 1967. After working as a congressional aide and running unsuccessfully for the House of Representatives, he won the following election cycle and served for five terms. When he arrived in the House, he heard about decoder boxes that would enable captioning for Deaf people so they could watch television. He worked with the National Captioning Institute to make prerecorded shows available for Deaf viewers. Harkin was very chuffed that he received one of the first five boxes for his brother Frank along with a collection of John Wayne movies that were captioned. When Harkin was a child, Frank had driven him to see movies at the RKO Orpheum in Des Moines in his 1949 Ford. The only movies they went to see were action films, since Frank couldn't understand the dialogue in more talky films. Harkin says that in recompense, "I got him the decoder box and the John Wayne movie *The Sands of Iwo Jima*, which was his favorite, and now as an adult, I sat in the house and watched it with him. That was an amazing moment to see him finally 'get' the entire film. He remembered the movie, but now with captioning, he could understand every line."

When Harkin was elected to the Senate in 1984, he became acquainted with Weicker and met with some of the disability people in Washington. Harkin also had a wake-up call when his own nineteen-year-old nephew Kelly, the son of his and Frank's sister, "was sucked down a jet engine on a plane on an aircraft carrier. He became a severe paraplegic, although he got his hands back." When Kelly tried to go to college, he was turned away. "I watched what happened to him," Harkin says. "Okay, so he went to Fort Collins. Colorado State—I guess that is Fort Collins. He found out that the classes he wanted to take he couldn't get to. Now this is all new to me. I had never heard of such a thing before. I went out there and heard Kelly's story. My reaction was, 'Jesus Christ. Why don't they change the classes?' I am on my high horse, and so, being a senator, I told him I would call people up. But when I did, all I heard was 'Well, we just can't do anything about it. We don't have the interpreters.' I heard all their excuses. This was all happening about the same time when I met Lowell Weicker, and suddenly light bulbs are going off in my head."

At that point, Senators John Glenn and Ted Kennedy approached Harkin. They each wanted him on their committees. According to Harkin, Glenn wanted him on the Government Operations Committee because both Harkin and Glenn had flown F-8 fighter jets for the navy. Kennedy wanted him on the Health Committee because Harkin was a reliable liberal vote. According to Harkin, when Kennedy asked Harkin to be on his committee, Harkin replied somewhat coyly, "Well, Glenn wants me on his committee." Kennedy insisted, "Ah no, this is *so* for you. You'll like this stuff. You're working on these issues."

Harkin had an idea: "So I saw Kennedy again, and I said, 'Ted I'd like to come on your committee, but I really want to work on disability issues that I've been doing with Lowell.' I wanted a subcommittee on disability. I said to Kennedy, 'If you could find something for me to do with disability issues and stuff like that, I'd like to come on your committee.' Within a day, he gets back to me, and says, 'Tell you what I'll do. I can put you on a disability subcommittee and you can chair it.' I said, 'OK, I'm on your committee.' That's how that came about. He put me on this Subcommittee on the Handicapped, that later became the Subcommittee on Disability. I was in charge of it."

Harkin now needed a key aide and advisor in the area of disability. He had a reputation as an impassioned and aggressive senator, but he was not deeply involved in the details of legislative composition, so he needed a person well versed in the details of legal language. He hired Robert Silverstein, universally known as "Bobby." Silverstein was trained in two seemingly contradictory schools of thought. While in high school, he took a short course with William Schutz, the sensitivity-training group guru from the Esalen Institute. Schutz promoted the use of what were then called *encounter groups*, in which strangers interacted without leaders to understand the dynamics of a group and to promote self-awareness. When in college at the University of Pennsylvania, he was involved in social justice and organizing. A weekend training session with the noted and notorious organizer Saul Alinsky taught Silverstein that both activism and organization were crucial. Alinsky, known for his raucous and aggressive approach to social change, seemed the exact opposite of the touchy-feely approach of sensitivity-training groups. But Silverstein managed to combine both philosophies, along with the strategy of "getting to yes," as articulated by Harvard Law School's Roger Fisher.

Though not disabled, Silverstein had a long history of fighting against injustice. After attending Georgetown Law School, he worked with David S. Tatel, who headed the civil rights division of HEW. There Silverstein was assigned to work with John Wodatch, who was working on the Section 504 regulations. In the 1970s, Silverstein was also involved with the National Lawyers Committee on Civil Rights Under Law. Of his move into politics, Silverstein says, "I got involved because of, as a Jew, you can summarize all the commandments into one phrase, 'Do justice and pursue acts of loving kindness.' And I heard that call to justice. But from there, after the Reagan administration came, this active, affirmative kind of law just disappeared, because the message to business and government was, 'You don't have to comply.' So at that point, I decided I'm not doing enough policy work. As a result of thinking that, I then went to work in the House." Silverstein was then counsel to the House Subcommittee on Select Education, where Representative Steve Bartlett was the ranking member. When Silverstein moved to the Senate, he was responsible for drafting a variety of legislation related to disability before he began on the ADA. Harkin had heard about Silverstein from other disability advisors and hired him on the spot.

Now that Weicker was out of office, the Senate was in good hands in terms of the ADA. Harkin was the chief sponsor, with Kennedy pushing a strong second. Bobby Silverstein would be Harkin's very capable advisor. According to Silverstein, "Harkin and Kennedy had to make a fundamental decision: do they reintroduce the NCD bill again, or do they introduce a new bill? Lots of folks in the disability community said, 'We can't compromise from the word go,' but Harkin and Kennedy, working with staff, working with the Pat Wrights of the world and the Chai Feldblums and others, decided, 'We've got to get a good bill but only, let's say, leave ten percent, fifteen percent, for compromise, because now, it's for real. And we don't want the opposition to frame the bill. We have to.'"

One of the things they were concerned about, from a public relations point of view, was that the bill should not be characterized by the opposition as "the bankruptcy bill," which is how the pro-business lobby characterized the NCD bill for its draconian bankruptcy provision. The easiest way for the opposition to kill the bill would be to reduce it to a matter of dollars and cents.

For the bill to succeed, it would need a Republican to push it through. Ted Kennedy and Orrin Hatch, Republican of Utah, had worked together on various bills. They were known in Washington as "the odd couple," but they liked each other and created bipartisan legislation together. Hatch was a logical choice for sponsorship since he had a nephew with a disability. Hatch describes his relationship with Kennedy: "We formed a partnership that was quite an interesting one. We would fight each other dramatically to the point where I'd be ready to punch him in the mouth because he'd start that screaming on the floor, as only he could do. Then when the debate was over, he'd walk over to me and say, 'How'd I do?' You couldn't get really mad at him. He was just such a character. We were good friends." There was some special chemistry between Hatch and Kennedy, but less so between Hatch and Harkin, whose leftist populism rubbed the conservative senator from Utah the wrong way. Nevertheless, they were able to work together through their shared sympathies for their disabled family members. Other Republicans who joined in on the bill were John McCain and Bob Dole, both with disabilities themselves.

Another important qualification for signing onto the bill as a supporter, Pat Wright had insisted, was that sponsors either had to have a disability or have a relative with one. She wanted the legislators to be personally motivated to avoid having the bill die before coming up for a vote as it had in the previous legislative session.

On the first day in December 1988, after the elections, Harkin sent Silverstein to talk to Hatch about redrafting the first ADA and what changes would be necessary to allow Hatch to come on board. On January 12, Hatch responded with his list of modifications.

Six days later, President Bush attended a preinaugural event organized by disability groups and held in the Hubert Humphrey Building. People milled about the modernist wood-paneled reception room designed by Marcel Breuer, the designer of the famous Bauhaus chair. Among them was Representative Bartlett. Although a booster for disability rights, he had been on the fence about his support for the ADA in its current form. He had had an earlier discussion with Tony Coelho and Paul Marchand, who were trying to convince him to be a sponsor. "I wouldn't do it," Bartlett says, "because for me as a Republican, it was just kind of a bridge too far. Because Republicans, both then and now, just abhor the idea of suing people. . . . And I knew once lawsuits would have to be brought under the ADA, it would be a big problem. So I didn't say no, but I didn't say yes. I said, 'I don't . . . I . . . I . . . I'm not there yet.' So they said okay! And I remember Paul Marchand looked at me, and he smiled, and said, 'Steve, you'll get there.'"

In that wood-paneled reception room, Bartlett remembers "standing next to Boyden Gray. George Bush comes in, and he's up at the front with Justin Dart. So Justin's introducing, and Boyden Gray kind of gives me a little elbow in the ribs, and says, 'Listen to this.' I said, 'What?' He says, 'Well, you'll see.'"

Bush looked out at the room filled with wheelchair users and other people with disabilities. He cleared his throat and began: "I said during the campaign that disabled people have been excluded for far too long from the mainstream of American life. And I still believe that this is an accurate statement. And I want to do what I can, working with those of you in this room that care too."

Bartlett listened to what the new president said and was both surprised and relieved at what he heard. "Once Bush said he was going to submit the ADA to Congress, then I realized two things. One is I had sufficient cover to make it happen, and second is that it was going to be a real bill now, not just a pipe dream." *Sufficient cover*, explains Bartlett, means this: "If you're a Republican, and you go around introducing bills that create lawsuits, well, the other Republicans get mad at you. So if it's George Bush, and me, then I can say to anyone who objects, 'Well I don't know. Hell, talk to George Bush. Don't talk to me!'" Bartlett would still need further encouragement to fully support the bill, and it would take another two months for him to come around.

While these positive things were going on, Silverstein sat alone one Sunday as his children attended lessons at Temple Rodef Shalom in Falls Church, Virginia. He was hunched over a worn conference table in the curved library, which was flooded with daylight from the wraparound windows and showcased exposed wooden beams cantilevered out from rusticated sandstone interior walls. Here Silverstein took the first stab at writing a rough draft of the ADA. That very building had been the site of a hate crime years earlier, when nineteen rifle shots echoed through the building, blasting windows and destroying property. Given Silverstein's respect for the Jewish credo to "do justice and pursue acts of loving kindness," he was now drafting a document that would, with the help of many people, become a law that would fight acts of hate and discrimination toward people with disabilities. Over many subsequent days, he sat in his office peering at legal paper through his thick glasses and drafting and redrafting the new bill, turning it from the thirteen-page NCD report that Weicker offered on the floor of the Senate essentially unchanged (except for removing insurance as a factor) to a thirty-six-page piece of legislation that would be proposed in May 1989. According to Frieden, "Bobby was a technician, and it's a good thing he was, because a lot of the things he added in the fifty-two-page draft that Harkin introduced were essential to making sure that the law lived on." One of the technical things that Silverstein and Carolyn Osolinik, Kennedy's aide, did in preparation for writing the ADA was to come up with a list of one hundred questions that needed answers. When they had the answers to those questions, they felt they could write the bill and that others could defend it.

A team was forming around the major push to get the ADA through. They divided the work into task forces. Wright and Neas were in the strategic task force, coming up with the big-picture plan and how to achieve it. Then there was the "paper" task force made up of those who were actually writing the legislation and constructing the legal language. On this job were Silverstein, Chai Feldblum, Tim Cook, Bob Burgdorf, Karen Peltz Strauss for the Deaf community, Bonnie Millstein for cognitive and affective disabilities, and Jim Weisman, known as "the transportation dude." Arlene Mayerson was telecommuting in from Berkeley. Others with specific expertise would be called on depending on the area being considered.

In addition to this insider game, there was the lobbying task force in contact with both the politicians and the larger disability community. Liz Savage headed up the lobbying effort, counting the votes of key senators and congresspeople and sending representatives from disability organizations to talk to those on the fence.

Members of this lobbying group included Paul Marchand, Becky Ogle, David Capozzi, Maureen McCloskey, Bob Williams, Denise Rozelle, Tom Sheridan, Lauren Sommers, Paul Hearne, and Jane West. This outreach part was so important because many of the more radical provisions of the earlier bill were being scaled back. The promoters of the new bill did not want to surprise the disability activists and organizations by creating a fait accompli that would be perceived as a major retreat or defeat. And it was important to get ideas and feedback as the bill was being written.

The feedback served a double function. First, it helped gauge the level of agreement or disagreement with proposed legislation and changes. But it also made the disability community feel involved in the process rather than feel like outsiders. To that end, weekly steering committee meetings jointly sponsored by the Leadership Conference on Civil Rights (LCCR) and the Consortium for Citizens with Disabilities (CCD) began on February 2 in the United Methodist Building on Capitol Hill to rally the forces. And there was a grassroots task force with Justin and Yoshiko Dart, Marilyn Golden, Lex Frieden, Judy Heumann, Jim Weisman, Sandy Parrino, Marca Bristo, as well as leaders of ADAPT and the National Council on Disability (NCD).

It was appropriate that the meetings for civil rights of the disabled were held here. The United Methodist Building, at 100 Maryland Avenue, is a triangular, five-story Italian Renaissance structure opposite the Supreme Court. The only nongovernmental structure on Capitol Hill, the United Methodist Building was constructed in the 1920s as a center for social justice. Orator and reformer William Jennings Bryan spoke at the dedication, and the building was used during the struggle for women's rights, the antiwar period, and the civil rights era as a staging ground for demonstrations, including Martin Luther King Jr.'s historic march on Washington. The ghosts and whispers of the past gave strength and encouragement to the new band of reformers.

These weekly meetings were chaired by Wright; Neas; Marchand of Arc, who was chair of the CCD and was considered the dean of the disability community; and Curt Decker of the National Disability Rights Network. The actual negotiations and decisions on what would go into the bill and what changes would be made were held more closely to the chest by an inner circle of Wright, Neas, Silverstein, Iskowitz, Osolinik, Feldblum, and Mayerson. According to Feldblum, "You make a decision such as 'We're going to have to get rid of the insurance. It's not going to fly.' Then you need to get the whole group along. At those meetings, I would then have to explain, 'Here's what the proposal is.' Pat has to manipulate at those meetings at so many different levels. Officially, she's just running these with Decker and Marchand. She has to make sure they're on board with whatever decision you now want them to 'democratically' agree to. Then she's got the larger group to convince." Savage added, "A lot of people came in from out of town, and one of the things we tried to do was really make them think they were—not make them think, but incorporate them in as part of the process."[3]

A number of disability organizations would send representatives to the meetings, and many activists would drop in if they happened to be in Washington. The aim was to get the groups to agree to language and changes in language. Then the representatives, in turn, would be sent out to lobby. While the meetings were very important in terms of community building, their ultimate function was less about democracy and more about outreach and perception. Savage noted that "the reality of Washington is you don't explain what's going on behind the scenes. I mean, there's a public message and there's what's actually happening." To reach a broad consensus among disability groups, according to Savage, "you get a couple of mainstream groups who have conservative boards, and if they agree to it then it's easier to get other groups to sign on; it gives you cover, and you know, that's how you form a cohesive message from a cross-section of the disability community. I mean that's the reality of how it happens."[4]

Decker says the process is "a very inside-outside game." He clarifies that "it is very helpful to have the grassroots groups to be pushing and demanding, 'We want the best deal possible; we will accept no compromise.' Then those of us who are the suits—the people who walk the halls and attend the meetings—say, 'Yeah, but we can accept this compromise if we can get your support.'"

Conflicts would occur. Feldblum remembers some of the meetings with disability groups as "horrible." Silverstein recalls: "I'll never forget the day that Caroline [Osolinik] and I had to defend the draft in front of the National Council on Independent Living. They beat the shit out of us. 'Why are you compromising before you even introduce?'" He added that "by the end of the two- or three-hour grilling they understood what was included and why and what was not included from the previous draft and why."[5]

One group that had its unique issues was the Deaf community. On March 8, a group of Deaf and hard-of-hearing leaders assembled at Gallaudet College, a year to the day after the uprising, to create a list of demands of the Deaf community concerning the ADA inclusion of accommodations like sign language interpretation and assistive listening devices. Karen Peltz Strauss, a hearing disability lawyer, was there as well. She recalls: "The list was very, very long. Everyone agreed that relay services was at the top of the list, but the second thing on the list, which was just as important, was closed captioning on TV programming."

The Deaf leaders were concerned that the politicians might not consider a relay system a "civil right" and might not want to include such a service in a nondiscrimination bill. As Strauss puts it, "We weren't real hopeful that Congress would accept that [relay system] as a civil right—that you couldn't just prohibit discrimination, you actually had to *do* something to remedy that discrimination." But relays didn't seem so different, after all, from lifts on buses. The relay service, moreover, would require a surcharge on everyone's phone bill. Because Senator John McCain had a Deaf person on his staff and had been on the board of trustees of Gallaudet, he was very sympathetic to the issue.[6]

However, staffers were very resistant to the idea of including closed captioning in the ADA, Strauss remembers: "We were told in no uncertain terms by staffers on the Hill, 'Over our dead bodies are we putting this into the bill.'" The Motion Picture Association of America had made it clear that it would kill the ADA if the bill had these provisions. Facing this roadblock, the Deaf activists decided to come up with their own stand-alone piece of legislation. The Decoder Circuitry Act of 1990 mandated that all new televisions with screens larger than thirteen inches had to have decoders to allow closed captioning. As with many disability accommodations, the benefits to this innovation apply to a wide range of people. So these captions are now ubiquitous in noisy bars and airports. And many people who have trouble understanding regional or national accents or who have minor hearing losses can use the technology as well.

Because the meetings were held for various groups, each group that represented a specific disability—cognitive disability, epilepsy, blindness, Deafness, and the like—would want to make sure its particular disability was represented. The job of the coordinators was to incorporate those concerns and at the same time look at the big picture. In the past, much disability legislation was particular and each of the disability groups would only be concerned that its specific disability was in the bill. Now with the ADA, that kind of individual disability lobbying had to broaden to include other disabilities. At various times, some groups objected to the representation of other groups in the bill—particularly the cognitively disabled, the mentally ill, and people with HIV/AIDS. The core group of leaders and especially Wright made it clear that all groups had to be included and that none could be carved out or thrown under the bus. The other core principle was that you could negotiate on time lines, but not on principals. As Marchand notes, "We decided that we all had to stick together."

EIGHT

A New Day, a New ADA

BY MARCH 15, 1989, Bobby Silverstein and others produced a draft version of the ADA that would be known as Senate Bill 933 (S. 933).[1] It had some bare bones of the earlier bill but was very different particularly in flexibility and scope. The word on the ground was that the earlier bill was a pipe dream and would never be passed. Republicans particularly didn't like the range of places that would be considered public accommodations. The earlier bill also demanded that all barriers be removed immediately—the so-called flat-earth provision. Conservatives didn't like the costs that businesses would incur both in having to retrofit and in legal penalties, including the very tough bankruptcy provision. Silverstein's newer draft was milder in most regards except in the range of public accommodations. The draft bill was circulated around Capitol Hill, the White House, and the disability community. Key Republicans who supported antidiscrimination and civil rights in the abstract now in reality had to swallow a bill that might have a major impact on business and the economy. Ripples of turbid uncertainty began to obscure the clarity that had seemed to surround the idea of civil rights earlier on.

Representative Steve Bartlett remained on the fence. While he liked the idea of civil rights for disabled people and now felt he had coverage with Bush's endorsement, he was not happy with giving individuals the right to sue. He was also concerned about the impact on business in the sections on employment and public accommodation. He had his assistant Pat Morrissey send out the draft to the Congressional Research Service of the Library of Congress with a "rush request" for an analysis of the difference between the old act and the new one.

On March 22, just a week after the draft came out, Morrissey received a seven-page report from Nancy Lee Jones, the legislative attorney for the Library of Congress. Jones acknowledged that both the Silverstein and Weicker versions of the new bill provided broader coverage than 504, which had only involved programs or activities receiving federal funding. Jones pointed out that the definition of disability in the Weicker version was quite different between 504 and the ADA. The Weicker bill only had the most general definition of disability, while the Silverstein version included the words "substantially limits" in the definition of disability. It referred to "a physical or mental impairment that *substantially limits* one or more major life activities" (emphasis mine). Thus, according to Jones, the Weicker bill was broader in definition because "substantially limits" narrowed down the kind of disability being discussed. (This difference would later come back to haunt the new law as courts began to quibble with the definition of disability.) As for the general provisions on discrimination, Jones pointed out that the Silverstein bill deleted the requirement that all barriers be eliminated (the flat-earth provisions). Jones also noted that "generally the draft bill contains less stringent requirements" for employment than did the Weicker bill and included carve-outs for private clubs.

A key term introduced in the draft bill was "undue hardship." If an accommodation would produce "undue hardship," then the accommodation would not be required. The Weicker bill had a stricter approach, saying that accommodation must be done unless it would "fundamentally alter the essential nature, or threaten the existence" of the business or program. Undue hardship is a much lower bar and more in accord with the rulings in *Southeastern Community College v. Davis* and in *Alexander v. Choate*—two cases that specified that businesses or state and local governments had to make only the changes that they could without causing undue hardship or burden. So the bankruptcy provision was gone.

In terms of transportation, Jones noted that the draft bill "would provide less coverage" than the Weicker bill. The draft bill divided transportation into public and private and gave private more leeway, requiring only a private party's "good faith effort" to try to "locate used vehicles" that are accessible. The Weicker bill only allowed transportation companies one year to ensure the accessibility of all new vehicles, and up to seven years for fleets. The draft bill required ten years for intercity, rapid, and light rail; five years for commuter rail; and three years to retrofit key stations, although the time limit on stations could be extended up to twenty years by the secretary of transportation.

Public accommodations in the draft bill were essentially the same as those in the Weicker bill, which itself looked back to Title II of the Civil Rights Act of 1964. But the draft bill added "undue burden" and "readily achievable" to the requirements. So under the new bill, places of public accommodation could discriminate if the cost of accommodation created an undue burden or was not readily achievable.

In terms of communications, the Weicker bill was stronger than the draft bill, in that the Weicker version specifically included "broadcasts, communications, or telecommunications," while the draft bill had no specific section on this. The Weicker bill required captioning, but the draft bill did not. Unlike the draft bill, the Weicker bill required the Federal Communications Commission to provide regulations on the prohibition or removal of communication barriers. And the Weicker bill required that broadcast programming increasingly be captioned, while the draft bill did not. As Strauss says, the Deaf lobby essentially moved all those requirements to a freestanding bill so that the ADA wouldn't incur the wrath of the entertainment industry.

Both bills said that their provisions should not override 504. The draft bill did this more deftly, avoiding a possible conflict between the application of the bill and its effect on 504. Jones concluded in her report that the newer bill "could be interpreted as expanding the existing coverage of section 504." Reading this report, Bartlett mulled over his still-wavering support.

At the White House, things were also becoming murkier. While President Bush had gone on record as supporting the ADA in the abstract, he now had to consider the bill as it presented itself in reality.

The White House at this moment early in the administration was chaotic, as things generally are with a new president. The draft bill was released a mere two months after Bush moved into the White House. Boyden Gray, as White House counsel, had been involved in pushing the ADA along, with the help of Evan Kemp. But now Gray was devoting most of his time to filling the approximately three thousand positions that a new president must appoint. Gray recalls: "It was something that took up a huge hunk of my time the first year. There were always nominees coming through, but the big bulge was in the first year. So I was so hamstrung, and I didn't have much time to devote to the ADA." In addition, the administration had to deal with the savings and loan crisis.

While Gray doesn't recall being particularly involved in the ADA, others recall that he was much more intimately involved. John Wodatch is somewhat dubious of Gray's claim: "Well, he probably may not remember, or he may not want to remember, because this is a pretty liberal thing he did." In fact, along with Dick Armey, Gray is currently cochair of FreedomWorks, an organization with ties to the Koch brothers and the Tea Party movement. Gray's brother Burton had founded the superconservative Federalist Society, of which Gray has been a longtime member.[2]

The next in the chain of command on the ADA was Roger B. Porter, a Harvard professor at the John F. Kennedy School of Government. He had met President Bush when Gerald Ford had invited him to play doubles in tennis, and currently served as Bush's assistant for economic and domestic policy. William L. Roper, a pediatrician, worked on health policy for Porter and would be chosen as the point man in ADA negotiations. Porter had a public reputation as a hardworking, driven Mormon who eschewed caffeine and alcohol. But some staffers in the White House whispered about "his predilection for avoiding controversy . . . his desire not to incur the wrath of Budget Director Dick [Richard] Darman, and his basic inability to make decisions or delegate authority."[3] Charles Kolb, a White House insider, said that Porter was one of the principals in the White House who were "basically decent people but essentially miscast in roles that required political action rather than endless analysis and reflection."[4] The confusion at the White House in this new administration might have been part of a larger inability to act decisively. Marianne McGettigan, who joined the White House staff in July, says about the earlier delays, "I don't think they knew what they were doing. None of them had any Hill experience."

Gray chose Ken Yale, the executive secretary of the Domestic Policy Council, to head the ADA working group within the White House. Yale was a green-around-the-gills staffer who had just graduated from Georgetown Law School the year before. Although he had no experience with disability, his wife's two brothers were cognitively disabled. Yale says that his job was mainly to write pro and con papers that would be presented to the president. He didn't see himself as having a political function. Yale says that when Gray tapped him to be in charge of this endeavor, "it was such a shock to me. I felt very uncomfortable because I am supposed to be the honest broker, and here I am chairing this [very political] thing."

One could speculate why Gray appointed such a greenhorn to chair a significant committee. In a sense, with Yale in charge, Gray could control the outcome and not get any untoward opinions. The first meeting of the ADA working group was held very early in Bush's term. Invitations were sent out to the appropriate people in the affected agencies, including the Department of Transportation, Department of Labor, and Office of Management and Budget. The OMB was represented by Janet Hale, the top person under the director, Dick Darman. Yale remembers: "The first meeting was enormously well attended. The first thing that really struck me was how adamant Janet Hale was against what we were doing. It only dawned on me that she was speaking for transportation interests that would have to accommodate disabled people." According to Charles Kolb, Hale's "chief role was to hold up action on a variety of initiatives."[5]

Yale remembers: "Well, the next morning, I get an e-mail from Tom Scully, principal associate director for health care, and he told me that Dick Darman heard from Janet Hale that Ken Yale had convened a disability working group. Darman threw a fit and hit his fist on the table. He yelled, 'What the hell is Yale doing starting a working group?!' Here I am, two years on the Hill, fresh in the White House, and I said, 'Oh man! I made the OMB director Dick Darman pissed off.'"

Anxious the rest of the day about his standing, Yale ate a nervous lunch at the White House Mess and was walking down the hallway in the West Wing when he saw Darman walking toward him.

Darman said, "I understand you chaired a disabilities working group."

Yale replied, "Well, yes, I did, as a matter of fact." And he added quickly, "I did it because I was asked."

Darman immediately replied, "Oh, and who asked you to do that?"

Cowering a little, Yale responded, "In fact, C. Boyden Gray."

Darman pulled up a bit. "Oh!" he said. "OK, but in the future, make sure you clear these things with me before you go ahead."

The powerful opposition developing in the White House was being established early between Darman and Gray. Yale recalls: "I realized that something was going on way above my head."

Yale proceeded with his task, thinking that he was conducting an inside-the-White-House maneuver that would translate Bush's campaign promise into a Republican-friendly policy of limited scope. But shortly after the first or second meeting of the ADA working group, Yale "got a call from this guy from the Hill named Bobby Silverstein. I had absolutely no idea who he was. He says, 'I understand you have this disability working group.'" Yale was astounded. "We had executive privilege, closed meetings, and here is someone on the Hill whom I never met who knows about this. The next words out of his mouth were, 'We have a bill up on the Hill that does what you are talking about.' How did he know that we had one or two meetings?"

Suddenly the lay of the land became clear. The Democrats had a bill, and the Republicans had done nothing. Silverstein's draft bill had beaten the House team to the punch. The idea of a limited Republican bill coming out of the White House now came crashing onto the reefs of political intrigue. For the next few months, the White House would be playing catch-up and doing so in a confused and chaotic way.

On April 5, Silverstein received a telephone call. On the other end was David Sloan, the White House liaison with the Senate. Sloan seemed relaxed, although clearly making things up on the spot, and said that the administration needed one to two weeks to vet

Silverstein's draft bill. Sloan was confident that there would be a very positive agreement. The White House would also decide which Republican senators and representatives would become involved.

The next day, Kennedy, Coelho, and Harkin wrote to the president saying that they had no problems with his taking an additional two weeks to review the draft bill. "We're on track," was the message to White House chief of staff John Sununu and Gray. Things seemed to be moving along with the velocity of the Amtrak Metroliner speeding into DC. In reality, the train hadn't left the station.

Four days later, on April 10, Gray seemed to have found time from his otherwise pressing duties to write a long memo to Sununu in response to the chief of staff's request for Gray's preliminary views on the ADA. Sununu was a newcomer to Washington, just arriving from New Hampshire, where he had been governor. Bush selected him for his loyalty. In the dodgy days of the primaries, when Bush was running a distant third behind Dole and Robertson, New Hampshire was the crucial state he had to win. Sununu was instrumental in Bush's winning there, along with the serendipitous snowstorm that sandbagged Dole. In return, Bush rewarded Sununu with the post of chief of staff. According to one aide, "Sununu was very intelligent and had a good grasp on domestic policy. These [issues] were not . . . Bush's strong suit."

Sununu, who looks more like a beefy prize-fighter than an intellect, is actually the brainy kind of guy who got perfect SAT scores and moved on from college to earn a PhD in mechanical engineering from MIT. He held the rather unpolitical positions of professor and dean of mechanical engineering at Tufts University before he ran for office. Brash, arrogant, and acerbic-tongued, he managed to make many enemies in a short time. The *Baltimore Sun* said, "Mr. Sununu's reputation for rudeness, arrogance and bullying was well known in New Hampshire when Mr. Bush tapped him for the top staff job in his administration."[6] The former governor made the May 21, 1990, cover of *Time* magazine as the "bad cop" of the Bush administration and as "the power to reckon with."

He apparently was known to hold a grudge. When Candy Thomson, a reporter who covered him as governor and now as White House chief of staff, was getting married, she received a surprise phone call from Sununu. He said, "I understand congratulations are in order." She replied that yes, this was the case, and thanked him. His response: "I didn't say I was offering them. I just said they were in order. What I really wanted to say was, 'Fuck you.'"[7]

When it came to the ADA, Sununu claims that in the early days of the administration, "I sat down with the President and we had ticked off a bunch of legislation he really wanted to get passed including the Clean Air bill, the civil rights bill, and the ADA. I had a specific interest in the ADA because I had worked with the disability community in New Hampshire." While governor, Sununu presided over a revamping of the mental health system, reducing hospital admissions and expanding the role of local community facilities. Gray's memo to Sununu was an attempt to get the chief of staff on board despite what might have been Sununu's skepticism concerning the financial impacts of the ADA. White House staffer Hans Kuttner characterizes Sununu's attitude toward the ADA as holding to the opinion that "this would be an economic disaster until evidence would arise to prove to him otherwise." Gray went through the history of the ADA and highlighted the problems the Republican White House might have with the new bill. "The most immediate concern is that nobody has any estimates of the costs that any of the provisions of this bill would impose on the private sector." But Gray quickly added, "The disability community properly points out that the savings that would result (in terms of welfare payments no longer required) should be offset in such a calculus."

Essentially, Gray worried that the draft bill was too ambitious and would hurt business. He wanted to increase the cutoff size of a small business from fifteen to fifty employees, which would carve out most of the small businesses in the United States. He wanted to limit the scope of public accommodations "only covering hotels with more than five rooms for rent, restaurants, places of exhibition or entertainment" and leave it at that. Gray wanted to protect businesses from lawsuits by limiting businesses' damages to only back pay and no further monetary damages. And he noted that "the unavoidable murkiness of the concepts of 'reasonable accommodation' and 'undue hardship'" would expose business owners and others "to the risk of punitive damages."

Sounding a theme that would be repeated by some conservative Republicans, Gray didn't like the way that drug addicts, alcoholics, and people with contagious diseases (by which he no doubt meant HIV/AIDS) were handled in the new bill. The current bill said that these groups would be protected if they did "not pose a direct threat to property or . . . safety." Gray didn't like that an employer couldn't use a drug test on employees with the aim of firing anyone who tested positive. Gray preferred the standard in the Fair Housing Act of 1988, which "permits exclusion of any users of controlled substances."

From the perspective of costs, he lamented that "the bill is presently structured so that its benefits go to the public as a whole but its costs are borne by employers." In the spirit of George Bush's promise in the debates—"Read my lips: no new taxes."—Gray preferred that the costs "were borne by the public at large by allowing a tax credit for making the accommodations." Republicans would take all of his objections up in the Senate and the House.

The final word that Gray had for Sununu was that "the Administration should participate constructively in the formulation of this legislation." Noting that the White House staff had two weeks from the date of the memo as wiggle room in negotiating, Gray told Sununu the staff should take advantage of that grace period to strategize.

This memo clearly shows that Gray was for the ADA but with serious reservations, many of which flew in the face of what the disability community wanted. Although many disability advocates now see Gray as the good guy facing off against Sununu's bad guy, Gray was basically pushing a somewhat conservative agenda while supporting the overall concept of civil rights for people with disabilities. He had to play off the disability community, which wanted everything, and the more conservative Republicans like Sununu, Sam Skinner (secretary of transportation), and Darman inside the White House and leaders of the Senate and Congress like Jesse Helms, Dick Armey, and others, who didn't want a liberal bill in the first place. As Wodatch says, "Of course they [key players at the White House] had a position. Boyden wouldn't let anyone else know it." The reason? The Republicans "were all opposed to the entire White House operation—I mean, you can picture, we would to go to the Hill and have a negotiation, and on one side of the table was Ted Kennedy, Harkin, and the president's staff. On the other side were all the Republicans. They were very uncomfortable with this. It was like the president was doing something with Ted Kennedy, and it was—it just made them uncomfortable, and Boyden kept them all at bay."

What game was Gray playing? While pushing for the disability bill and being singled out by the disability community as an in-house savior, he was clearly articulating a much more business-friendly approach than he would let the group know about. It was a subtle game that appeased the conservatives as well as the liberal activists with disabilities. In that sense, it was a bit of a feint since, ultimately, you couldn't be riding both horses at the same time.

By Sununu's account, he, Sununu, wasn't driving the White House policy—Gray was. Sununu recalls that he, the chief of staff, was chosen to be the heavy hand of the administration—the bad cop— to Bush and Gray's good cop: "I sat down with Boyden and [Dick] Thornburgh [the attorney general] . . . and got from them the critical, technical issues. There was a lot of serious concern about specific wording. I think that such a big piece of legislation depended on two or three handfuls of words in terms of what would be acceptable to the president." Putting it bluntly, Sununu declares, "I was the bad guy on everything in that administration. I may have been the executioner, so to speak, on what was okay or not okay at the table, but I received all my guidance and would be told what could be accepted and couldn't be accepted by Boyden and the attorney general. It's an important point. I'm not a lawyer. The issues that made it a difficult negotiation were legal nuances. I may have gone down to do battle. Maybe they perceived I had a better personality to do battle, or maybe I was being thrown to the wolves."

Other observers have different takes on Sununu. Roper has this to say about Sununu: "He was the White House chief of staff, and part of that job is to cut deals and make the trains run on time. He was depending on others to be the people of substance who were able to talk about it." Senator Durenberger puts it this way: "John was the kind of guy you needed to have at the table if you were going to impress the Kennedys of this world with the fact that there's going to have to be some change here, some change there. There's a point beyond which we don't go."

But the then secretary of transportation, Sam Skinner, has a clarifying take on Sununu's role: "John and I and others slowed the ADA down a little bit because we knew you couldn't do all this quickly. I think some people probably perceived that [we were being obstructionist], and I think we probably took some stuff out and stopped some stuff from going forward that would have had very little effect on people's accessibility. It would have [however] had a major financial drain on resources that could be put in other directions." The thought on the part of Sununu, Skinner, and others in the White House was that the ADA couldn't be stopped, since it had Bush's approval, but it could be changed in ways that made it less liberal and more conservative.

On April 21, another memo, "Development of Administration Disability Policy," was carried to Sununu, kicking off what people thought would be the two-week grace-period discussions. The memo registered the importance of the ADA and the speed at which it was progressing: "Attorney General Thornburgh has put together a Domestic Policy Council Working Group on Disability Policy." In addition, within the White House, the Council of Economic Advisers would form a working group to "discuss problems and issues . . . with the business community" while Gray's Office of the White House Counsel was to "contact disability community leaders." The Office of Legislative Affairs would coordinate contacts with Congress, and the Office of Intergovernmental Affairs would have discussions with state and local authorities. Obviously, formulating the administration's position was going to be a complex affair. In fact, it became so complex and took so long that the effort almost failed to affect the Senate as the legislature formulated the bill and moved toward the markup of the legislation. *Markup* is the way that committees and subcommittees can make amendments to a piece of legislation that has been introduced on the floor of the House or Senate. While the committee doesn't actually make the amendment, it votes on recommending amendments to the full House or Senate.

Now the two-week grace period had come and gone without any action from the White House. There was still the general feeling that an agreement was forthcoming, and a press conference to announce that agreement was arranged by Coelho and Sununu and scheduled for May 1 in the Rose Garden. At the conference would be Harkin, Kennedy, Coelho, and some Republicans that the president would select. An accord was going to be announced amid White House pomp.

But the conference was not to be. One of the problems was that Hatch, fearing that the White House–Senate bill would be too liberal, decided to write a bill of his own. Hatch was the ranking member on the Labor and Human Resources Committee and had already given Silverstein a list of the changes he wanted made to the ADA, including the usual Republican limitations and an exemption for religious groups. As a Mormon, Hatch had reasons for including the latter carve-out. Generally, he had been a positive force working with Kennedy and Harkin on earlier disability-related legislation and was certainly motivated by his brother-in-law who lost the use of his legs to polio.

Because of Hatch's initial reservations, though, he did not cosponsor the bill. That's when he came up with the idea of creating his own legislation. Mark Disler, his aide, wrote up the alternative bill, titled "To Establish a Clear and Comprehensive Prohibition of Discrimination on the Basis of Handicap." Disler remembers that Hatch was "concerned that the Republicans on the Labor Committee and in the Senate should neither be to the left nor the right of Bush. . . . [Hatch] wanted the Republicans to be in alignment with the administration." In other words, Hatch wanted the White House to produce a document in line with core Republican beliefs. Disler adds, "When the bill was introduced, the Bush administration was just formulating itself. People were being named to different positions. . . . The concern was that there was all this expertise in the Bush administration, at some point they would be organized enough to take a position."

But when would this moment happen? Gray had alerted Sununu, telling him, "Senator Hatch has also prepared a bill, but will defer to the administration on whether to introduce it or cosponsor a modified Harkin bill." Hatch eventually gave up his own bill and threw his support behind the ADA, but he seems to have also used the threat of his own bill as a convincer. Hatch himself recalls: "By raising the prospect of an alternative bill, I hoped to get some leverage in the effort to move the bill more to the center."

Clearly, the White House and the disability groups were aware of Hatch's bill. Disler recalls a meeting in Silverstein's office: "I just happened to mention we might have an alternative, which we hadn't decided what we would do with. I just kind of dropped it. Bobby turns around and pulls it [Disler's draft of Hatch's alternative bill] off the shelf. I thought that was really funny. I understood immediately the administration was also working with [Silverstein and his disability group]. I assumed that's where he got it from. In other words, I had drafted something, shared it with the White House, [and Silverstein] had a copy of it." What this incident shows is that the supposed disconnect between the White House and disability groups was illusory. Someone in the White House, most probably Gray or Kemp, was leaking information. This secret liaison would come back again with significant results.

The other key Republican player was Dole, the Senate minority leader. His support was crucial. Dole too was considering writing his own bill. His aide Maureen "Mo" West had a background in disability-related subjects, having been a nurse before becoming a political aide. She also had good contacts with some of the key players in the disability camp. She kept checking in with Dole to see how intent he was on making his own bill. At one point, she asked him, "Would you mind hearing out some disability activists?" He agreed, and Dole and the activists had a fireside chat in the whip's office. Wright, Feldblum, and David Capozzi were present. They talked for an hour, going through what his act would do and what the draft ADA would do. They asked for Dole's support. According to Mo West, "he just sort of mellowed after the meeting. He said, 'Let it work through the committees, and I won't do my own bill.'" Dole wanted to put his mark on the bill, so he and his aides came up with a provision to include technical assistance. Since he had already authored a tax exemption in the federal tax code for making facilities and transportation accessible, West suggested to Dole that he could expand that tax exemption toward further accommodations, technological, or communicative aids. She notes approvingly, "I was certain all impacted parties of this legislation would welcome such an exemption." Dole thus could have a major effect on the disability community without having to produce his own bill. He went along with the idea.

Dole recognized that his approval of the bill would be important. "I don't want to sound braggadocio," he says, "but I think I offered cover to a lot of Republicans, and a lot of Democrats, because I don't believe a liberal Democrat or even Ted Kennedy without some solid support on our side would have been able to get it passed. So it truly was bipartisan, which we need a little of now." And he adds ruefully, "It wasn't all easy. You know, we got a lot of heat, too. It wasn't all, 'Thanks for what you did.' A lot of it was, 'I'll never vote for you again.' All that stuff."

A couple of weeks later, on May 9, the Council of Economic Advisers within the White House sent around a memo on the policy implications of the ADA. The council had clearly been debating whether to pursue a more Republican style of approach using tax incentives or to go with the preexisting approach that focused more on regulation. As the White House staff engaged in its complex and sometimes confusing attempt to craft a bill that would prevent Bush from looking like a liberal and would appeal to Republican core values, the clock was ticking. The joint press conference to be held on May 1 in the Rose Garden to announce the launching of the ADA was suddenly and unilaterally canceled.

Without White House support, then, on May 9, Harkin introduced the Silverstein draft bill, now officially the ADA, on the floor of the Senate before obtaining White House approval. The earlier agreement of "We're on track" had clearly gone off the rails. Harkin, speaking for those who sponsored the bill, but not for the president, said, "To this day, federal law still does not prevent an employer or an owner of a hotel or restaurant from excluding people with disabilities. Today, under our nation's civil rights laws, an employer can no longer say to a prospective employee, 'I will not hire you because of the color of your skin or because you're a woman or Irish or Jewish or Catholic.' If the employer did, that person could march to the courthouse, file a lawsuit, and win. Yet to this day, the courthouse is still closed to Americans with disabilities. I consider this the final frontier, the final barrier we must break down in our society." He added, for people with disabilities, "This is their Emancipation

Proclamation." Kennedy supported the bill, saying it "will end this American Apartheid."

In the House, Coelho introduced the ADA: "This is a good bill, but it will take more than good intentions to get it passed. There needs to be a commitment from the public, a commitment from Congress, and a commitment from the President, to see this bill become a reality." While these words were true, it was clearly going to be difficult to line up those constituents successfully.

Also on May 9, the first Senate hearings for the ADA were held in the Dirksen Senate Office Building. Here Hatch offered his ultimatum to the White House to support the bill by June 19 or else the legislation would go forward without the White House's input. In the House, Coelho, who had been elected majority whip in January, had significant power to move the bill forward. The majority whip is charged with assuring that a bill has the necessary votes, and Coelho had been tasked by the majority leader to push the bill to passage. In his testimony on that day, he urged Hatch, "We would prefer that you not introduce your own bill." Hatch demurred, saying, "I would love nothing better . . . but in its present form I cannot."

At this hearing, Justin Dart wheeled in a box of "discrimination diaries" he'd collected from his travels around the country. He also showed the committee an unoccupied wheelchair, saying, "I submit to you this brand new empty wheelchair. . . . On January 24, 1988, last year, my youngest brother, Peter, was faced with the necessity to use [it]." Instead, according to Dart, his brother said, "I'd rather be dead." The wheelchair was such a powerful symbol of oppression and discrimination, posited Dart, that his brother committed suicide several days later rather than be "confined" to a wheelchair.

Meanwhile, Republican Steve Bartlett in the House was still dallying. Although he felt Bush's speech had given him cover, like Dole and Hatch, he still had serious reservations. By this point, Lex Frieden, Bartlett's fellow Texan, had left the NCD and gone back to Houston for several reasons. The main reason was that as a member of the NCD and a federal employee, he was not permitted to lobby for the ADA, and Frieden, a very good talker and persuader, wanted to actively move the new bill forward. One of the first things he did when he got to Houston was to set up hearings to convince some wavering Republicans and Democrats that the ADA was a bill whose time had come. He recalls: "We asked Major Owens if he would bring the House Committee on Labor and Education to Houston for a hearing, and he did." Bartlett, as a member of the committee, would be attending. Frieden, sensing that Bartlett was on the fence, told him to come to the hearing, where he could ask any questions he wanted.

The session was held on August 28 in the gym of the Metropolitan Multipurpose Center, where disabled athletes play wheelchair basketball and other sports. Bartlett remembers: "A lot of the attendees left for the Houston Astros game, but I stayed for the entire time." Bartlett was impressed by the people who testified: "You know, you go to hearings, and oftentimes, witnesses just come in and they're cheerleaders, and that doesn't really help you . . . solve [anything]. But every one of these witnesses, though, was direct and specific. First of all, they explained with some graphic detail what happens in their real world that can only be solved by a civil rights law. Then secondly, they described ways to make it work."

The convincer that day was the testimony of Bob Lanier, the chairperson of the Texas Highway Commission and of METRO, Houston's transit authority. A child of working-class parents and of the Great Depression, he was nonetheless a businessman and, in Bartlett's view, "on the right." As Bartlett recalls, "here he was, [the transportation secretary] of a big city, and on a real-time basis, he had to deal [with] and make work all of the various things about disability rights, some of which could get extremely misunderstood and controversial and litigious. Here was a guy who had to make it work in the real world, and he was not only willing but also eager to impose a whole new super law on top of it. That was very impressive because I knew he was a hands-on politician. He knows what it takes to build a highway. He knew that these changes were not going to be without cost. He was not only willing, but also enthusiastic. He was also a conservative, a businessman."

But what moved Bartlett to tears was when Lanier got to his feet and began to recite a poem. It was Thomas Gray's "Elegy Written in a Country Churchyard." The verses that moved both Lanier and Bartlett were about the rural poor buried in an English country cemetery.

Lanier's Texas twang gave new meaning to the words of the British poet extolling the unremembered lives of poor country people:

> *Full many a flower is born to blush unseen,*
> *And waste its sweetness on the desert air. [...]*
> *Some mute inglorious Milton may rest,*
> *Some Cromwell guiltless of his country's blood. [...]*
> *Here rests his head upon the lap of Earth*
> *A youth to Fortune and to Fame unknown.*

Lanier added, "And the notion I guess is that who knows what in this little country churchyard a Cromwell might lie, a Milton might lie, to whom society never gave a chance to contribute, not just for themselves, but to all of society." The idea in the poem was that the lives of disadvantaged people should not be ignored or dismissed "with disdainful smile," that their existence was as important as those with beauty, power, and wealth. Lanier's recital of the poem hit home for Bartlett. "It was a very convincing hearing, and that was the day I decided to be for the bill."

NINE

WHITE HOUSE BATTLES SENATE

MAY 25 WAS A perfect day in Washington with temperatures idling in the low seventies. It was less than a perfect day within the White House. With demonstrations in Tiananmen Square revving up and the first formal meeting of the Soviet and Chinese leaders in Beijing ending a thirty-year rift, Bush's attention was not sharply focused on the ADA. Bush had just sent nineteen hundred troops to Panama to protect US interests, in a lead-up to his subsequent order for the United States to invade Panama at the end of the year. As the former head of the Central Intelligence Agency, Bush always had his eyes focused beyond the borders of the United States. While the ADA was important to him, it probably wasn't his top priority at the beginning of his first year. White House staffer Roger Porter notes, "The principal focus was the budget, Excellence in Education, and the Clean Air bill we finished up in May." So the White House continued in its somewhat rudderless confusion concerning the ADA. Neal Devins describes the lack of focus: "He provided no direction himself, nor did his appointees speak in a single voice. Civil rights policymaking was instead discordant and often self-contradictory."[1]

If the White House staff members were looking to Bush to lead them on the issue of civil rights, they would have had a problem. Certainly, he was temperamentally and emotionally forged in the tolerant smithy of New England Republicanism, and in 1948 as a Yale senior, he took a leadership role in the United Negro College

Fund. Yet, although his father, Senator Prescott Bush of Connecticut, sponsored legislation to protect voting rights, desegregate schools, and create an equal employment commission, first-term congressman George H. W. Bush voted against the Civil Rights Act of 1964. Having shifted from New England to Texas and running as a Goldwater conservative, he believed that he would never be elected if he supported civil rights. Thus while electioneering, he said that the very provisions his father had proposed were unconstitutional. As he put it in April 1964, "We all deplore the hatemongers of this world. The only thing I hate to see is our Constitution trampled in the process of trying to solve civil rights."

After Johnson signed the 1964 act, Bush was concerned. "The new civil rights act was passed to protect 14 percent of the people. I'm also worried about the other 86 percent." In a letter to a friend, he later regretted taking "some of the far right positions I thought I needed to get elected. . . . I hope I'll never do it again."[2] But on several occasions, political expediency trumped ideology. Although he ultimately voted for the Fair Housing Act of 1968, he earlier spoke out against open housing and initially voted to kill the bill and send it back to conference, expressing a concern that the bill would hurt real estate agents. When asked about his contradictions, a close friend of Bush summed it up: "pure politics."

In Reagan's administration, Bush had good relations with civil rights leaders and was one of the only members of that administration to keep such contacts. But when Reagan was going to veto legislation to overcome *Grove City*, Bush demurred, saying, "I'm not going to start differing with the president after 7½ years into the vice presidency."[3] According to Ruth Marcus, who covered Bush for the *Washington Post* concerning civil rights, "Caught between the two sides on a significant national issue, Bush managed to please neither, leaving considerable doubt in their minds—and the public's—about what he really believed."[4]

The White House staff was caught between the horns of a dilemma—trying to maximize political advantage and minimize political loss without clear guidelines from the president. Staffers were still reeling from Hatch's May 16 ultimatum that the administration had to come up with its own bill by June 19. If it failed to do so, Hatch would stop running defense for the Republicans and therefore would not hold up the full-committee markup and floor action before the August recess. That gave the White House about a month to respond.

In response to the White House's pace, Pat Wright and Liz Savage thought it might make sense to bring in the activists. The National Council for Independent Living (NCIL) was holding its annual conference in Washington, DC. Wright and Savage called a meeting with members of the conference about holding a rally at the White House for the last day of the conference—May 14. Since the conferees were already in the capital and the White House appeared to be slow-walking its support, a demonstration seemed like a good idea. The several hundred conferees marched that Mother's Day from Capitol Hill to the White House at night, carrying candles for a vigil there and chanting "Where's George?" and "ADA now!" As the mass of wheelchair users and others crowded into the street facing the White House, NCIL president Marca Bristo had an idea. She placed a call to the Domestic Policy Office, where she got an appointment with William Roper. Bristo along with Dart met with Roper, Gray, and Kemp the following morning to protest the delays.[5] It seems unlikely that this meeting was in fact spontaneous, given the connections that Wright and Dart had with the White House. Janine Bertram recalls that it was actually Kemp who organized the march: "I remember the Sununu faction was gaining power, and Evan called Marca and said, 'Can you march to the White House?' People marched to the White House and demonstrated against the president, and it was to tamp down the Sununu factor."

Ken Yale remembers: "There were also some protests that came to the Old Executive Office Building next to the White House, but we didn't get impacted by that very much. When we were at the White House, there was a protest every week. You'd see them and just shrug your shoulders."

Ten days later, on May 25, Daniel Heimbach, associate director for domestic policy, wrote a memo to Yale beginning with a section titled "Problem." He outlined the negatives succinctly: "Administration strategy on the ADA currently suffers from a lack of clear direction and specificity."[6] Porter recalls that part of the problem was that Bush had spoken about job discrimination in the State of the

Union and elsewhere, but he didn't focus on other issues until later. The draft bill had sections devoted to employment, but it was also dealing with accommodations, telecommunication, and transportation—the complexity of which threw off the newly minted White House staff. With deadlines approaching, "agencies still have not been given a clear idea of what we are trying to achieve, or what they should be helping us preparing [sic] for."[7]

Heimbach outlined three options in the memo: (1) wait and see, (2) attack and replace, and (3) negotiate and modify. Waiting would be valuable, because ultimately it would result in "the best possible factual information, not on politics." But of course, the problem was that "we do not have the luxury of time needed . . . [and waiting] ignores Hatch's ultimatum that the Administration will be left on the side lines. . . . [It] is simply impossible under the present circumstances." The "attack and replace" option would have the advantage of setting up "an independent Administration ideal [that would] likely be popular with the business community." However, such an approach would be "divisive [and] difficult to win [involving] a serious fight likely to generate heated animosity [and] will lose support of disability communities gained in the campaign." The memo also mentioned that the administration could opt for the draft Hatch bill, still in play, and that doing so would give "sufficient time" to meet Hatch's ultimatum. Such a chess move would obviously buy off both Hatch, who was using the threat of his own bill as leverage with the White House, and those pushing for a more radical ADA bill. But this option for the White House would result in a "pyrrhic" victory, Heimbach wrote, as "we are likely to lose more than we stand to gain."

The final option was to negotiate and modify, which the memo described as "the only realistic choice," although it risked criticism from the business sector. And this option could make Bush "lose political capital" if the negotiations failed and he had to veto the bill.

THE WHITE HOUSE had three weeks to arrive at a consensus.

During that period, Majority Whip Coelho called John Sununu at the White House to inform him that he, Coelho, would be calling

President Bush directly. At the height of Coelho's power and given the confusion in the White House, Coelho stood in a good position to push the ADA through the House. But history produces odd and unexpected diversions to courses that should run straight. At that moment, Coelho had become involved in a financial scandal that was seriously unraveling. He was the third-most powerful Democrat in the House and was slated to become the majority leader if the also-besieged Jim Wright stepped aside. Wright was struggling with financial and sexual scandals and would eventually leave office. As majority leader, Coelho would then have had a straight shot at becoming Speaker of the House, third in line behind the president and the vice president. His presence and enthusiasm were more than reassuring for the major players pushing the ADA. Yet, as events unfolded, it became clear that Coelho was to face a House investigation for financial transactions that tacked very close to an illegal wind.

As the walls began to close in on Coelho, he was mindful of the agony of an eighteen-month-long investigation of Speaker of the House Jim Wright. Considering the downside of toughing it out, Coelho opted to leave quickly. Ralph Neas remembers a meeting with Coelho and Pat Wright just before the resignation: "It was emotional because he was leaving, and he's the author of the bill. We lost the Senate author [Weicker] in the election, and we were losing Tony."

It took almost another month before the White House's Disabilities Working Group came out on June 20 with a memo titled "The Administration's Position on the Americans with Disabilities Act." This was a mere two days before the Hatch deadline. Roper recalls that he was the main author of this report sent to Dick Thornburgh, Skinner, Darman, Sununu, and Michael Boskin, the chair of the Council of Economic Advisers. The memo outlined the administration's concern about the "substantial costs" and the bill's "ambiguous and overly ambitious legal standards of what constitutes discrimination, and the bill's imposition of substantial burdens on small businesses." The aim was to "endorse a course of actions somewhat more modest than that followed by the ADA within its present form." This "more modest" tactic, the memo noted, might be a problem since "some in Congress and in the disability community may criticize this approach because it is not as generous and far-reaching as the current version of the ADA and because it does not exactly parallel existing coverage for minorities and women."

Indeed, the idea that the scope of the proposed bill should be limited and the parallelism between disability and civil rights for other minorities should be mitigated would not play well at all to those involved in creating and pushing it. As Wright had stated all along, and Neas reiterated, the two most important things that they would not compromise on were breadth and parity. The Civil Rights Act of 1964 had a rather limited scope, covering only federally financed entities and a very limited set of public accommodations—lodgings, restaurants, movie theaters, gas stations, and other places of public service. That was pretty much it. The new ADA had a much wider sweep. The White House strategized that by imitating the 1964 act, "85 percent of small businesses qualifying as public accommodations under the ADA approach would be exempted." The other big exemption that the White House wanted was a complete and total exemption for religious institutions.

Like a skilled scrimshaw carver, the White House memo would "endorse" the ADA by whittling it down to a minuscule version of itself. Regarding public accommodations, the memo proposed a "small establishment exemption": for public accommodations with fifty or more employees, the rules would go into effect two years after enactment; for companies of twenty-five or more, it would take four years. The calculus of this move was that in the first case, only 7 percent of the firms that were covered by the Civil Rights Act would be affected, and in the second case, only 20 percent would be covered. This proposal would be a neat disappearing act staged by the White House. Another nick would be carved out of the bill by limiting the scope of accommodations, so that, say, only wheelchair access, but no other accommodations, would be required in restaurants. As the memo cautiously noted, "This limitation would, however, likely be resented by persons with visual and hearing impairments."

For employment, the whittling game would change the Senate bill's requirement that employers with fifteen or more workers be subject to antidiscrimination requirements. Instead, the White House proposed a formula that employers with fewer than fifty workers would be exempt for two years, and in four years, the limit would drop to twenty-five. That would leave uncovered 28 percent and 20 percent of workers, respectively.

In the realm of what would constitute adequate accommodation, the administration wanted the least encompassing language, the by-now well-known "undue hardship" and "reasonable accommodation." These terms would provide much wiggle room and deniability if a worker brought a case against an employer, who could argue that the accommodation the employer had provided was "reasonable" and that any further would cause the business "undue hardship."

Considering the fraught terrain of health insurance, the memo wanted clarification that employer insurance plans "are not affected by this legislation." In one copy of the memo, a White House staffer had crossed out that phrase and written "doesn't mandate insurance coverage for preexisting conditions." Obviously, a disability would be a preexisting condition. That proviso would save employers upward of $1.5 billion, noted the memo approvingly, adding that such a move "would help ensure support of [the] business community for the bill."

On the thorny issue of remedies and damages in court, the memo recommended simply following the Civil Rights Act, which provided injunctive relief and restitution of out-of-pocket expenses and back pay. But the White House would not want punitive damages, compensatory damages, or the right of a private citizen to sue an employer.

To understand which remedies were in or out, it might help to grasp which remedies were available in general. There are several options in play: The first is to get a court to rule that a person or an entity should stop the discrimination (injunctive relief). The second option is to mandate the payment of back pay and incidental costs like legal fees—a preferable option, because these costs are often determined in a bench trial only involving a judge (since juries tend to award bigger cash settlements). The third is to compensate monetarily the aggrieved person for the pain and suffering of discrimination (i.e., compensatory damages), an award usually determined by a trial jury. The fourth option is to fine a company for its discriminatory activity (punitive damages). And the fifth is whether individuals have a right to bring a lawsuit on their own (right to private action) or whether only a governmental entity like the Equal Employment

Opportunity Commission (EEOC) or the attorney general can sue the discriminator.

In general, Republicans are for very limited remedies and very limited private rights to sue. Since Republicans tend to represent the interests of business owners and corporations, they want to limit these parties' liability to lawsuits, which Republicans often term "frivolous." Democrats, who in principle tend to represent the interests of workers and consumers, often want to maximize the types of remedies available. That ideological rift was fully at work in the White House's memo, which pointed out that the bill "overemphasizes litigation seeking extraordinary remedies as a central means of achieving results, rather than encouraging cooperation and voluntary compliance."

Another tricky issue that reared its head in the memo was the idea of who should be covered by the ADA. While the disability community sought a definition that would be broad enough to cover the largest number of people, the White House wanted to restrict the protected group. One of the ways that critics of the bill did this was by focusing on outlier cases. The White House wanted to carve out those who "use or [are] addicted to illegal drugs, or those who have been convicted of drug trafficking." With this carve-out, the White House was highlighting its support for Reagan's drug-free workplace legislation.

The memo concluded that "many in the House and Senate who are not cosponsors of the Harkin Bill . . . are looking to the White House for leadership." With the clock counting down to the June 22 deadline in forty-eight hours, the president had to act. "If we fail to do this, we lose the opportunity to be credible players in shaping this landmark legislation for disabled persons."

The person who brought the White House's position to the Senate was Thornburgh. He was a tested conservative and could be counted on to keep an eye on the bill and stop it from moving too far to the left while maintaining good contacts with disability organizations. Thornburgh's commitment to disability was profound, but it would not alter his vision of the way government should function. Gray and Kemp would remain éminences grises. Kemp is best seen as the conscience of disability issues, telepathically communicating from his position at EEOC to Gray, who gazed into the crystal ball, applying what he heard to realpolitik.

But Thornburgh had until recently not been kept in the loop by his staff. His managerial style was one in which he interacted very little with department heads and relied on memos, which he often returned marked up in red ink. For various reasons, staff had kept copious notes on the various meetings related to the ADA, but Thornburgh had not been informed of this, according to Grace Mastalli, who worked at the Justice Department. In fact, on Memorial Day weekend, when everyone had left town, she received a call from Jane Hale at OMB asking about the ADA. Since no one was in the office, Mastalli tracked down a folder that was filled with meticulously taken notes of all the previous White House meetings—notes that had not been available to principals like Hale and Thornburgh. In addition, the most knowledgeable person in the Justice Department, John Wodatch, who had written the Section 504 regulations, had been excluded, up till this point, from participating in the discussions at the White House. Mastalli phoned Thornburgh and told him about this screw-up. Thornburgh asked her to get all the information for him and to include Wodatch forthwith in all the White House meetings. The following few weeks would be crucial in getting the attorney general up to speed and ready for his official speech outlining the administration's position.

On June 22, the very date that Hatch held over the White House's head, Thornburgh finally brought the administration's position to the Senate. While he endorsed the bill in principle, he presented the reservations now specified in the closed-door meetings at the White House. Thornburgh apparently was going to postpone his testimony because he didn't like the version of his speech that the White House was insisting on. Silverstein recalls: "Nobody knew what he was going to say, because there were two drafts [of his statement], from what we understood, the good draft and the not-so-good draft."[8]

Mastalli, working with Thornburgh, says, "Roger Porter couldn't believe that Thornburgh was going off the deep end. He delegated Bill Roper to get the attorney general in line" with the OMB position, which was for keeping the bill to the bare minimum. Mastalli recalls being summoned to Sununu's peach- and celadon-hued office: "I kept on being called over to the White House and yelled at for not getting the attorney general to fall into line." The White House sent over a draft of the testimony that it wanted Thornburgh to read, but as Mastalli says, "there were huge differences between them. Literally the night before the attorney general was scheduled to testify, we were fighting over every word of his testimony." Along with another Thornburgh aide Alvin Schall, Wodatch and Mastalli were on the phone going over details with Thornburgh, with his wife Ginny in the background. Mastalli describes the conversation: "Thornburgh drew the line in the sand: 'I won't say this' and 'I have to be able to say that.'" Finally, after midnight, negotiating with the White House, Thornburgh came up with a speech he could stand behind the next day.[9] Mastalli recalls that the meeting ran so late that she had to send a friend to get a change of clothing because there wasn't time to go home or sleep.

That day, Thornburgh outlined the compromise proposed by the administration, and he pledged "full support for comprehensive civil rights legislation for persons with disabilities." He asserted that many disabled people "still lead their lives in an intolerable state of isolation and dependence. . . . [Legislation is needed to] end the anomaly of widely protecting women and minorities from discrimination while failing to provide parallel protection" for the disabled.

Thornburgh recalled: "There were three things in my mind. One was . . . [to] establish a mood . . . to get people's attention . . . [and] let them know what we're talking about. . . . Secondly, . . . overcoming a kind of knee-jerk skepticism about further civil rights legislation. 'Don't we have enough civil rights?' . . . And the third was to address the concerns specifically of the business community, especially small businesses who really were haunted by the notion that they would be obliged to make enormous outlays of resources."[10]

When the testimony was over, Neas turned to his wife, Katy, and said, "We're going to have an Americans with Disabilities Act." At the same time, Silverstein, bringing in his getting-to-yes mentality, approached David Sloan of the White House and said, "We are ready to meet anytime, anywhere to resolve any differences." He said the same to Mastalli.

The same day, a well-placed story in the *New York Times*, by Kathleen Teltsch, touted the advantages of hiring disabled workers. The story led with a quote from Wright about how children who benefited from disability rights legislation in the 1970s were now entering the workforce: "There is no question they expect to work, and it does not dawn on them that society has a mind-set to think of them as different or dependent." The theme of the news story was that the ADA would be good for business. Teltsch cited unnamed "advocates for the disabled" who use Department of Labor projections that the workforce would be dwindling by the year 2000 because of the retiring baby boomers. Teltsch further cited dutifully the Harris poll conducted by the NCD to show that disabled people want to work.[11] Clearly, the article was timed and placed by influential disability advocates, echoing as it does the language and statistics of those now pushing for the act.

The article represented a shift in the public relations outreach of the ADA proponents. Whereas the initial goal had been to introduce the bill and get the White House on board, now the thrust would be to convince conservative Republicans and wary Democrats who feared the liberal bias of the bill. The argument being orchestrated was that disabled people would now be taken off the welfare rolls and placed into the workforce. Thornburgh remembers using this argument with his reluctant Republican colleagues: "This is a Republican initiative. It's designed to take people who are now disabled and not part of the workforce and give them the tools to make them productive citizens, get them off of public assistance, let them earn a living, let them pay taxes. And sometimes that worked."

Looking through the "retrospectroscope," we can see that this argument did not predict the future accurately. Clearly, there has been no worker shortage in the twenty-first century; in fact, unemployment has reached record highs through the period. Further, the ADA was singularly ineffective in affecting the unemployment rate among people with disabilities. Even today, the unemployment rate of people with disabilities remains as high as, if not higher than, it was before the ADA.

TEN

SECRET MEETINGS
AND BAGEL BREAKFASTS

SHORTLY AFTER THORNBURGH'S testimony and Silverstein's offer to meet anytime and anywhere, negotiations between the White House and the Senate began in earnest. On June 26, Kennedy staffer Osolinik called up Mastalli and set up the first meeting for the next day to establish the ground rules. David Sloan at the White House agreed. Osolinik and Iskowitz would represent Kennedy; Silverstein would represent Harkin; Mark Disler, Hatch; and Mo West, Dole. The Democrats wanted the disability and civil rights community to be involved, so they invited Wright and Neas.

The first proposed rule was that if an agreement were reached, both sides would be bound to that agreement for the duration of the bill in both the Senate and the House unless both sides agreed to an amendment. In other words, neither the White House nor the Senate would allow any amendments to what each entity had worked out. This tactic made sure that rogue Republicans would not be able to alter the bill or fill it with weakening amendments. The second ground rule was that the current negotiations had to come up with a complete bill without any loose ends that might snarl things up as the legislation proceeded. So in short, complete agreement—no amendments. In addition, the Democrats wanted to have the disability community and the business community at the table and wanted the House to be invited as well. The logic was to get all the stakeholders together to sign on to the inviolable pact. And the disability activists along with the Democrats literally wanted everyone to sign a promise to abide by the agreement. However, the administration was, predictably, not ready to sign on to these stipulations.

At the White House, there was a meeting that same day. Hans Kuttner, a twenty-seven-year-old Princetonian, decided to keep a diary of all that happened. On that day, he recorded, "The story starts Monday [June 26] in Roger Porter's office. His weekly coordination meeting with David Bates and staff focused on who should represent the Administration in negotiations with the Hill. The answer, probably at Roger Porter's suggestion, was Bill Roper." Roper, a pediatrician and health expert who a year later would become head of the Centers for Disease Control (CDC), seemed like a logical person to go to the table with the Democrat's ADA team. It is perhaps ironic that a doctor was seen as the appropriate point person, given the antithesis between the view of disability as a civil rights issue and the view of it as a medical one, but in this sense, the White House was continuing a long-standing misperception of what disability is—the administration considered it a disease rather than an identity.

Kuttner continued: "[Porter] would have been equally happy with Grace Mastalli, but [Department of] Justice internal politics and other factors . . . conspired to prevent this." Mastalli, an attractive woman with brown hair cut in bangs and, at the time, a distinct preference for jackets with dramatic shoulder pads, had come to the Justice Department recently from OMB and had been assigned by Thornburgh to be his second in the disability negotiations. The attorney general referred to Mastalli and Wodatch as "the dynamic duo"; they would be handling all the disability issues for him.

As the Justice Department was part of the White House, Mastalli could easily have been chosen over Roper to be the key negotiator, but as Kuttner noted, internal politics got in the way. First, she was a career employee as opposed to a politically appointed one. As such, she might not have passed an ideological litmus test since many in the Bush administration were still active Reaganites looking to continue the imprimatur of deregulation and tax reduction. The second reason was somewhat more personal. Her superior, Carol Crawford, held a grudge against Mastalli. As Mastalli says, Crawford would allow her to be the representative from Justice "over her dead body."

On the morning of June 29, Silverstein received a call from Sloan. Silverstein was preparing for a fight but was surprised to hear Sloan say he believed that the White House was fine with the mutually agreed-upon conditions. "I told him that was not what Roper said," Silverstein noted. Sensing an opportunity, Silverstein added that they would need to have the disability community in on the negotiations as technical experts. Sloan said that this might work.

There was no further contact the following day. Silverstein called the office and was told that Sloan was "gone for the day."

After a few days, there was a need for the principals to get involved in the negotiations, and so Sununu called Kennedy over the July 4 weekend. Sununu had heard that Osolinik was proving a difficult chair. Sununu said to Kennedy, "Get rid of Osolinik, and we can get this done." Obviously, Kennedy did not agree.

Kennedy called Thornburgh to see if the attorney general could jump-start the stalled talks. Thornburgh admitted that he was "out of the loop" and was going to try to get back in the process, adding that he thought the idea of a complete bill—no amendments—was "reasonable." Finally, on July 6, Kennedy and Sununu talked on the phone. They agreed to the idea that "both sides would stay together for the duration" and not allow amendments unless the changes were mutually agreed upon. In exchange, the ADA proponents agreed to exclude disability community representatives from the negotiating table. This was no small concession, given that the bill was about the disability community. The final proviso—that no one would talk to the press—was added. The agreement would be written up and signed by all concerned.

Meetings now began almost daily. There were several big topics for discussion. First was the issue of private bus transportation and whether the vehicles would be made accessible with wheelchair lifts. The private bus companies were extremely concerned that retroactively fitting buses would be an enormous expense that would bankrupt the companies. The second issue was whether the bill would affect state and local governments, as well as their buildings and facilities. Obviously, a standard Republican core issue was to limit the scope of "big government" and its regulations, supporting state's rights whenever possible. Another issue was telecommunications, which included relay services that the White House wanted paid for with a surcharge on all phone customers rather than with government funding. The Deaf community was reluctant to see that happen, according to Karen Peltz Strauss: "What we absolutely didn't want was for there to be a line item on people's phone bill that said 'Services for the deaf' or whatever."[1] A final issue was raising the limit on small businesses to fifty employees, as Gray had wanted, which would essentially cut out almost all small businesses in the United States.

Kuttner's diary reflects that things were going well: "Today marked the fifth negotiating session with the Senate staff. The task has turned out surprisingly easier than expected. With a minimum of obfuscation and search for tactical advantage that is 'negotiations,' we have found ourselves plugging away at a list of resolvable items, leaving things that will take really doing to later on and probably the principals."

On July 18, there was a meeting for White House staff only. Porter brought on a new person with whom he had worked in the past, lawyer Marianne McGettigan. Born and raised around working-class Boston, she claimed she had never met a Republican until she graduated from law school in 1975. But before law school, while she was staffing the office of Senator Warren Rudman of New Hampshire, McGettigan participated in a panel at a conference. Roger Porter, then at Harvard, approached her and, impressed by her performance, suggested that she might want to enroll in Harvard Law School. She did so. Later, when Porter was at the White House, he ran into Mc-Gettigan again and simply asked her if she was a registered independent. McGettigan thought this might have been a job offer, but didn't have the hubris to assume it was. The question about how she was registered to vote was a probe about her working at the White House, which vetted political appointments and only took registered Republicans. But since she had been working in Washington State, which did not require a person to have a party affiliation, she could say she was not an independent, which made her at least acceptable for the White House position.

Justin Dart was, more than any other person, the spokesperson and inspiration for the disability activist movement.

Tom Olin

Then vice president George Bush receiving the influential *Toward Independence* report in January 1988, which contained an early version of the ADA. By Bush, left to right: Sandy Parrino, Lex Frieden, Jeremiah Milbank Jr., C. Boyden Gray, and Justin Dart.

In St. Louis, on March 17, 1988, a group of ADAPT activists protested Greyhound's unwillingness to put lifts on buses.

The historic strike in March 1988 of the Deaf President Now movement, in which Deaf students at Gallaudet University took over the campus to protest the appointment of a hearing president chosen over qualified Deaf candidates. The strike resulted in the appointment of the first Deaf president, I. King Jordan.

A spirited group of marchers heads to the US Capitol to protest the slow pace of the ADA legislation in Congress. Front row (left to right): George Roberts (one of the original members of the Atlantis community and ADAPT); Stephanie Thomas; Frank Lozano; and Jennifer Keelan, pushed by her grandmother Eddie Olin, next to her sister Kaiilee; second row (left to right): Evan Kemp; Jay Rochlin (former head of the President's Committee on Employment of People with Disabilities), pushing Justin Dart's wheelchair; and Michael Winter. Janine Bertram can be seen between Rochlin and Lozano.

President Bush (center) leaves the White House followed by his major advisors (left to right): Chief of Staff John Sununu, counsel C. Boyden Gray, and Attorney General Richard Thornburgh.

White House chief of staff John Sununu, who acted as the "bad cop" for the White House in negotiations with ADA advocates.

White House counsel C. Boyden Gray, whose West Wing maneuvers gave disability advocates influence inside the executive branch.

Attorney General Richard Thornburgh, who headed the Justice Department and whose leadership pushed the ADA through the White House.

Rep. Stephen Bartlett, Republican from Texas, who shepherded the bill through the House along with Rep. Steny Hoyer, Democrat from Maryland.

Iconic photograph of demonstrators with disabilities who abandoned their wheelchairs and dropped their assistive devices to crawl up the Capitol steps in protest of the slow progress of the ADA legislation, March 12, 1990.

Tom Olin

Tom Olin

On March 13, 1990, activists stormed the US Capitol building, chained themselves together in the Rotunda, and demanded to speak to legislators. More than a hundred protestors were arrested.

Ralph Neas (second from left), the head of the Leadership Conference for Civil Rights and a key lobbyist and insider, with his wife, Katy Neas, aide to Sen. Harkin, along with Sen. Ted Kennedy (left) and Rep. Steny Hoyer (right).

Sen. Bob Dole (R-KS) during the Senate reception following passage of the ADA, along with other celebrants.

On Capitol Hill, Rep. Steny Hoyer (D-MD), left; Sen. Orrin Hatch (R-UT), wiping a tear of joy; and Justin Dart, in cowboy hat, head of the President's Committee on Employment of People with Disabilities, celebrate the passage of a bill guaranteeing a full range of civil rights for disabled Americans, July 13, 1990.

On the day of the ADA bill signing, DREDF members posed with Sen. Kennedy. Back row (left to right): Pat Wright, Deborah Doctor, Jennifer Steneberg, Lynn Jehle, George Steneberg, Ted Kennedy, and Michael Torpey; front row (left to right): Diane Lipton, Pam Steneberg, Arlene Mayerson, Faith Robinsong, Linda Kilb, Nora Pont, and Liz Savage; in front: Marilyn Golden.

Courtesy of the George Bush Presidential Library and Museum

President George Bush signs the ADA after calling for the "shameful wall of discrimination" to come down. Standing (left to right): Rev. Harold Wilke and Sandra Parrino; seated (left to right): Evan Kemp, Bush, and Justin Dart.

Courtesy of Chai Feldblum

Chai Feldblum and John Wodatch. Feldblum worked extensively with Reps. Hoyer and Bartlett on the House portion of the legislation. Nevertheless, she was not invited to the signing ceremony. Wodatch worked on the ADA in the Justice Department and wrote the regulations for Section 504 and for the ADA itself.

Sen. Tom Harkin, cosponsor of the ADA, along with Bobby Silverstein, who drafted most of the bill, at the celebration immediately following the White House signing ceremony.

However, McGettigan had decided she had had enough of Washington, DC, and so set her mind on being a "beach bum" for the entire coming year. She decamped to her brother's house on Cape Cod with some friends from the Kennedy School to begin her beachcombing experience. Porter came up to the area for the July 4 weekend and again asked her to come to the White House. His appeals were hard to resist, and so she agreed.

In a mere two weeks, on July 18, with sand still clinging to her soles, she arrived at her new job. She was just settling in on her first day in her office in the Old Executive Office Building and admiring the dramatically high ceilings, when she was called into a 4 p.m. meeting on the ADA. She says she asked, "'What's that?' And I was told it was the Americans with Disabilities Act, and that I was appointed to be the person for the White House" in the ongoing meetings. McGettigan noticed that Mark Disler, Orrin Hatch's aide, was at the meetings because he was the only one who had experience working on the Hill. "I said, 'Wait a minute; we're a separate branch. He has to go.'" Disler was from the Congress, and this was a White House meeting.

The second issue McGettigan addressed was the problem of John Wodatch, the civil servant whom Thornburgh had insisted join the meeting because he had worked on the 504 regulations. Someone said that if Disler had to go, then Wodatch had to go as well because he was a career appointee and wasn't political—wasn't even a Republican. McGettigan recalls that she got out the proposed ADA and picked out a section: "I said, 'Which of you here can define "undue hardship"?' There was silence. I said, 'John?' He had the answer. So Wodatch remained since no one else, apparently, could go through the legislative process and knew in detail what the act meant."

McGettigan says that the third issue she tackled was the current White House strategy, which was to "piss off Kennedy and wait till after the August recess. I knew exactly what Kennedy wanted to do. He wanted to bring it to the [Senate] floor when the recess was over and then get it to the House right away." Mastalli adds that the administration had been "stonewalling" in a process of "avoidance and denial." McGettigan analyzed the situation and advised the White House not to continue to delay: "I said, 'You have the optimal leverage on Kennedy right now. You better do it now.' They were going to just stop it. I said bring it forward now. That was the most significant thing I did in the whole thing." Because McGettigan was "extremely savvy in the ways of the Senate, having worked for Senator Rudman," according to Mastalli, her approach was heeded.

On July 20, the meeting of the grand potentates of politics took place. Kennedy and Sununu met in the evening of a cloudy day that had been pushing ninety humid degrees. Although Sununu called the discussions "constructive," and Kennedy says the meeting represented the "productive development of the issues," there was still a long way to go. Roper says of this meeting, which he attended as Sununu's staffer along with Osolinik, who was there as Kennedy's person: "The four of us sat on the couch in the White House chief of staff's office. For a time, Kennedy was just really pushing Sununu about, 'You guys are way off course here. We need you to be reasonable. Come on, and let's meet each other in the middle.' Those kind of things." Thinking about this meeting, Roper adds, "Then what happened was Sununu responded in kind. He was equally aggressive back at Kennedy. Finally, these two guys, they both said their piece, and they started dealing."

Kennedy later recalled that at this meeting, one of the sticking points was the continual thorn of remedies. Writing to Sununu later in the process, Kennedy said, "At our first meeting on the ADA on July 20, 1989, you said that Attorney General Thornburgh would handle the remedies issue."[2]

Sununu wrote the next day, "The President and his Administration are anxious to make progress this year on disability rights legislation." But he cautioned, "We seek sound legislation developed by consensus, not confrontation." The same issues that dogged the bill thus far remained stubbornly unresolved. Striking a pragmatic note, Sununu admitted that there might be no White House–approved bill that would go to markup. Instead, "we have to recognize that these differences may eventually have to be resolved through the subsequent steps in the legislative process." That move, a carrot and a stick, essentially said, "If you want the White House to be on board to approve this bill in the markup process, then you'd better accede to our demands. If not, we'll use the political process in the House to get what we want." Kennedy replied in gracious terms, saying that the ADA "offers Congress and President Bush an historic opportunity to end the widespread discrimination against people with disabilities. . . . I'm more hopeful than ever about achieving a landmark bill that we can all support with great enthusiasm." Both men were kicking the ball to the next yard line.

On July 24, Kennedy and Harkin met with Thornburgh. There had not been a breakthrough; the administration was buying time and slow-walking the ball in part to avoid having the Senate deal with the bill before the August adjournment of Congress. Thornburgh asked to postpone the markup in the Labor and Human Resources Committee that had been planned for July 26. In exchange, he promised to send over a bill of particulars by the next morning. But the next day, there was no bill of particulars forthcoming from the White House. Silverstein speculated that the list of White House objections did not come, "because the draft prepared by the Attorney General was opposed by camps within and outside the administration." The same day, Kemp wrote an impassioned memo to Thornburgh with the subject line "Break down in negotiations on the Americans with Disabilities Act."[3]

Kemp clearly bought the good guy/bad guy scenario that Silverstein articulated, seeing Thornburgh in the pro-ADA camp and Sununu in the anti-ADA group. Kemp pleaded to Thornburgh, "Without your immediate intervention, I believe that the Bush Administration is very close to providing the Democrats with a campaign issue and to alienating millions of disabled voters and their families." Perhaps having heard of Sununu's threat to Kennedy to let the parties duke it out in Congress without the White House's endorsement of the ADA bill, Kemp front-loaded the political message inherent in such a strategy. The Republicans, via the White House, would look like the naysayers to an important piece of legislation. Eschewing the gentlemanly senatorial language of the Kennedy-Sununu letters, Kemp cut to the chase: "At this point the Administration is perceived as refusing to negotiate in good faith. . . . I urge you to contact the President and, with his approval, to personally lead the negotiations." Kemp added, "Time is critical." He ended the memo saying ominously, "I am concerned that failure now, when we are so close, will have serious consequences for the President, the Republican Party, and yourself."

On July 26, Thornburgh finally sent his letter of particulars.

So close yet so far, the parties remained deadlocked on key issues that represented the core beliefs of each group. Mastalli describes the negotiations: "[They] felt on some days like armed combat." The two sides were facing each other, eye to eye, and now the question was, who would blink?

ON JULY 28, there was a three-hour meeting with Harkin, Hatch, Durenberger, Dole, Kennedy, and their staffs. That meeting, which opened this book, was the one held in Dole's office in which Sununu yelled at Silverstein and in which Kennedy, in turn, yelled back at Sununu. The scene, as described, could provide a cinematic and easy way to explain how the deadlock between the Senate and the White House was resolved. Kennedy's ire made Sununu back down, and the rest is history. But that isn't really what happened.

INDEED, THE COVER story of the success of the ADA is widely known. On August 2, the White House put out a triumphant and celebratory memo stating that "the Administration had reached a consensus with key Senators from both parties" on the ADA. Jonathan Young, one of the most reliable commentators on this history writes, "On July 31, Kennedy and Harkin and Attorney General Thornburgh resolved the handful of remaining issues and closed the negotiations . . . [with a] breakthrough compromise."[4]

But the hidden story is a more complex one that had been concealed for years. Rather than an impromptu "breakthrough" in one magical meeting of the contending forces—like the story of Kennedy yelling at Sununu and Sununu yielding—there were many secret, behind-the-scenes negotiations that painstakingly worked toward a grand compromise.

The prenegotiation ground rules agreed upon and signed in blood were that the only people allowed at the negotiating table would be representatives of the Senate and the White House. The House staff,

the business community, and the disability community would not
be allowed to attend. The reasons for this stricture were clear from
the White House perspective. To allow the lefty disability activists
from Berkeley like Wright and the Washington liberal lobbyists like
Neas to sit in on the discussions would forever taint the bill as a
radical ploy to expand big government. The political costs would be
too great to have that liberal shadow cast on the conservative Republican White House. Specifically, the White House had a vendetta
against Neas, seen as a turncoat Republican who, as the head of the
Leadership Conference on Civil Rights (LCCR), had spent much of
his time shooting down White House nominees, including Reagan's
1987 nomination of Robert Bork as Supreme Court justice. Bork
was anti–civil rights and anti-abortion, and Neas worked cease-
lessly to get Bork's nomination thrown out. Obviously, Neas was no
friend of the White House, and the idea that he would be directly
involved in negotiations was anathema. According to Mastalli, no
one at the White House was even permitted to take a call from Neas.
To the White House, Neas was "kryptonite."

It appears, as John Wodatch says, that all the memos, the hard
work of the White House, and all the engagement of lower-level staff
were "a cover." Gray's claim that he wasn't very involved was likewise a cover. Charles Kolb, who was Roper's successor, wrote that
the Bush's White House "was essentially an Administration where
people went to considerable lengths to conceal things from each
other . . . [a] systematic denial of the truth about what was actually happening around George Bush and his senior aides."[5] Many
of the memo writers and table negotiators were operating on false
premises, thinking they were helping to construct a viable bill. In
reality, the truly contentious parts of the bill were being horse-traded
in off-site locations.

Gray, as the main mover of the ADA in the upper echelon of the
White House staff, had to operate stealthily. His main contacts in
the disability community were Wright and Kemp. It was mainly with
Wright that he had substantial back-channel communications. Mc-
Gettigan notes that "as a lawyer, Boyden Gray was remarkably sup-
portive of [the ADA], although his staff were all Federalist Society.
I don't think they were [as supportive]." Gray's second in command

was John Patrick Schmitz. A scion of a wildly conservative family, Schmitz clerked for Supreme Court Justice Antonin Scalia. Schmitz's father had the dubious honor of having been expelled from the John Birch Society for holding views that were too far to the right of that extremely conservative organization. Gray's associate counsel was Lee Liberman, a brilliant lawyer with a tight-lipped, monotone speaking style who was close to Bradford Reynolds and who also clerked with Justice Scalia. She, along with Gray's brother Burton, was one of the founders of the Federalist Society. She is married to William G. Otis, who is also an expert at the Federalist Society and who was special counsel to George H. W. Bush. Otis publicly and successfully urged George W. Bush to grant a pardon to I. Lewis "Scooter" Libby for his conviction of a felony in the Valerie Plame affair. All these participants in the meetings were and are friends of Supreme Court Justice Clarence Thomas. It is completely understandable that Gray would want to conceal his active involvement with Wright from such coworkers.

As he recorded in his diary, Kuttner suddenly came to realize: "As the process wends its way forward, the cast of meaningful characters shrinks. Perhaps it never was large or close." In fact, the cast of real characters and players was extremely limited—in the White House, Gray, Porter, and Roper; in the Justice Department, Thornburgh; and presiding, Sununu and Bush. But Roper, Porter, and Sununu were left out of the crucial machinations around the grand compromise. This was really Gray's show, with the cooperation of Thornburgh, done through proxies.

Here's how this went: As the negotiations in July stalled, several crucial issues needed to be resolved: the scope of public accommodations, the range of remedies available, the exemption of religious groups, and the sticky issue of transportation, particularly whether there would be "local option." As explained earlier, the local option would allow cities and towns to determine whether they would use paratransit systems instead of the law's requiring that all localities make their transit systems accessible. The local option was a feature that disability activists and groups like ADAPT loathed, likening it to separate-but-equal laws under segregation. The other issues were the carve-out for religious organizations and the issue that dogged the negotiations and caused Sununu to blow up at Silverstein: whether an elevator had to be installed in a barber shop, for example, on a second floor. That is, a serious issue was the problem of how far accommodations had to go, especially in preexisting buildings and with small businesses.

The difficulty for disability advocates like Wright and the DREDF folks was that they had sworn resolutely that there would be no compromises once they had come up with their draft bill. ADAPT activists had fought long and hard on issues around transportation, and they would see any compromise on issues like the local option as a complete and total sellout. Meetings had to take place, but they had to be completely covert—out of the eyes of all the parties concerned because the disability activists were banned from the negotiations.

Mastalli, who was given wide latitude by Thornburgh to act as his second, suggested that the White House representative McGettigan come to her house and, over a series of "bagel breakfasts," they might try to work out a compromise with Osolinik of Kennedy's staff, along with the forbidden contingent of Wright and Neas. Wodatch from the Justice Department would be there as well to help with the language and the law. In other words, the signed-in-blood barrier separating the White House–Senate negotiating team from other interest groups would be breeched by allowing the disability community to secretly slide into the active negotiations. All this would be done undercover at Mastalli's house. Mastalli says that all the participants "swore to go to their graves" that they would not reveal that these off-site negotiations were being held. She notes, "While . . . key staff of both the White House and the Justice Department had many competing interests, policy views and priorities, nearly all appreciated the value of making a deal." The top players, like Gray and Thornburgh, wanted "plausible deniability" and knew that "the structure of an enactable law could not be achieved through the formal White House–Domestic Policy Council [route]. In short, they knew—as did I, Marianne [McGettigan], Patrisha Wright, Ralph Neas, and key senators and their staff . . . the art of behind-scenes/off-camera deal making."

Mastalli points out that while the politicians "engaged in the highly stylized and somewhat shocking public statements and exchanges [directed to their political bases], the deal makers worked out the proposed compromise and vetted issues through informal networks and channels." Referring to the old saw "Laws are like sausages; it is better not to see them being made," Mastalli adds, "The correct metaphor was not the overused sausage-making [one], but rather like Kabuki theater," in which actors make grand gestures in very slow motion. Silverstein backs up this theatrical metaphor in a somewhat different way. He sees himself as the conductor in the pit in the opera: "All you see is my bald spot. The senators are on the stage, and they're doing all of the heavy lifting, but I'm facilitating communication" and coordinating what is being done.

One important excision was the almost-complete exclusion of the OMB, run by Dick Darman. According to Charles Kolb, Darman had "elbowed aside Porter" and "was near centering his lock on policy with Sununu."[6] Paul Blustein of the *Los Angeles Times* described Darman this way: "Perhaps no Cabinet officer since Henry Kissinger has earned such a reputation for strategic wizardry and Machiavellian cunning as has Darman."[7] Mastalli says the secret negotiations were a way of turning the tables on Darman: "OMB is, in fact, infamous for cutting backroom deals against the wishes of cabinet officials. One way to look at the ADA is that the attorney general and White House counsel . . . turned the tables a bit on OMB." Given the White House factions, Gray might well have wanted to drive this deal without involving Porter, Sununu, or Darman. At this point, both Darman and Sununu were beginning to form the power duo that would later be criticized during the disastrous budget negotiations the following year. Maureen Dowd described them as "the two men, who both glory in a haughty intellectualism and an open disdain for Congress."[8] John Podhoretz noted that when one talks about "being in the loop," "Sununu and Darman and their trusted aides were the loop."[9]

From the Senate side, Kennedy was known as someone who was very well prepared and his main goal was to get to a deal. Durenberger, who cosponsored the ADA on the Republican side, says, "Kennedy's goal, on everything I worked with him on, was [that it was] more important to pass a bill than for it to be what he wanted it to be." Kennedy also had a strategy that fit in with that of Gray, which Kuttner commented on: keep the number of people making the decisions to a few. Durenberger describes Kennedy's tactic: "One of the first things I remember was a small meeting with a few senators and a few staff at the very beginning of the process with Ted Kennedy. He told us that drafting a bill like this was like playing the accordion. First you pull it open, fill it up with air, and then you squeeze it out. He was saying we would bring in a whole lot of people in the beginning and then slowly reduce the number in the room until we reached the final few decisions."

IN REALITY, WRIGHT and Neas had not really been out of the loop in the July negotiations. There was a "constant interchange," according to Feldblum, between Wright and Neas and the Senate negotiating team, although the interchange was done before or after each table negotiation. But the disability and civil rights people were never directly in contact with the White House negotiators before the bagel breakfasts.

The people who met in Mastalli's house all had connections with each other and with key people in the Senate and the White House. McGettigan and Neas were political allies. Wright had a direct line to Gray and Kennedy. Silverstein was intimately connected to Harkin and others on the Hill. Mastalli spanned the Justice Department and the policy side of the White House. Wodatch knew everyone in the disability community and everything about all the laws and regulations that had been enacted and enforced. In short, this was the A-team of ADA negotiators—the elite of those who managed and spoke for the political elite.

Silverstein was only permitted to attend one of the final bagel meetings because people were concerned that his tendency to keep extensive notes in his voluminous binders might compromise the secrecy all wanted and needed. In fact, these bagel breakfasts were so secret that Silverstein even to this day was unaware that there was more than that single meeting he had attended. In reality, there had been seven or eight, according to Neas, spanning the crucial month of July.

The meetings had to be kept secret, according to Mastalli, because "people were putting their careers and credibility at stake."

For McGettigan, meeting like this was a betrayal of White House trust and the trust of her mentor Porter. Thornburgh may have given Mastalli tacit permission to hold these meetings, but he clearly wanted plausible deniability. That was because Thornburgh wanted to have nothing to do with Neas, with whom he was sparring on other issues and who was persona non grata at the White House. Both Thornburgh and Neas are quick to point out that despite other disagreements, they worked willingly together on the ADA.

For the month of July, this group met on a regular basis and finally achieved a grand compromise. It involved a trade-off between limiting remedies while expanding the scope and range of public accommodations. In exchange for letting the range of institutions and entities increase way beyond that of the Civil Rights Act, the group agreed to let the remedies remain at the level of those of the Civil Rights Act—in other words, only injunctive relief and back pay for lost wages as well as repayment of legal fees. Left out would be those annoying features to Republicans—compensatory and punitive damages. Whereas the Civil Rights Act opened a few selected stores on Main Street—hotels, restaurants, theaters, and the like—the ADA theoretically opened every shop in town. Additional compromises involved allowing the onerous local option so that paratransit systems could be a part of the mix in urban and intra-urban transportation. Also, the timeline for compliance by over-the-road buses like Greyhound was pushed into the future, with various kinds of exceptions and releases to be determined by the secretary of transportation. The exceptions included having train stations comply with the ADA but with a get-out-of-jail ticket to be determined by the secretary of transportation as he or she saw fit. Finally, only larger businesses would be affected.

On July 30, a comfortably cool Sunday morning, Gray lay asleep in his Georgetown house, his pot-bellied pig snoring somewhere on the premises. It was quite early in the morning when the phone rang loudly. Gray turned over in bed and wearily answered it. On the other end of the line was Wright, who had attended the last bagel breakfast, which had finally sorted out all the details. She wanted Gray to be the first White House official to know the results. Wright was accustomed to calling Gray in a pinch. She recalls: "Whenever we were stuck with whatever the negotiation was, I would place a call to Boyden." In this early morning phone call, Wright detailed the grand compromise, and Gray penned it down on a bedside envelope. Wright later recalled that there were three documents in his personal papers that Gray thought particularly important to save for the Library of Congress, and this envelope was one of them.

The next day, Monday, July 31, a huge gaffe almost blew up the bagel breakfast secret. The idea was that Wodatch would pretend that the grand compromise had been cooked up at the Justice Department. He was unaware that Wright had already called Gray. Wodatch recalls: "I was supposed to go to the usual Monday meeting at the White House and say, 'Well, how do you all feel about this?' Boyden was going to then say, 'Hmm, that's not a bad idea,' and try and sell it." That way, there would be no whiff of a conspiracy between Gray, the disability advocates, and the White House.

That was the plan, but it didn't go as they figured. Wodatch walked into the West Wing, rehearsing the script in his mind. "I go in. Boyden is not there. I make my pitch to Roper and the other people who are there. Boyden comes in and makes the same pitch twenty minutes later. I'm sitting there going, 'Well, okay, there goes any [plan].'" It was obvious now to all concerned that all the work, the memos, and the planning had been irrelevant, since Gray had been secretly cutting the deal. As Wodatch remembers, then "a strange thing happened. Boyden was the boss, so now everyone knew that this was a deal that had been worked out, and that they didn't have anything to do with it. They also knew that the boss had done it, so then they all said, 'Well, okay, we'll go with that.' Boyden was the person who engineered that, and the rest of the White House was not really involved."

Kuttner's version in his contemporary diary supports Wodatch's recollection: "We also learned of Boyden Gray's Sunday morning phone call with Pat Wright of the Disability Rights Education and Defense Fund. She outlined to him a position that came uncannily close to [the one] that Justice had cooked up." Gray was clearly trying to claim that his knowledge of the compromise came from Wright alone, although his involvement ran much deeper.

Mastalli recalls that this "uncanny" moment was "the one that almost blew everything out of the water." Roper realized immediately that the proposals were too similar to be a coincidence. Someone had to be talking to Wright. There was a breech or a leak. Coming to this conclusion, he looked at McGettigan and said, "Have you been talking to Pat Wright?" McGettigan dissembled. Her reputation and integrity were on the line with this story.

On the same day, Kennedy called Thornburgh and proposed the bagel breakfast compromise. The Democrats had been arguing for an increase of remedies by including both the limited protections of the Civil Rights Act along with an older and more expansive Section 198 of the Civil Rights Act of 1866, which had been passed to protect the rights of African Americans after the Civil War. That nineteenth-century law allowed for punitive damages and even jail sentences for people who discriminated and denied civil rights. Kennedy agreed to "drop the Section 198 remedies from the ADA." His logic ran thus: "From my perspective, our deal was made on the basis that the remedies in the ADA would be parallel to the remedies in Title VII [the employment section of the Civil Rights Act of 1964]; persons with disabilities would be no better off, and no worse off, than other persons protected by Title VII."

When Kennedy called Thornburgh, the senator offered the deal that Thornburgh already knew from his back channel with Mastalli and Wodatch—that the ADA remedies would parallel Title VII for employment. For public accommodations, the ADA would parallel Title II of the Civil Rights Act but would also add provisions of the Fair Housing Act when it came to repeated patterns and practices of discrimination. In that case, the attorney general could bring a lawsuit, and punitive damages would apply. The deal ramped up the monetary penalties for first-time offenders from $27,500 to $50,000 and, for repeat offenders, from $55,000 to $100,000—and this would include legal fees being repaid to victims who prevailed. Thornburgh called back that night to agree to "almost all the remaining issues, including remedies," according to Kennedy.

On the issue that had exasperated Sununu—the barbershop on the second floor of a preexisting building—Kennedy and Sununu personally worked that one out on the phone on August 1. Only new buildings of three stories or more, and with more than three thousand square feet per floor, would be required to have elevators, as would all shopping malls and professional offices with health-care services.

Now that a deal had been reached, there was a series of meetings to confirm the results on both sides. It seemed as if the White House, with all the players in constant motion, suddenly had to come together to agree on something it may not have agreed on in the first place. Kuttner recalls that "Bill [Roper] accepted the logic of Grace's [Mastalli's] argument and tried to raise Roger [Porter] via the White House's telecommunication network." Roper reached Porter just before Bush's speech to the National Governors Association in Chicago. Suddenly, the political situation changed dramatically. Bush got on the phone and said he was cutting short a longer trip to the West because grisly video footage of the hanging of Colonel William Higgins, captured by the Hezbollah in Lebanon, had just been released. According to Kuttner, Roper spoke to Porter over the phone, "conveying the information that the attorney general [Thornburgh], Boyden Gray, and he thought it [the ADA] was an acceptable deal." Porter had agreed to raise the issues with Sununu on the way back from Chicago.

Bush flew back to the White House, landing by helicopter. Looking grim-faced in a dark suit, he walked briskly across the lawn with Sununu and Porter in tow.

With the White House in turmoil over the Higgins hanging, the message now was "take the deal and run," according to Kuttner, who further notes: "Senator Kennedy, we became aware, was, or at least his staff was, meeting with the disability group. There Pat Wright probably argued a similar line to that advanced with Boyden Gray: 'take the deal and run.'"

Roper and Porter then met with Sununu shortly after he returned from Chicago. Sununu told them to call Secretary of Transportation Skinner to let him know about the deal cut concerning buses and trains. Then there were meetings with Sununu, Porter, Roper, and Gray. They all reached agreement, and Bush, in the midst of a National Security Council meeting, signed off on the bill. The staff of Kennedy and the White House met all night, finishing up around 3 a.m. with language that turned the agreement into legislation.

The next morning, on August 2, the administration sent out its triumphant press release proclaiming, "The Administration has reached a consensus with key Senators from both parties on legislation that would expand the reach of this country's civil rights laws to include disabled Americans."[10] A mere page and a quarter, the announcement was short on details. It uses the words "President," "Administration," and applicable pronouns in almost all paragraphs—conveying the impression that the bill was essentially a White House and presidential document. It included wiggle-room statements that would allow Republicans to continue to amend the bill, even though the White House had signed an agreement not to allow amendments. For example, "We will continue to analyze the full ramifications of the legislation and look forward to working with the Senate and the House to complete the legislative process this year."

The following day, the press covered the story and did it in a way that the White House had hoped. Kuttner gloated, "The press apparently wrote from the White House statement more than other sources. Most stories began in a manner similar to the *New York Times*, 'President Bush and . . .' The press play was adequate—front page in the *Times*, *CBS Evening News*." The *Washington Post* had a less breathless report, mistakenly headlining the agreement as "Accord Set on Disabled-Worker Bill." The article continued: "The business community, however, expressed strong reservation. Despite compromises negotiated by the White House, 'It's still a bad bill,' said Fred Krebs, manager of business and government policy for the US Chamber of Commerce." Susan Perry of the American Bus Association, quoted in the article, was more blunt, calling the bill "a virtual death sentence for private bus systems. . . . The industry is in very fragile condition."[11] Marianne McGettigan, who now had to deal with the business community, reports that its basic message was, "This means war!"

ELEVEN

"THIS MEANS WAR!"

WHEN THE COMMITTEE VOTE was finally taken on bringing the bill to the floor, the motion passed unanimously, 16 to 0. The secret meetings, the days of negotiation, the deals and raised voices, the backslaps and handshakes, the cries and whispers, all culminated in this significant moment. The White House and the Senate ostensibly agreed. Further, they agreed in principle not to allow any amendments or other changes to the bill as it stood unless the White House and Senate themselves endorsed those changes.

But two factions were now unhappy. Some disability groups, including ADAPT, thought that the negotiators had conceded too much. And the business community believed that the White House had sold its interests down the river.

Influenced by the lobbying on the part of business, another group was also unhappy. The House held that the Senate had largely ignored it in these negotiations. According to Feldblum, the House was "pissed off." Particularly left out of the process had been Major Owens, the African American congressman from New York who had been an early supporter of the Weicker bill. In addition, because of the scope of this bill, it would have to pass through four major committees, with a total of seven subcommittees in the House. Normally, a bill only goes through one committee. The chairs of each committee are like minor potentates who control everything that goes on in committee. While all of these chairs were part of the Democratic majority, they still had reasons to object to various aspects of the bill. Democrats might be suspicious, as well, of the Republican White House's agenda. Republicans would be suspicious of a liberal bent to this civil rights legislation, and both Republicans and Democrats would be sensitive to the complaints of business owners in their districts. In other words, the newly born bill still had many growing pains to go through.

At this point, you might think of the ADA as a bill to protect the civil rights of people with disabilities. But you could also see it as a bill to protect businesses from frivolous lawsuits and sweeping government regulations. Each debate and amendment that would occur in the House could be seen as trying to effectuate one of these two imagined bills—one that protected citizens or one that protected businesses. In some cases, these two goals might coincide. In others, they might be very far apart.

On August 4, the day the Senate packed up and went on summer vacation, what was called a "Dear Colleague" letter was sent out, detailing the fifty-seven cosponsors of the bill. The letter was signed by a bipartisan group of legislative stars: Tom Harkin, Edward Kennedy, Bob Dole, John McCain, Paul Simon, George Mitchell, Jim Jeffords, and Dave Durenberger. The letter stressed the importance of the bill but also sounded the Republican theme: "The ADA will save the government and society billions of dollars by getting people off the dependency/social welfare rolls and into jobs, into restaurants, into shopping centers and into community activities."[1]

The next steps in the legislative process required the writing up and filing of a report by the Senate committee. The report is supposed to document the opinions and history surrounding the redrafted legislation, why the committee wants the bill passed, and the rationale for the amendments and other changes to the original legislation. Since Kennedy, still set on speeding the bill through Congress, advocated an early vote before the Senate as soon as the August vacation was over, Silverstein and colleagues swiftly created a draft report by August 22 and circulated it for comments among all concerned, including the administration, the entire business community via the administration, and disability groups.

The following week, Kuttner sent a memo to Roper and Porter about a briefing to placate the business community, explaining, "You can expect consternation over some of the things we did not get in the negotiations." Kuttner then organizes talking points under two headings: "Desire Fulfilled" and "Goal Unmet." In the "Desire Fulfilled" category, he notes, "Employment remedies follow what they wanted." This statement specifically meant that only back pay and legal fees would be levied in a successful suit. Also pleasing was that the EEOC would act as a gatekeeper to prevent frivolous lawsuits. In the downside column of "Goal Unmet," we find a concern about tax relief and the requirement that there be wheelchair lifts on all new buses. Kuttner singles out Fred Currey, the chairman of Greyhound, who said that he "may portray the lift requirement as the death knell of his firm."

Currey is a trim man who looks like a cross between Burgess Meredith and Ross Perot. Like the two, he had the razzmatazz spiel of the Music Man and could sell you anything. He was so adamant about his company because he had just pulled off what he thought was going to be a shrewd financial investment that was now rapidly going nightmarishly wrong. Currey had unwisely hyper-leveraged himself by borrowing a huge amount of money—three times what Greyhound was worth—to buy the company in the first place. He had hoped to turn the company public with an initial stock offering and then reap millions. The only problem was that the SEC had refused to let Greyhound go public. Now Currey was sitting on a property built on quicksand, and the ADA was going to hasten its demise. Currey was fighting for his economic life but was disguising that self-interest as a noble attempt to save the intercity bus system. The ADA was the Grinch that would ruin his hoped-for Christmas.

Given the agreement that there would be no amendments to the bill, the White House was making a not-so-subtle attempt to get around that restraint. The business community was being encouraged to influence the legislation in the House (with behind-the-scenes coaching of administration officials). Just as the agreement had been broken in the bagel breakfasts by the disability activists, now the White House was deploying a strategy of seeming to agree with the no-amendments promise, while signaling to Republicans and the business community that the administration gave free rein to change the bill as it worked its way through the House.

Early the next morning, on August 11, President Bush met with members of the disability community. The group was "generally pleased" with the legislation, according to a briefing paper for the president.

Business community members who had been giving the White House input throughout the negotiations arrived a day later and gathered around a long oval table in the windowless Roosevelt Room of the West Wing. This room, situated across the hallway from the Oval Office, was made during Franklin D. Roosevelt's redesign of the West Wing. FDR had shifted the Oval Office closer to the president's residence and increased the privacy of his office. Being closer to the residence was an obvious advantage for a mobility-impaired person, and the increased privacy helped Roosevelt get around without being seen using his wheelchair.

The meeting began with Bush entering the room and engaging in photo ops with businessmen (and just one businesswoman—Susan Meisinger of the American Society for Personnel Administration). After brief remarks, there was a general discussion in which Bush participated but then left in short order. The rest of the hour-long discussion continued with Gray, Roper, and Porter. At the table was the insistent and omnipresent Currey of Greyhound, as well as representatives of the American Institute of Architecture, the American Retail Federation, Associated General Contractors, the National Restaurant Association, the National Federation of Independent Business, the Hotel and Motel Association, Food Management, Inc., the National Association of Theater Owners, and the US Chamber of Commerce. Those who owned businesses were happy with the limited remedies that the White House had negotiated. But they were unhappy with the issue of public accommodations, which the White House had traded off. There were too many places considered public accommodations—exponentially more than in the Civil Rights Act of 1964. Also, the attorney general's action against a public accommodation would go beyond the 1964 act and include limited civil penalties, including monetary damages. The White House told the businesspeople to hang on, that their interests were duly noted.

Two days after the meeting, the *New York Times* carried a carefully placed story no doubt instigated by the business lobbyists who had sat in the Roosevelt Room. The headline blared the cautionary warning: "Bill Barring Bias Against Disabled Holds Wide Impact." The opening line said that the ADA "is likely to cost businesses hundreds of millions of dollars a year, representatives of trade and industry groups say." The article continued lamenting that the bill "would almost certainly invite a wave of lawsuits, business lobbyists said." The political reality was, as Nancy Fulco of the Chamber of Commerce said, "No politician can vote against this bill and survive." She was also worried: "We're going to see litigation all over the place." Rather than appear to be Scrooges throwing Tiny Tim off the bus, these businesspeople could not oppose the bill but would have to try to weaken it by a thousand cuts in timing, remedies, and how high or low the bar would be on accommodations.

The public relations message of the business lobby thus spun from trying to weaken the bill's effect on business to trying to protect the taxpayer from the abuses of overly zealous disability advocates. Currey, in his Cassandra-like fashion, lamented, "Any increase in our costs results in a decrease in our service to small towns." Instead of claiming, as he did in the White House meeting, that Greyhound would go under financially, he shifted his public tactics to emphasize that the ADA would hurt small-town America. Robert S. Morgan of AT&T expressed concerns about the relay system for the Deaf: "We are not sure how this service is going to be paid for. . . . Ultimately the . . . consumers will end up paying."[2]

A new and contentious issue also began to crop up in the ongoing meetings and the run-up to filing the report: would drug addicts be covered under the ADA? If drug addiction is a disease and not simply a bad habit, then drug addicts or recovering drug addicts should be able to claim protection under the ADA along with alcoholics and other substance abusers. The current rules concerning drugs at the workplace were determined during the Reagan administration and were very strict. Employers had the right to test their employees for drugs and, if they found traces of drugs, could fire their workers. Zero tolerance for drugs in the workplace was the Reagan signature put on the drug laws. Now all this heavy action would seem to evaporate into thin air with the ADA.

Kuttner wrote on August 28: "Our discussions with the Senate staff over the report to accompany the Americans With Disabilities Act have come down to one issue: coverage of drug addicts. . . . [T]hese are things of which controversies are formed." Drug czar and larger-than-life personality William Bennett had weighed in on this issue, along with his supporting staff of conservatives. Bennett's position was that while it wasn't such a bad thing for an employer to give a drug addict a break, this should not become federal policy across the board. He feared that the least worthy people would benefit the most from this provision—that is, those who every six months would claim they were beginning rehab or those who would say they were drug addicts just at the moment of giving a urine sample. The Kennedy-Harkin people were focusing on rehab, standards for urine tests, and the research finding that former addicts with steady jobs were the least likely to relapse.

As the report was being handed in, Kuttner gloomily assessed that the argument over the drug addicts was forbidding. He began to see and perhaps regret the behind-the-scenes maneuvers with the business community—maneuvers that in effect violated the initial agreements made with the Senate staff. Now the White House was encouraging business-friendly amendments that would "spontaneously" arise as the bill moved through the House. Kuttner described these concerns in his diary: "It seems we [at the White House] have never come to a real meeting of the minds over the one issue that opened the negotiation, the duration and strength of our commitment to the agreement we reach with the Senate." The sticky issues of the drug addicts, the telecommunications issue, the height of buildings requiring elevators, and the "regarded as" clause, which says that not only people with disabilities would be covered but also anyone who was "regarded as" being disabled (e.g., a gay person who was thought to have AIDS but didn't and was fired or not hired). Kuttner saw these unresolved issues as land "mines in the open field. We will discover them only [when we run into them in] the field."

On August 27, Roper updated Sununu that the ADA would be the order of business when the Senate reconvened on September 6. He told Sununu that he or Bush might have to "contact recalcitrant senators" to speed the process along. Roper reiterated what Kuttner had said and what disability activists might not have wanted to hear: "The Kennedy and Harkin staffs were most accommodating in the development of the committee report." This accommodation involved seventy-three changes requested by the business community and others in a ninety-page document. The Kennedy-Harkin staff accepted sixty-eight of the changes, which means the disability folks agreed to 93 percent of the changes—not something that the larger disability community would be happy to hear about. To justify these compromises and others, Kennedy said, "It was worth the trade-off because the concept was so important."[3]

The one issue that remained open was drug addiction. All agreed that the addicts who were detected by a drug test and whose performance was impaired because of addiction would not be covered. But it was the "self-confessed" drug addict under treatment that the business community wanted to rule out, while the Senate staff wanted that person covered.

Ironically, the week that the ADA came to the Senate was also a national antidrug week. On the evening of September 5, Bush broadcast to the nation a half-hour address from the Oval Office outlining and kicking off his antidrug campaign. The next morning, the ADA came crashing onto the Senate floor.

The same day, the *New York Times* came out against the ADA. In its front-page editorial titled "Blank Check for the Disabled?" the newspaper noted that the bill was moving through Congress with "narrow public scrutiny." Indeed it was, and that was the plan of the disability negotiators who wanted to go below the radar to avoid critiques such as this one. Liz Savage commented, "We didn't seek out press attention. . . . [T]he law never would have been enacted [if there had been a great deal of publicity]."[4] The editorial worried that the "the legislation is vague" and the "costs could be monumental." It wanted to see the language like "readily achievable" and "burdensome expense" made more precise and cost projections more accurate. "Congress and the Administration now have a . . . responsibility to stand back, to weigh, to calculate. . . . It requires little legislative skill . . . to write blank checks for worthy causes with other people's money."[5]

While the Senate was about to debate the bill, grassroots organizers like Marilyn Golden summoned disability activists around the country to write letters and make phone calls. Wavering senators were contacted by their constituencies. Cyndi Jones recalls: "During this time period, we're working to keep people calling and sending letters. . . . Anytime they wound up in Washington, they were doing lobbying." This hidden army largely invisible from the public eye was significant in writing letters and making phone calls, which could be done by people who otherwise would have trouble traveling to a demonstration or exerting influence in other ways.[6] The disability lobbying, including the very effective visits made to legislators by Justin Dart, had an impact. As Randel "Randy" Johnson, legal counsel to the Republicans, notes, "The disability groups were very effective lobbyists. Still are, you know, when they show up in the hallways . . . it's tough to say no."

When the ADA came to the floor of the Senate, it was a historic moment in so many ways, but one was that this was the first Senate debate simultaneously translated into American Sign Language. For the first time in history, a Deaf American citizen could watch the floor debate directly. As mentioned earlier, widespread captioning was one result of the ADA. Before the act, politics, along with sports, drama, and comedy—in fact, almost everything on TV—was off limits to the Deaf community. It was the first time Deaf people could be part of the twenty-four-hour news cycle.

The initial order of business was to make clear that the White House had agreed that the compromise bill should not be changed in any way. Senator Harkin said, "Senator Kennedy and I are committed to this compromise. We will oppose all weakening amendments. We will also oppose any amendments that are intended to strengthen the substitute, if these amendments do not have the support of the administration and Senator Dole. We are pleased that the administration and Senator Dole share this commitment. We hope other Senators will understand how fragile this compromise is and will support it." Harkin was clearly under the impression that the White House had agreed to avoid all amendments, but he appeared to be unaware that, as Kuttner had said, this agreement had already been broken.

Senator Hatch, who had initially wanted to write his own bill, as did Senator Dole, outlined his reservations about the details of the bill while continuing to support and cosponsor the overall project. Hatch's first objection concerned small businesses and the scope of public accommodations, which he found to be much broader than that of the Civil Rights Act. What bothered him, though, was that the bill exempted small businesses from the employment provisions but not from the public accommodation ones, which produced a paradox: "Thus, the bill creates the following anomaly: a mom-and-pop grocery store is not subject to the bill when it hires a clerk as a new employee, but it is subject to all of the bill's requirements in its treatment of customers, as well as to an extremely onerous penalty scheme when it violates any of those requirements."

Hatch also noted that the expenses of the ADA would be costly to small businesses: "This is a crucial difference between a disability civil rights statute and a civil rights statute in the race area. In order to provide equal treatment to racial minorities, a business need only disregard race and judge a person on his or her merits. To provide equal opportunity for a person with a disability will sometimes require additional actions and costs than those required to provide access to a person without a disability."

Hatch next complained that the remedies were excessive: "Our purpose here should not be punitive." And, under the impetus of the unflagging Currey, Hatch introduced the idea that the ADA would penalize bus companies. Channeling Currey, Hatch warned that smaller and less profitable rural bus routes would have to be abandoned if the costs went too high. As it turned out, Greyhound was so financially insecure that it filed for bankruptcy even before or perhaps in anticipation of the passage of the ADA. Greyhound did also eventually cancel rural bus routes in favor of more profitable, intercity ones. However, Greyhound still exists today and is the major interstate bus carrier in the United States (although it is now owned by a Scottish corporation).

The major amendment Hatch offered was for a tax credit to help small businesses. This credit was opposed by Dole and by Senator

Lloyd Bentsen, who called it a "killer amendment." Hatch was offended by that suggestion and said, "Do not tell me it will kill this bill. I would not let it kill the bill. Before I let that happen in conference, I would have stripped it out myself." Dole suggested that there already was a tax deduction he had authored in the tax code for removing architectural barriers. When brought to a vote, Hatch's amendment failed.

The heat began to be turned up over the issue of how disability was defined and who was to be included in the category of disabled. Senator William Armstrong brought up the issue of drug users and alcoholics. Senator Jesse Helms, a superconservative who would go on to be one of the eight senators to vote against the ADA, immediately got into a verbal spat with Harkin:

> MR. HELMS: Does the list of disabilities include pedophiles?
> MR. HARKIN: What?
> MR. HELMS: P-e-d-o-p-h-i-l-e-s?
> MR. HARKIN: I can assure the Senator, no.
> MR. HELMS: How about schizophrenics?
> MR. HARKIN: Schizophrenics, yes.
> MR. HELMS: Kleptomania?
> MR. HARKIN: Well, I am not certain on that.
> MR. HELMS: Manic depressives?
> MR. HARKIN: Manic depressives, yes. I can state that . . .
> MR. HELMS: How about a person with psychotic disorders?
> MR. HARKIN: I am told, yes. I am informed by staff it covers that.
> MR. HELMS: Homosexuals?
> MR. HARKIN: No; absolutely not.
> MR. HELMS: The Senator is certain about that?
> MR. HARKIN: I am absolutely certain.
> MR. HELMS: Transvestites?
> MR. HARKIN: Absolutely not.

The catechism is telling because the very imprecision of the ADA would go on to be its Achilles' heel in court, as justices attempted to determine who was or was not in the protected class. Eventually, the ADA was amended to exclude a list of manias and paraphilias like some of the ones discussed. A more telling issue revolved around homosexuality. Although homosexuality had been clearly excluded from protection under the ADA by legal precedent and definition (i.e., since the American Psychiatric Association declassified it in 1973, homosexuality was not considered a disability or a mental illness), socially conservative senators wanted to have a specific exclusion of homosexuality. Harkin and Kennedy readily agreed to this exclusion, since homosexuality was not considered a disability in the first place. But there was a too-easy slippage from homosexuality to AIDS. Helms slipped this way in his questioning of Harkin:

> MR. HELMS: But the Senator says that—well, the committee report says, as a matter of fact, if I recall correctly, that those who are HIV positive or who have active AIDS disease are covered. Does that mean that an adoption agency cannot inquire about HIV infection under this bill? I apologize for raising all these questions but I need to know the answers.
>
> MR. HARKIN: Again, I would ask what is the relevancy to an adoption agency whether or not a person has tested HIV positive. What is the relevancy of that to whether or not they can be good parents?
>
> MR. HELMS: If I understood the Senator's question, I hope he is not serious. What is the relevancy of somebody who tests HIV positive or who has AIDS with respect to the adoption of a child, is that what the Senator is asking me? . . .
>
> MR. HARKIN: Maybe I should ask the Senator, and again I ask the Senator why it would be relevant if someone tests HIV positive? Maybe there is something I do not understand.
>
> MR. HELMS: I think the Senator does understand.
>
> MR. HARKIN: No. I do not understand.
>
> MR. HELMS: You want to put a child up for adoption and subject him to a terrible risk? Bear in mind, Senator, that approximately 85 percent of the HIV-positive people in this country are drug users and/or homosexuals.

Helms made this point more bluntly: "If this were a bill involving people in a wheelchair or those who have been injured in the war, that is one thing. But how in the world did you . . . get into this business of classifying people who are HIV positive, most of whom are drug addicts or homosexuals or bisexuals, as disabled?"

An amendment by Helms that specifically excluded homosexuals, bisexuals, and what Helus termed "morally objectionable" conditions was approved. These included transvestism, pedophilia, transsexualism, exhibitionism, voyeurism, compulsive gambling, kleptomania, pyromania, gender-identity disorders, current psychoactive substance use disorders, and current psychoactive substance-induced organic mental disorders. In the process, a new concept was introduced—the "rehabilitated drug user." That person would be covered under the ADA while the ongoing drug user would not be. As Ruth Colker explains, "The language achieved under [this amendment] was key to the passage of the ADA because it offered a compromise between those who wanted drug users to be unprotected by the statute and those who wanted drug addiction recognized as a disability."[7]

Though Helms was obviously acting in homophobic and biased ways, his objections would have some resonance later on. When he got up on his soapbox, he was not entirely wrong: "The bottom line is that every question I have brought up is going to be decided in a Federal court after thousands of employers are sued under this act if it becomes law." Focusing on the terms "reasonable accommodations," Helms noted, "The Lord only knows what that means because that will be decided in court." And on "undue hardship": "That is a bunch of senseless verbiage."

The senators were clearly getting punchy after this all-day debate, and by the late evening, Senator Wendell Ford cautioned in colorful language about the dangers of rushing to a vote when not every head was clear: "I understand that we are pushed for time. It is quarter of 10 at night. So we want to get it over with and go on and make a mistake and hope that we can take care of it at the conference. . . . Apparently my colleagues are so anxious to get the bill passed tonight, they will swallow camels and choke on gnats."

Gordon Humphrey, another of the diehard opponents of the bill, also waxed both eloquent and histrionic: "Mr. President, the bill before us is one of the most radical pieces of legislation I have encountered in my 11 years in the Senate. . . . [T]his bill treads so heavily on individual liberty, private property rights, and the legitimate concerns of employers that I cannot support it." Employing one of the themes that would be used in the House deliberations, Humphrey said that the bill was badly written: "Frankly I am astounded that this bill has arrived on the floor in the shape we find it. . . . Clearly, according to the committee report the bill in its original form . . . is intended to create benefits for drug addicts, right at a time when we are trying to fight this scourge of drugs in our society." Recalling his role working for the House Republicans, Randy Johnson reinscribes this point of view: "[The Senate bill] wasn't all that well written when it came to the House. Then we really drilled in on improving the way it was written." While there may have been poorly written elements that would lead to confused legal decisions, the subtext of the "poorly written" argument also meant that the bill was not business friendly. That problem would be taken care of when the bill reached the House.

Late that night, after swallowing camels and choking on gnats, the Senate finally voted on the ADA—seventy-six in favor and eight against (with sixteen senators "not present"). The bill took four months from introduction to approval in the Senate with essentially only one day of debate; the next phase would take about a year to get through the House with months of debate.

TWELVE

BUILDING THE ACCESSIBLE RAMP TO
THE HOUSE OF REPRESENTATIVES

WHEN THE TEXAN Congressman Steve Bartlett watched President Bush give his inaugural speech, he realized that the ADA would become a reality. Bartlett, a Republican, now saw that his job would be to make the ADA conform to his own and his fellow Republicans' ideas. He recalls: "I was trying to avoid a law that would just get so litigious as to be disruptive to the lives of people with disabilities. Just to use an example, employers wouldn't hire people with disabilities, because they were afraid of lawsuit or other kinds of problems."

Lying in wait before the bill were four committees, seven subcommittees, and eleven hearings that would be working on different titles of the bill. According to Coelho, "It got to the point that leadership in the House, the Democratic leadership, was concerned that there would be a public negative reaction to the ADA because we had just gone through the Medicare Catastrophic Coverage Act debacle." That act was supposed to be a boon to senior citizens, protecting them from devastating health-care costs. However, when a percentage of Medicare recipients learned that they would have to foot the bill, they revolted so dramatically that the chair of the powerful Ways and Means Committee, Dan Rostenkowski, was chased out of a meeting in his own district by placard-wielding, angry senior citizens. The law was rescinded the same month the hearings on the ADA began.

Coelho says that the House was leery of making the same mistake twice: "What they did in the House was to refer to many committees with all the subcommittees, and that was a deliberate attempt to slow down the process and to make it next to impossible to get the bill out. So the ADA went to Judiciary, it went to Commerce, it went to Education and Labor, it went to Transportation, and so forth. So it gave the opposition all kinds of opportunities to kill it."

In fact, some of the committees went further and decided not to act just on the title relevant to the committee but to vet the entire bill itself. Each committee, according to Bartlett, was "ruled by a quite ferocious autocratic combination of committee chairman and ranking Republicans, as well as, in many cases, subcommittee chairman and ranking Republicans, and they each had their own territory." Because each committee was working on a specific title of the bill, the groups had no general reason to coordinate with each other. That seemed like a recipe for disaster and disagreement. Further, the House was frustrated that it had been excluded from the White House–Senate discussions. Tempers were heating up, and the bill had a long way to go.

To avoid this incoherence, Coelho, banished from the official halls of the legislature, nonetheless continued to play a role in helping to shepherd the bill through the Scylla and Charybdis of the House committees. Coelho and Newt Gingrich were seemingly as far apart on the political spectrum as they could be—one a liberal Democrat and the other a superconservative. Gingrich, a conservative Republican with a reputation for pushing the envelope, had just been involved in ousting Democrat representative Jim Wright for financial irregularities, and Wright's fate, as a result, had pushed Coelho himself to resign. Yet Coelho and Gingrich, like Kennedy and Hatch, had a good legislative working relationship. As Bartlett describes it, "It was a relationship based on wanting to achieve success. They were both willing to let the other guy, meaning the other party, achieve their success, as long as you could get yours. Newt and Tony had a way of doing business that was pretty successful and pretty unique, and on the outside of the House, people didn't know that."

Gingrich, then minority whip, came to Bartlett and said he had heard about the ADA from Coelho and he was eager to cosponsor it. Bartlett was a bit stunned because Gingrich actually had no idea what the bill contained. Bartlett felt that the bill was not "ready for prime time" and cautioned his colleague: "Well, Newt, I appreciate your enthusiasm for it, but if you cosponsor it, then there will be no more negotiation or conversation about making changes that need to be made to make it work."

Gingrich replied, "That's fine for you, but I've reached my own conclusion."

Bartlett recalls: "I always knew that when Newt would get this way, he was like a dog with a bone. When he wanted to do something for political purposes, he would go after it. He said, 'I really want to do it, and Bob Michel [minority leader] wants to do it too.'"

Bartlett replied, "Well, Newt, okay." He quickly added, "It's a yes, but in order to make this happen, you need to give me some authority to negotiate the bill so that it can be the bill you can be proud to cosponsor, as opposed to cosponsoring just because it has a nice title."

Gingrich furrowed his brow and said, "Let me talk to Bob Michel." He came back in a while and said, "Okay. Bob says that you're going to be in charge. We are designating you as our representative, as a leadership representative."

Bartlett points out that "this particular technique was almost never used in that era. . . . The technique is to have a leadership appointee who is going to manage the four committees." Gingrich specified, according to Bartlett, "We're going to designate you to negotiate the final terms of the bill in all four committees, and Tom Foley [Speaker of the House] is going to designate Democrat Steny Hoyer to be your counterpart across the aisle."

Hoyer recalls: "Speaker Foley assigned me and gave me the responsibility of coordinating [the ADA], because it was in, as you know, a number of committees and subcommittees in the Congress." Hoyer's role was unique since he had no appointments on any of the committees involved, while Bartlett was a member of at least one committee. Melissa Shulman, Hoyer's aide and a seasoned Hill staffer, says, "It was extraordinary" to have someone like Hoyer guide the bill through all four committees. Without that guidance, Shulman says, "the bill would not have happened." She also recalls that within days of Coelho's resignation and Hoyer's replacement of him, "Pat Wright and Ralph Neas showed up at my office, and it pretty much went from there . . . and they never left."

Major Owens was the Democratic chair of the part of the Education and Labor Committee that would hold meetings in September. He felt doubly shunned—first having been left out of the White House–Senate negotiations and then having been put in second place to Hoyer, a fellow Democrat who was not even on this committee or any other relevant committee that would vet the bill. Nevertheless, Owens remained supportive if miffed. In fact, the idea of beginning with Owen's subcommittee was part of the disability advocates' larger strategy. According to Coelho, "we orchestrated the assignment of where the bill would go to build up a momentum of getting it passed out of committee. So first we went to Labor because it was easy to get it out of the Labor Committee."

Bartlett had his own plan—a bit of legislative subterfuge. He recalls responding to Gingrich's request: "[I said,] 'Okay, Newt, I'll do it, but I need you to do two things. First of all, I want you to personally tell the four ranking Republicans of these four committees that I'm your representative. Secondly is [that] you and Bob [Michel] do not under any circumstances cosponsor that bill or even act like you're going to cosponsor until I say so, because that will be my leverage.' That way, I had Newt and Bob Michel. Their cosponsorship was my big-ticket item. No one really cared if I was a cosponsor, but to have Newt and Bob Michel in my pocket ready to cosponsor when I said so gave me real power. Newt said, 'Well okay, but don't take too long.' I said, 'Newt, I'll take as long as it takes, but don't get ahead of me.' That was our agreement."

It would take nine months for the bill to work its way through four committees, seven subcommittees, and two conferences. Bartlett foresaw that if he waited for each committee to take up its issue, the process would be drawn out even longer. So he hatched a plan to go to the Republican ranking members on the committees and discover their objections in advance. He knew they'd be pressed to pass the bill by the Democratic chairs of each committee since the Democrats controlled Congress at this time. As Bartlett notes, the objections "were mostly coming from the business community."

After hearing their objections, Bartlett went to Hoyer and said, "OK, I'm ready. I've got in my pocket what these four ranking members want to achieve." Hoyer knew what he wanted to achieve, so they went into intense negotiations that lasted well over a hundred hours. These sessions were held in a conference room on the same floor as Hoyer's office and, according to all involved, were grueling and involved many late nights and a lot of pizza. According to Bartlett, "that's when I told Gingrich and Michel they could now go ahead and be cosponsors."

Bartlett and Hoyer agreed to bring in experts. On the Democrat-disability side was Feldblum as lead legal advisor and whom Hoyer referred to as "my lawyer." Also attending were Wright and Shulman. Occasionally Neas might show up. On the Republican-business side were Randy Johnson, Pat Morrissey, and Jeff McGuiness. Morrissey recalls: "The negotiations were civil, no one stormed out of the room, and everyone wanted to get to yes. Everyone learned all the constitutional issues, everyone dove in. People spent so much time on something they didn't know a lot about, and by the end of the day, they were experts on [it]. I never thought about the Greyhound buses. I never thought about trains. It was an extraordinary effort." Jim Weisman was the expert on buses and trains. He recalls these sessions as "fun. . . . We were always laughing." Well, perhaps not always, but it was a memorable marathon of negotiations to those involved.

Bartlett, as part of his plan, realized early on that the White House had agreed to the concept of no amendments. Given his canvassing of Republicans, he also saw that the House would never pass the bill without major alterations. So he went to his aide Morrissey and said, "Pat, we want to make a list of what we want. It's got to be short, only ten things, focus on the employment part, and we're going to see Roper. Yep, you and me." Morrissey recalls that they got into Bartlett's beat-up Chevy Camaro. Morrissey noticed that the car "was falling apart. You could actually see the road through the floor. On the floor where I was to sit, there were probably fifty V-8 [juice] cans that he had consumed on the way to work over the course of a month. I have cerebral palsy, and getting into his car was a real challenge. When we got to the White House and the marine guard opened the door, the guy was clearly in a state of shock when he saw all the tomato [juice] cans on the floor. And I practically fell into the guy's arms trying to get out of the car, because I couldn't stand up with all those cans."

As Morrissey recounted, when they went to the White House to see Roper, Bartlett drawled in his direct Texas way, "[Roper said,] 'There's no way this son of a bitch is going to get passed unless the House gets to influence the final product. It's not perfect, and here's the ten things I want.' And that changed the whole dynamics in the House. His credibility was at that moment established." According to Morrissey, Roper agreed to their list and thus signaled yet again that the White House was never really committed to the no-amendments policy.

Hoyer for his part was so involved that when the Food Marketing Institute approached him about the issue of retrofitting supermarkets, Hoyer drove out to a shopping mall in Hyattsville, Maryland, in his district, to see how the bill would work. Morrissey accompanied him to see "how you would move shopping carts in and out. They wanted to show us what the practical impediments were about what the public accommodations sections would require. You know, when you go to the supermarket and there are the gates they use to block the carts when you go to the parking lot. Also, an older facility might not have wide-enough aisles, so how do you do the accommodation?" Hoyer stood in the large parking lot, surveying the situation, and took it all in. Later he worked on compromises that allowed for reasonable accommodations without committing supermarkets to do major retrofitting. The Food Marketing Institute supported the bill.

Feldblum remembers drafting language over the month of October as the Hoyer-Bartlett negotiations continued. It was a time-consuming and herculean effort, and a lonely one for Feldblum at that. "I just worked—I worked so many hours, it's even hard to describe. I think the only reason why it just didn't seem particularly weird to me is I worked so many hours, as a law clerk to [Chief Justice] Blackmun a year or so before. So working eighty hours a week, pulling all-nighters, if need be." Shulman was working so hard on the bill that her fiancé said to her, "If the bill isn't passed soon, we're not getting married!"

With the start of the House phase of negotiating, the disability advocate group that included Wright, Neas, Silverstein, Savage, and others began meeting every morning at the cafeteria in the Rayburn House Building, a Washington-insider location famous for its breakfasts. In addition, weekly meetings at the United Methodist Building continued with the coalition of disability groups to inform them what was going on. Feldblum noted that there might be pushbacks from various subgroups—the Deaf community, blind people, transit advocates, drug addiction groups—when they felt their interests were being sacrificed. Another purpose of the United Methodist Building meetings was so that Savage could organize the week's lobbying using local and national representatives to martial the troops. According to Feldblum, Savage would "figure out who in their [the congressional members'] district they listen to. Getting that person to call or to set up a visit when the member was back in the district—those are one-by-one lobbying efforts."

As the lobbying efforts continued, the disability team made its first strategic move in the House. It brought the bill to Education and Labor, the "safe" committee.

It was chaired by Gus Hawkins, the first black US representative elected from west of the Mississippi. Within that committee were two subcommittees that would have purview—the Select Education Subcommittee, on which Bartlett sat and which was chaired by Owens, an African American congressman from New York, and the Employment Opportunities Subcommittee, headed by Matthew Martinez. The latter committee, in the interests of efficiency, ceded its rights to hold hearings to the former. Significantly, all three committees were headed by minorities directly affected by the earlier civil rights legislation and now proponents of this new one. And of course, Bartlett was the ranking Republican on the Select Education Subcommittee. Plunging into the fray a few days after the Senate vote, that committee held its first meeting on September 13. There were many speakers, most notably Evan Kemp, who described the shock that people had upon seeing him, a disabled wheelchair user, and making assumptions about him, to then find out that he was a commissioner at the EEOC.

The House Judiciary Committee's subcommittee on Civil and Constitutional Rights had already jumped ahead of all the committees by meeting on August 3. Its initial hearing opened with James Brady, Reagan's press secretary who had been rendered paralyzed by a gunshot during an assassination attempt on the president. He highlighted an important point about being disabled—that unlike other minorities, any person can become disabled. "I never thought I would be in the disability community. I joined it in an instant 8 years ago, somewhat against my wish. . . . Disability is a fact of life, like being white or black or Hispanic." Echoing that theme, Don Edwards, the chair, said, "You know, when I was growing up, I never thought my family would be connected with disability. . . . Now I have found that of my four grandchildren, two have serious disabilities, and one of my sons has a serious disability." He recounted how his son, a lawyer, couldn't get a position at law firms because of his disability. Brady went on to praise the ADA as a Republican bill, written by a Republican agency, headed by the Republican Justin Dart, supported by a Republican president, and so on.

The next speaker was a Vietnam veteran who argued for the ADA. Upon completing his testimony, Representative William Dannemeyer asked him how he felt about drug users being included, as protected in the bill. The veteran's riposte was that all Americans should be protected. Badgering the veteran, Dannemeyer wanted to know if people with HIV should be allowed to be pilots. "How about the airline pilot who is HIV positive and we know that 40 to 50 percent of persons in that category exhibit dementia, deterioration of the brain. Do you believe that person should be flying an airplane?" Conservative Dannemeyer, one of only twenty members of Congress to ultimately vote against the ADA, was reading from the talking points that would be used throughout the House hearings: attacks based on alcoholism, drug use, sexual orientation, and HIV status.

When Feldblum testified, she too was questioned aggressively by Dannemeyer, again on the issue of people with HIV and drug addicts. He also questioned what he called the overly broad definition of disability. "As you describe the act," he said, "it's possible that there isn't anyone in America who doesn't come within the coverage. It's a brilliant move about which you are engaged. We are all disabled. . . . You should hear some of the things people say about me. I mean, people have not only questioned my judgment but my thinking capacity. Wouldn't you agree?"

Feldblum dodged the bullet: "You would have to prove that you were mentally disabled in order to get under protection. I don't know if you'd want to come into court and do that."

Amid general laughter, Dannemeyer jokingly replied, "It's obvious, really, isn't it?"

The humor, however, didn't hide what Dannemeyer might be trying to do. By asking such questions, the congressman, perhaps sensing that the ADA would pass even with his opposition, was trying to create legislative history that could be used in later court decisions that might rule in favor of his more conservative position. In fact, when Feldblum consistently refused to offer yes-or-no answers to complex questions posed by Dannemeyer about people who were HIV positive or drug addicts, the representative said, "Are you telling me you don't know?"

Feldblum replied, "No, I'm telling you the way it often is in law."

Dannemeyer snapped back, "Or you don't want to say?"

Feldblum quickly replied, "No, no. The way it is often in law, that the question is not, for example, a yes or no issue."

Dannemeyer revealed, perhaps, the reason for his adamant grilling: "Are we finessing legislative history for some judge to resolve [later]?"

Feldblum, then twenty-nine years old, was obviously being very aggressively questioned. She had been suffering from anxiety attacks that began in the previous year, and although she handled herself very well, this was clearly a stressful situation. Dannemeyer perhaps felt he could intensely grill a young female lawyer in a way that he might not question a more seasoned member of the administration.

On September 20 and 28, the House Committee on Public Works and Transportation held its hearings. Norman Mineta, the subcommittee's chair, called for bipartisanship. As a close friend of Coelho, Mineta had been primed to push for the ADA as it stood. Mineta is an Asian American of Japanese descent. During World War II, his family had been torn from its comfortable life in San Jose and sent to an internment camp with twelve thousand other Japanese Americans crammed into barely heated barracks in Wyoming. As the victim of these harsh policies, Mineta had been in the forefront of fighting for a US apology and reparations for Japanese American citizens. Coelho recalls: "When we had the legislation dealing with the reparations for the Japanese, because of the internment of the Japanese, I as the whip was very helpful to him in getting that legislation through. So I basically just went to him and said, 'You know, I was helpful to you. I need you to be helpful to me.' But he came through for us big time, and we got through [his committee] by one vote."

Seemingly in that spirit of bipartisanship, the ranking Republican, Bud Shuster, revealed that he had a special interest in the bill because his mother was a double amputee. "I have banged up my knuckles more times than I can remember trying to juggle a wheelchair through a door that was too narrow or trying to get a wheelchair up a flight of stairs or into rest areas." Although superficially sympathetic, Shuster was also close to Fred Currey, according to Coelho, and thus echoed the Republican concerns about the cost of wheelchair lifts. In fact, Shuster would kick out James Weisman, who worked on transportation for the Eastern Paralyzed Veterans of America, from his congressional office more than once before calling the police to arrest thirty-five wheelchair users demonstrating outside his office the following March. Later, with political Pavlovian conditioning, he called the police on a group of wheelchair users who he thought were coming down his hallway to protest again when they were in fact simply visiting Hamilton Fish's office next door.

That day, the testimony split on party lines. The Republicans like Shuster and Dennis Hastert hammered away at people who were testifying. Coelho remembers that Shuster "fought us all the way." Their point was that wheelchair lifts on buses were expensive. Having to provide both these and paratransit would be a burden on communities. The Republicans argued that places where the winters were bad and had much snow would also be unable to use those wheelchair lifts, because most users could not really get out of their houses and through the snow to the bus stops. Moreover, they said, lifts malfunctioned more in the snow. These interrogations were reminiscent of a TV legal procedural in which an aggressive prosecuting attorney attacked a hapless witness. At one point, Hastert cross-examined someone who was advocating universal accessibility on buses:

> MR. HASTERT: Now, you say there are some buses that [only] get 10 or 12 pickups [of wheelchair users] a day. That means that you have buses that are equipped, that are riding the routes, that never get a rider?
>
> MR. JENKINS: No not necessarily so. With the 27 vehicles that we have, you have to remember that at least 3 of those vehicles are used for spares. . . . Out of those buses that are out there, there are some that get one lift, but there are some buses that get more than one lift.
>
> MR. HASTERT: A day?
>
> MR. JENKINS: There are some days when you have holidays and when you have—
>
> MR. HASTERT: Well, the numbers work out, sir, that say you get one lift every three days, average. So, evidently, you have buses out there that never get lifts.
>
> MR. JENKINS: No. Each and every one of our buses gets lifts at some time or another. There are some buses that get more lifts than others.
>
> MR. HASTERT: Every day? Every week? Every month?
>
> MR. JENKINS: I would say on a weekly basis . . .
>
> MR. HASTERT: [discussing costs] So, it is a 3 percent local share. Who is that? Is [it] the other riders who pick that up or is [it] the taxpayer[?].
>
> MR. JENKINS: The county government.
>
> MR. HASTERT: The taxpayers.
>
> MR. JENKINS: The taxpayers.

You can feel the witness squirming and sweating as Hastert hones in on his main point, repeated by many other Republicans, that this bill is costly and excessively broad. In this case, Hastert's talking points are to push for a local option that would countermand the idea of universal access on buses and trains. Local option, of course, was anathema to disability activists.

These interrogations might look like they are about trivial technicalities, but at base, the argument is about how broad the federal government's reach should be. On the liberal side is a central government regulating private businesses, states, and localities; on the conservative side is the free market and states' rights. This is an old argument dressed up in new clothes for the occasion. When it came time for the bus owners to testify, one congressman not on the committee made a special trip to the hearing to testify about the chair of the board of the American Bus Association and the owner of three bus companies (one in Pennsylvania): "Frank Henry represents the essence of the free enterprise system and the success of that system not only in Pennsylvania but nationally." The stakes were that high—the essence of free enterprise versus the force of federal regulation.

Chuck Busskohl, the owner of Arrow Stage Lines and the director of the United Bus Owners of America, was blunter: "This bill, by requiring full accessibility on all buses would weaken, if not kill, the bus industry. Jeopardizing the industry's economic survival threatens to leave as many as 10,000 communities without any intercity transportation service."

The omnipresent and irrepressible Currey achieved the high point of the session. Irascibly, the chief executive of Greyhound began by reframing the idea of discrimination: "The bill as proposed by the Senate discriminates against inter-city bus companies. I know that is not a very popular thing to say, nevertheless, it is true." He made a prediction: "This bill will initiate and conclude with the collapse of our rural service at Greyhound." Currey mentioned in passing that 50 percent of his ridership were poor, earning below $15,000 per year. In other words, intercity buses were the affordable option for poor people traveling long distances. His strategy, then, was to pit the poor against the disabled. But he forgot that the disabled are themselves mostly poor—twice as likely as the nondisabled to earn $15,000 or less for a family of four. Currey's was a false opposition.

Nonetheless, his solution was that the bill should be changed so that instead of mandating that the entire fleet be accessible, the system would be made accessible by the use of a special chair (not a wheelchair lift) that would elevate the person to the bus level. Each terminal or bus could maintain one such chair, and therefore the costs would be much less than installing and maintaining wheelchair lifts in an entire fleet of buses.

One of the reasons that Currey came up with this plan was that the vast majority of buses in the Greyhound fleet were leased from third-party companies. Greyhound actually is a service provider without a fleet and acts more like a middleman than an owner. So the cost of retrofitting buses would be borne by the company leasing the bus to Greyhound and would, of course, be passed along to Greyhound. Much simpler would be to buy the Buck Roger chairs that would catapult the hapless disabled person onto the bus.

Currey was using strong-arm tactics outside the hearing rooms. Senator Sherwood Boehlert was directly pressured. Greyhound said it would abandon service to the Utica, New York, region that Boehlert represented if he did not vote against the bill. "And if it is you who votes for it, Congressman, it will be you that loses the service. Explain *that* to your constituents . . . why they lost Greyhound."[1]

After these hearings, the subcommittee would not meet again until the markup in April 1990. However, because of overlapping jurisdictions, it was not only Mineta's subcommittee but also the Energy and Commerce Committee meeting that would oversee aspects of transportation since the latter had jurisdiction over Amtrak. John Dingell, considered one of the most powerful members of the House, headed the Energy and Commerce Committee. He ruled the committee with a strong hand, and while supportive of the ADA, he was also a strong advocate for Amtrak and didn't want to endanger its already shaky financial foundations, which had been routinely deprived of funds by successive administrations. President Bush, like Reagan, had recommended stripping all federal funds from Amtrak, and representatives like Dingell were against such actions. Anything that might weaken Amtrak was viewed with suspicion. Wright recalls that Dingell's committee was the hardest to get through. The subject of preventing mentally disabled people from riding the trains came up. Wright said, "Well, if we set up a test for mental stability probably no one would be riding Amtrak." At which point Dingell's staff person threw a pen across the room at her.

The Subcommittee on Transportation hearings began almost surreally with an immediate move by the chair, Representative Buz Luken, to attack the bill for issues related to drug addiction. Following the usual talking points, Luken badgered witnesses from the Department of Transportation, avoiding issues directly related to accommodations for people with disabilities by focusing on whether drivers of trains would be randomly tested for drugs. Luken himself could hardly afford to take the high ground, having just been convicted for soliciting the sexual favors of a sixteen-year-old girl and then trying to appease her mother with the compensation of a government job. He would subsequently be convicted of financial crimes and do jail time after being forced to resign from Congress in 1990. He was replaced by the present Speaker of the House, John Boehner.

The representative from Amtrak, Graham Clayton Jr., felt that the rail line was already in compliance with the bill as far as railroad cars were concerned and the requirement that at least one car per train be accessible. But he did not like the provision that all new cars had to be accessible, and he proposed that only 20 percent of new cars be compliant, as long as every train had one accessible car. Also, one of the greatest concerns was that railroad stations themselves be made accessible. Of 499 Amtrak stations, only 88 were accessible. Like Greyhound, Clayton threatened to close small stations rather than make them accessible. "We would just discontinue the station, which we have the right to do in most cases." And like Currey, he put the future in dire terms: "We cannot possibly survive and I don't think we will survive unless we reduce our need for subsidy." The implication was that retrofitting stations would lead to the end of Amtrak, which of course did not happen. (Yet, after twenty-five years, the majority of Amtrak stations are still not compliant.[2]) Finally, he added that Amtrak's current requirement that travelers with disabilities give Amtrak notice twelve hours in advance should be retained.

The next speaker, Phillip Calkins, a wheelchair user and director of public affairs for the President's Committee on Employment of People with Disabilities, headed by Justin Dart, objected to this twelve-hour advance requirement. Mentioning that his boss was sitting in the hearing, Calkins wondered, "Suppose for a minute he gets a request for someone to be in a meeting in New York this evening or tomorrow, which is not at all inconceivable, and he decides that I am the person to go to that meeting. . . . [I]t would certainly impair my usefulness to the President's Committee if Jay [his boss] could not make the decision to send me to that meeting, which of course would require me to hustle down to Union Station, get on the train and go to the meeting."

Luken reacted angrily to Calkins and Tim Cook, both disability advocates, saying that they were "lecturing" him without paying attention to the costs: "You don't mind if I become a little impatient." Luken's frustration comes from the fact that Amtrak would need funding to become compliant, but Reagan and now Bush had pledged to end federal subsidies for Amtrak. In fact, Bush would veto but Congress would sustain a funding package for Amtrak the following May.

From the perspective of twenty-five years later, the strong pushback by bus and train companies concerning their fears about the cost and effect of the ADA now seems unwarranted. Today, we routinely see kneeling buses and buses with wheelchair lifts as a part of the urban landscape. It is an aspect of the success of the ADA that many of its accomplishments are now invisible to us since they are so much a part of our lives.

Some members of the Judiciary Committee met again on October 11, this time with representatives from the business community. First up was John Motley of the National Federation of Independent Business. He wasn't shy to point out that his organization took a poll in which 87 percent of its more than a half million members opposed the bill. They would prefer a bill that was much weaker and didn't tell businesses what to do. Rather, they would like legislation that would encourage voluntary change. His reasoning was that unlike other civil rights legislation, the ADA "access for the disabled comes at the expense of others."

When James Sensenbrenner, a member of the committee, questioned those testifying, he added a personal note. His wife, Cheryl, he said, was a paraplegic and her sister had Down syndrome. Sensenbrenner's son Frank also had attention deficit hyperactivity disorder (ADHD). Although Sensenbrenner was a staunch conservative on many issues and grew up as an heir to the Kimberly-Clark fortune (his grandfather invented Kotex), he was nonetheless an advocate on many disability-related issues. He addressed the pro-business panel and noted that Republicans supported the ADA and so did a Republican pro-business administration. Sensenbrenner suggested the opponents of the bill act in a constructive manner "rather than trying to nitpick the bill to death." Indeed, an angry colloquy developed in which Sensenbrenner condemned one speaker for his tone and his attempts at all costs to limit the bill.

The committee met again on October 12, but this time it was the full Judiciary Committee, called together in a grand summit to hear Attorney General Thornburgh. Questions addressed to him were mainly concerning the expansive public accommodations title and specifically this title's lack of an exemption for small businesses—an exemption that the employment title had. Thornburgh pointed out that it was a matter of practicality—the small-business exemption in employment exempted about 20 percent of employers. But if there were a similar exemption for public accommodations, it would exempt almost 90 percent of locations and 100 percent of doctors and dentists offices, drug stores, laundries, and so forth.

After Thornburgh's testimony, Paul Roth, the chair of the National Association of Theater Owners, spoke about the costs to small rural theaters where low-income people go for entertainment and how those theaters would have to close. In arguments against some of the ADA's requirements, it seems that pitting the poor against the disabled was the standard strategy.

Most of the hearings were finished by the end of October. Some committees had written up reports and voted on the results. Now the effort would all take place between staff members trying to work out details. These backroom negotiations would go on until the spring of 1990. As they continued, major events dominated the news cycle. Bush and Mikhail Gorbachev officially announced the end of the Cold War, as McDonald's opened its first restaurant in Moscow. Nelson Mandela was freed as the world celebrated. At home, Greyhound drivers went on strike, to Currey's consternation. Freedom and justice were in the air. In quieter rooms and hallways, the disability crew was working on its own attempts to negotiate freedom and justice to attain consensus on the ADA.

THIRTEEN

THE CAPITOL CRAWL

WHENEVER PEOPLE THINK about activism and the ADA, one image comes to mind. A black-and-white photograph of people with disabilities crawling up the steps of the Capitol. Composed of people of all ages and disabilities, the gritty look of the crawl brings out the power of activism in the face of power. On March 12, 1990, three dozen ADAPT members who planned to stage one of their rambunctious, in-your-face in actions converged on Washington. Bob Kafka, an ADAPT leader who wore his curly hair long and sported a beard, recalls in his thick Bronx accent that "those that were doing the legislative work pretty well kept it as an inside-the-loop activity. They were doing lobbying in the traditional sense."

Kafka was part of a more action-oriented mind-set. Having grown up in the Bronx in a family in which his grandparents lived in what was known as "the Coops," a housing cooperative built by Communists, he had social protest running through his veins. After serving in Vietnam and then becoming disabled in a crash that happened after he had one too many beers, Kafka now had little patience for the slow pace of negotiation and legislation. Members of ADAPT were the Hell's Angels of the disability movement—speeding around on wheelchairs rather than Harleys, wearing headbands, blocking nonaccessible buses, and chasing transportation executives around town. Getting arrested was their red badge of courage.

Kafka describes his take on ADAPT's involvement with the ADA: "I believe that what occurred was the ADA went through the Senate pretty easily. It got bogged down in the House, and it really looked like it was going to die. That's when Pat Wright, Marilyn Golden, and Liz Savage contacted ADAPT." If Kafka's view doesn't exactly get the course of the ADA absolutely right, that is because, as he says, the grassroots were often left uninformed of inside-the-Beltway happenings. In fact, the ADA was far from being on its deathbed, but many in the disability community received that truncated message. And that's why they showed up at the Capitol steps in March.

The ADAPT members were joined by members of the National Rehabilitation Association who were in Washington for their annual convention. Upward of five hundred people first attended a rally in front of the White House to protest what they perceived to be the slow pace of the ADA through the chambers of the House. They were going to march to the Capitol, where they would hold their political action. Boyden Gray, informed by Evan Kemp and Pat Wright, came down to address the crowd at the White House, saying, "If it seems slow, remember how slow things were twenty years ago [when the Civil Rights Act of 1964 was being negotiated]."[1] In fact, time-wise, the Civil Rights Act of 1964 took about a year from introduction until passage, about the same time for the current version of the ADA to go from introduction to passage. Yet despite the parallel, the perception on the ground was that Congress was slow-walking the bill. A demonstrator along the way said, "They are stalling the bill that is going to give us equal rights, and we aren't asking for civil rights. We are demanding them *now!*"

The crowd then marched to the Capitol, where their numbers were increased by a couple of hundred more people. Gathering at the front steps of the otherwise accessible Capitol building, they listened to speeches by members of Congress and by Dart, I. King Jordan, James Brady, and then ADAPT leader Mike Auberger, who exhorted them to take equality seriously. ADAPT members, having planned their Saul Alinsky kind of direct action, got out of their chairs, dropped their canes and crutches, and began to crawl up the eighty-two steps of the Capitol Building. Tom Olin, who has documented many disability events, snapped away with his camera, as did a few news reporters. Michael Winter, the newly elected head of NCIL and a rather heavyset, bearded man with a sense of humor, crawled up the stairs with great difficulty on the warm day. Winter recalled: "After the speeches, we started chanting 'What do we want?' 'ADA!' 'When do we want it?' 'NOW!' The chants became louder and louder, and ultimately my good friend Monica Hall told me that it was time to get out of my wheelchair and crawl up the steps to the Capitol Building. Monica took my wheelchair, smiled and said, 'I'll meet you at the top!' I started to climb step by step towards the top." He began sweating and the climb was difficult. "At the very beginning," he said, "I looked up and thought that I would never make it. But right below me was a [young] . . . girl who was making the same climb, step by step. . . . I felt an obligation to be a role model for this girl and we ultimately made it to the top together."[2] Winter added that he didn't want to look "stupid" and mentioned that not everyone thought the crawl was such a good idea.

The star of the show was indeed photographer Olin's spunky, blond eight-year-old niece Jennifer Keelan, who had cerebral palsy. She was having difficulty climbing the steps as well, but with great determination she announced, "I'll take all night if I have to!" Later, as a young adult, she recalled the day: "I said to Wade Blank [founder of ADAPT], 'I want to climb the steps. I need to climb the steps.' It was the hottest day of the month of March, and I'm dripping in sweat. And I said to myself, 'I'm going to do it for myself and for my friend Kenny [Perkins, five years old], who died a few months before.' All these cameras are on me. . . . I had international, national, and local news on me. It's a big climb—eighty-two steps, and I have the pamphlet I have in my pocket that we were supposed to hand to the politicians. They say that it was the image of me that was [what caused] the final decision to get the ADA passed. I knew that I was not only representing myself, I was representing my generation. If I didn't do it, then no one from my generation would be represented."[3]

Tammy Gravenhorst was a pretty, raven-haired eighteen-year-old Colorado College junior with a winning smile and bangs that made her look like Audrey Hepburn. Gravenhorst had cerebral palsy and used forearm crutches to get around. She was able to secure a grant that took her to Washington, DC, to find out what the ADA was about as well as look into job prospects working as a linguist in the military. Before she traveled to Washington, she had arranged a meeting with Bob Dole. When she got to the Capitol and entered on foot through a fairly accessible entrance, she found out Dole couldn't make it to the meeting. Instead, she met with one of his aides, who dryly told her about the ADA and, from a technical and legal perspective, how a bill becomes a law. It wasn't exactly what she came to Washington to hear. She left the meeting disappointed and confused about what she was even doing in the nation's capital.

"I must have slid around on the marble floors under the rotunda for ten minutes trying to figure out which door to take," she remembers. "I really just wanted to get the hell off of those floors. I recall such relief at reaching an exit door because I knew gritty, navigable concrete would be on its other side!" In her haste to get off the polished marble floors that made walking with crutches so difficult, she "left through the wrong door [the one that led to the eighty-two steps], and I saw, my god, so many people. It didn't strike me right away that I was looking at so many people with disabilities. They were singing 'We Shall Overcome.' I had no idea this was going on. I was planning on just meeting with nondisabled white guys. It took me a long time to figure out what I was seeing. I thought, 'This is fantastic.' I asked someone what was going on, and they said, 'We are having a protest, a planned protest, that they didn't make this side of the building accessible.' I had no idea why they were climbing up the steps. I thought, 'The only way through this crowd is through it.' And I started down the steps, and everyone started cheering for me like I was making some political statement about the steps. I had no idea what was going on."

Gravenhorst goes on: "The next day, I had an interview with the Department of Defense, and the person said, 'We don't usually hire political dissidents.' I said, 'What are you talking about?' She said, 'Did you watch the news last night? You were on the news.' I had no idea."

Gravenhorst, whose married name is Berberi and who is now a professor of French literature, describes what happened to her as her *Charterhouse of Parma* moment—when the main character of Stendhal's novel wanders dazed and confused through the crucial historic battle of Waterloo without realizing where he is or what the import of the event was: "It became this watershed moment in disability, and I was there because I went out the wrong door. Sometimes, history only becomes history later."

That was certainly the case with this event. Although there was coverage in a few newspapers, the event came and went, little noticed at the time. Weisman, a lobbyist on transportation issues for the disability side, was in the Capitol on that day. He says, "The day they were crawling up the steps, the ADA was passing. It didn't matter whether they crawled up the steps or not. I was in the House listening to one of the hearings. And I knew they were crawling up the steps. I said, 'This is silly.' I didn't realize how significant it was. It was completely wasted on me. I thought these people are killing themselves. It's hot out. And the bill is going to pass."

In fact, Weisman had been at the Energy and Commerce Committee meeting that began at 10 a.m. in room 2123 of the Rayburn Building, across the street from the Capitol. The committee was in the midst of approving ten bills, including the ADA. The latter passed by a vote of 40 to 3 as the demonstrators crawled up the steps.[4] Thinking about the event, Weisman adds, "Their demonstrating was more self-empowering than it was constructive when it came to the legislation. But it was effective in the sense that you need warm bodies that legislators have to see." Weisman went on to mention that many groups did not like the tactics that ADAPT used. For example, the Paralyzed Veterans of America (PVA) specifically banned the use of the organizations' funds for demonstrations by the chapters of the ADAPT.

Kafka, in fact, had angrily left the PVA over its reticence. According to Kafka, "ADAPT's standing at that time [among other groups] was, 'We support your goals but we don't like your tactics.' Many in the, quote-unquote, 'traditional disability' communities really had a standoffish position about direct action. People forget that [now that ADAPT] is kind of accepted and looked to for leadership." Wade Blank, the founder of ADAPT, explained the more radical tactics: "We're taking the strategies of the 60's that helped get rights for black and brown people and women, and using them for people with disabilities."[5]

Keelan's recollection that it was her picture that launched a hundred votes for the ADA was a bit of an embellishment. In fact, the media coverage of her was actually a problem for the editor of the *Disability Rag* magazine, Mary Johnson, who wrote: "One might question why a movement intent on showing that disabled people are adults, not children, would make their central media image a child? One might wonder why people who repeatedly complain that TV and newspapers report on them only as courageous, overcoming barriers, were grunting up steps while reporters were asking them if they felt like heroes?"[6] Since so many telethons have used disabled children to arouse sympathy, Johnson's comments make sense. On the other hand, no one arranged for Keelan to crawl up the steps. It was the press that made her an icon, since the story was touching and "inspiring," which is the media's usual modus operandi concerning disability issues in the news.

The following day, ADAPT organized another controversial event. A tour of the Capitol had been arranged for a group of disabled visitors. The same ADAPT demonstrators in wheelchairs showed up and chained themselves together in the rotunda in front of a confused tour guide who thought she was there to show off the building. The police in riot gear were called, and it took two hours to cut the heavy chains and arrest 104 demonstrators and those accompanying them, taking them one by one out via the tiny elevator that provided wheelchair access. But before the police took action, the demonstrators were addressed by Foley, Michel, and Hoyer. Although the Associated Press characterized the meeting of the demonstrators as a "confrontation," according to Kafka, these addresses were arranged well in advance through the agency of Wright and Kemp.[7] Wright had helped stage this event to give cover to any hesitant House members who could now be convinced to support the ADA. Instead of looking weak before their constituencies and peers, the representatives would now look as if they were influenced by this impressive display of zeal for justice and quality.[8] In addition, Kemp and Wade Blank had become close friends not over the game of bridge but through a mutual and obsessive support of the Cleveland Indians. When Wright and crew had asked ADAPT to come to Washington, they had secured the appearance of the House politicos, as they had for Gray at the White House the previous day.

Nevertheless, the demonstrators were not really up on the details of the ADA. They did not know that the politicians were already committed to speaking with them when the demonstrators demanded to speak to representatives. And the ADAPT members were clearly uninformed in the ways of Congress when they demanded that the bill be passed in twenty-four hours. As the AP reported:

> Before the arrests, Foley assured demonstrators that he and other congressional leaders were pushing the bill. His words were met with skepticism. "It is a priority for passage in this session of the Congress," the Washington Democrat shouted over catcalls. "I am absolutely satisfied it will reach the floor, we will have a conference with the Senate and it will become law. Will it be on the floor in 24 hours? No," Foley added. A chorus of boos greeted the remark.[9]

Hoyer next spoke and urged patience: "Sixty days is not too long" to wait. But he too was jeered at with "We've waited too long already." Michel called "unreasonable" the demand by some of the protesters for passage in twenty-four hours. He told them that he knew they felt "frustrated."[10] Atlanta activist Mark Johnson, sensing the kind of condescension that felt like an infantilizing pat on the head, yelled back, "We're not frustrated. We're pissed off!" The demonstrators roared as Michel fell silent. Not everyone thought these tactics were wise. Bob Dole walked by the demonstrators shaking his head and muttering, "This doesn't help us at all."[11] Mary Johnson complained about the lost opportunity to inform the public: "Many individuals simply got the story wrong. They told reporters the wrong facts. They told reporters contradictory facts. Or they were able to tell them nothing at all."[12]

While the demonstrators were full of zeal, the possible disconnect between what they thought and what was happening would eventually lead to a rewriting of the history of ADA. The Capitol Crawl and the mass protest in the rotunda came to be seen over time as the equivalent of the Battle of Lexington and Concord, the Ride of Paul Revere, or the Battle of Bull Run—decisive events in an historical process. As one website now puts it: "To present-day disability activists . . . the 'Capitol Crawl' is seen as one of the single most important events that finally pushed for the passage of the ADA into law."[13] The crawl and rotunda arrest became, retrospectively, two of the three most iconic moments in disability history along with the occupation of the HEW building in San Francisco. The importance of these events to building disability identity and consciousness cannot be underestimated. But sometimes, as Gravenhorst noted earlier, history only becomes history later.

Before the Capitol Crawl took up some attention, a series of events truly did threaten the passage of the ADA. On February 7, Kennedy introduced a bill along with Hawkins to correct what civil rights groups saw as six major Supreme Court decisions that limited the right of African Americans and other racial minorities to win monetary damages for job discrimination. The court decisions regarded Section 1981 of an 1866 law of the post–Civil War era. Because the 1964 Civil Rights Act provided only limited remedies—essentially injunctive relief, back pay, and attorney's fees—many lawyers started suing after 1976 for job discrimination under the nineteenth-century law because it was much broader in scope and damages. When in 1976 the Supreme Court ruled in *Runyon v. McCrary* that Section 1981 could apply to private businesses, a flurry of cases was brought to court. But in June 1989, the court narrowed the application of the law to hiring and not to on-the-job discrimination or harassment. Kennedy and Hawkins then introduced their bill to countermand that court decision. In effect, the bill would also expand the 1964 Civil Rights Act and, by implication, the ADA.

The White House was unhappy with this state of affairs. Since the White House–Senate agreement had essentially traded limited remedies (desired by the president and Thornburgh) for a wider concept of public accommodations (desired by the disability community), it seemed that all was well. This deal had been the one struck in the final days of negotiating between Sununu and Kennedy.

Suddenly, it looked as if there had been a double-cross. In a stunning chess move, Kennedy had previously agreed to let the ADA parallel the 1964 Civil Rights Act—a desideratum for the White

House—but then in a bait-and-switch move, he was now proposing to change that very 1964 Civil Rights Act. This change of the hallmark legislation would, like a Rube Goldberg device, drop a ball that would set in motion a game-changing reversal in the remedies for the ADA. Specifically, the change would revamp the very restricted remedies that the earlier act allowed—only limited back pay and legal fees under limited conditions. Those limited remedies were to have been heard only before a judge and only after the EEOC had first tried to broker a settlement out of court. In effect, the deal would protect businesses from large damage settlements and other punishments under the ADA as they were under the 1964 Civil Rights Act. Suddenly, with the Kennedy-Hawkins bill, those bringing suit under the Civil Rights Act (and thus under the ADA, which paralleled the Civil Rights Act) could sue for compensatory and punitive damages and do so before a jury (since the Seventh Amendment assures the right to a jury trial for damages greater than $20).

On March 12, the same day as the Capitol Crawl, the *New York Times* ran a story about the Civil Rights Act and the ADA, with the headline "Measure Barring Discrimination Against Disabled Runs into a Snag": "Officially, the White House has not withdrawn its support for the bill." Marlin Fitzwater, Bush's press secretary, said, "We do support the legislation. . . . We're very supportive of their rights and their cause." But the article added, "President Bush was reluctant to support the disabled rights measure as long as the penalties were tied to those of the Civil Rights Act."[14]

In fact, the White House support, while strong on the Gray and Kemp side, seems to have slipped a bit after the initial agreement with the Senate. The White House had given the go-ahead to House members to add the weakening amendments that the Bush camp had sworn it would not add. And despite an eleventh-hour plea from Kemp, no mention of the ADA was in Bush's State of the Union message this year. Was Bush's interest in the ADA declining as business ramped up its protests? An internal White House memo on February 21 to Kuttner and McGettigan detailing the House Committee on Small Business Hearing emphasized business's concern that "the bill was too ambiguous" and thus left "it to courts to decide what is 'undue hardship' and that businesses do not have the resources or expertise to interpret the language. . . . [A]nother primary concern was cost." The take home-message was, "Business is worried."[15]

What's worrisome to General Motors is worrisome to a Republican administration. At that same hearing, James P. Turner, from the Civil Rights Division of the Justice Department, said, "The administration's support for the ADA was premised on the agreement reached expressly with its sponsors that the remedies" for employment discrimination would be the same as under the Civil Rights Act of 1964.

Also on the same day as the Capitol Crawl, Thornburgh wrote an annoyed letter to Hoyer: "A very critical element of this bill was that, as under Title VII of the Civil Rights Act of 1964, the remedies it made available for violations of the employment title were limited to non-damage remedies that can be obtained in a trial before a judge. . . . In return, the administration agreed to broad coverage under the public accommodations title . . . much broader" than in the 1964 law. That was the deal. Thornburgh emphasized the firm stance the administration was taking, backed by conservatives in the White House like Lee Liberman, who took an active role in this issue. "We will actively support a clarifying amendment" to limit the ADA.[16]

At the White House, there was general consternation. The usually placid Thornburgh was angry with Kennedy and Neas for pushing the bill to overhaul the original 1964 Civil Rights Act. But he was also upset that the Senate–White House deal was being undermined. Sununu was irate and felt betrayed. He had earlier said, "We're struggling to build into it [the ADA] provisions that the business community was desperately coming to us with concerns about."[17] Kennedy wrote a four-page Dear John letter to Sununu on March 30, reiterating his reasoning. Kennedy's aim in the letter was to "set out more fully the issue as I understand it." Kennedy continued: "During our discussions, there was never any suggestion, or even a hint, from your side to my side, that the Title VII remedies should be 'frozen' for persons with disabilities as of the date of our deal." Kennedy created a gotcha moment when he pointed out that Thornburgh had emphasized the parallelism between the ADA and the Civil Rights Act in his testimony the previous June. The ADA, Thornburgh had said, "uses existing civil rights laws for minorities and women as its model, the remedies under this bill should parallel these existing laws." Hatch too had said that the ADA "should parallel" the 1964 law. Perhaps in a stinging reminder of the time Kennedy yelled at Sununu, the Massachusetts senator reminded the chief of staff of the very meeting where they "met for three hours in Senator Dole's Capitol office to discuss the remaining key issues." Kennedy then essentially reenacted that scolding once more in writing: "To me, the Administration's current attempt . . . is flatly inconsistent with our deal and with the spirit of the ADA. . . . This approach would consign individuals with disabilities to second class status under our employment discrimination laws—exactly what we are trying to prevent under the ADA." Kennedy cleverly added, "Consider this final point, John. . . . [I]f remedies for other minority groups and women are ever cut back . . . people with disabilities would have greater remedies . . . than other groups."[18]

By April 3, the full Public Works and Transportation Committee approved the bill by a vote of 45 to 5. The bill had earlier passed the subcommittee on March 6. All the nays were Republican. Bud Shuster continued to complain, saying that the ADA was "feel-good legislation," and without the government providing new funds for transportation, "we could end up creating problems rather than solutions." Republicans complained that the bill favored Democrats in large urban areas. Republican John Paul Hammerschmidt of Arkansas rued in somewhat ableist language that most of the changes "came from your side of the aisle, while our efforts have fallen on deaf ears."[19]

One of the crucial issues resolved by the committee concerned buses. Compromises had been made, some of which angered the ADAPT activists. One compromise allowed a feasibility study that would decide whether over-the-road buses had to be accessible. That idea was brokered in a booth at a bar at the Mayflower Hotel close to where J. Edgar Hoover dined every day for twenty years. Present were Wright, Coelho, Currey of Greyhound, and a representative of Peter Pan Bus Lines. Wright describes the thought processes that went into negotiating the feasibility and the phase-in of various requirements: "Now, I don't know how many people actually ride over the road coaches, but it's a principle for me, which is [that] all public transportation should be accessible. . . . And that's the compromise that we proposed to the Greyhound people, which is to give them more time, even though I didn't necessarily think they needed it, but as long as they kept that, they had to be covered and had to find a way to make themselves accessible. You'll see the House version has sliding effective dates all over the place. You can tell that the longer the date goes out, the harder it was to negotiate." And this negotiation was one of the most difficult. Coelho says that he wanted to put a plaque up in the booth in the Mayflower Hotel to commemorate the importance of this particular compromise.

Now, at last, it was only the Judiciary Committee left to weigh in on the bill. The big issue was the one that Kennedy and Sununu were wrangling over. Ranking member Sensenbrenner offered an amendment to decouple the ADA from the Civil Rights Act—an amendment endorsed by the White House—saying without this change, "the deal that got the ADA passed in the other body would be undone." The chair of the subcommittee, Don Edwards, rebutted Sensenbrenner: "If your amendment passed . . . you would have the disabled with [fewer] rights than those covered by" the Civil Rights Act. Sensenbrenner ended up voting for the bill, which passed 7 to 1, with Dannemeyer, who perpetually objected to the bill for drug addicts and homosexuals, casting the only negative vote.

The action now moved to the full Judiciary Committee, which was headed by Jack Brooks. Bartlett says of him, "Jack Brooks, as you may have heard, is not someone that you'd want to negotiate with. His moniker was 'The Meanest Man in Congress.'" Lex Frieden remembers that Savage and Wright told him to go and lobby Brooks, who was a fellow Texan, because they felt Brooks was not cooperating, despite being a Democrat. Shulman, Hoyer's aide, recalls: "Jack Brooks was a very, very tough, old-style chairman. He wasn't going to do anything just because Steny Hoyer asked him to. They were not uncomplicated conversations." But despite his crustiness, Brooks wasn't beyond a certain old-school sexism. Shulman says, "I will never forget at one point Jack Brooks [was] literally pinching my cheek and saying, 'Don't worry; it's going to be fine.' It was just so old school guy, right?"

Brooks, delivering on his squeezed-cheek promise to Shulman, got an overwhelming vote of 32 to 3. Frieden recalls Brooks throwing his legislative weight around to do so: "It came up before their committee, and some of the members were not too sure they wanted to be on record as supporting this piece of legislation. The bell rang for a vote [on the House floor for another bill], and about half of the members got up to get out of there so they didn't have to vote on the ADA, and he [Brooks] ordered the sergeant at arms to lock the doors. He told them, 'I don't care how many times that bell rings, we're going to take a vote on this matter before anybody leaves this room.' He got them on record in favor of the bill, and that's how it got through that committee."

Now the last stand was fast approaching. The House would take up the bill on May 17. The day before that, a secret memo for the eyes of the Executive Office of the President only was sent out by the Legislative Reference Division, a part of Darman's OMB. It said, "The Administration has expressed serious concerns about the scope of employment discrimination remedies provided under the ADA, which are tied to the remedies available under Title VII of the Civil Rights Act of 1964." It added somewhat shamefacedly, "The Administration was unsuccessful in its efforts to work with the House Judiciary Committee to sever the link between the ADA and the Civil Rights Act." And the memo praised the Sensenbrenner amendment and recommended that it be put forward on the House floor the following day.[20]

Meanwhile, yet another problem was brewing. Randy Johnson, the lawyer for the business side of the Education and Labor Committee, was reading through the draft report of that committee. It had been routine for these reports to be printed up well in advance of the full House action, but this report was still in process a good six months after the markup. The House Rules Committee had given permission for the report to be printed two days before the bill came to the floor (three days was the usual minimum). Yet just three days before the report was supposed to be handed out to representatives, Johnson suddenly noticed that Hoyer's people had apparently been changing the language of the report in what appeared to be unilateral ways to support the disability side in the argument over civil rights remedies, among other issues.

Johnson remarked that this "is a blatant attempt to resolve the current controversy over the remedy linkage" by making it seem that there had been agreement to the Kennedy side of the debate. The language that had been added said that the remedies "as they exist now or as they may be amended in the future" are the ones enumerated for people with disabilities. Johnson scolded, "Since no staff or principals of the Education and Labor Committee were parties to the Senate negotiations, we have a hard time understanding how this Report can honestly resolve this issue. Was there some discussion of this issue at the November markup that we missed? The fact is, is that it never came up and it borders on the fraudulent to attempt to use the Report as a vehicle to bootstrap the result desired."[21] After going through more egregious additions, Johnson wrote to Feldblum and the others on the Democrat side: "Well, it's now 8:55 pm, May 12. We are tired of playing hunt the peanut and no doubt other 'nuggets' of substance will slip by in the short time we have to review. Perhaps this is the strategy which explains the need to rush this bill to the Floor in a hurried, chaotic process which is an insult to both the merits of this legislation and the bipartisanship which led to its development."

Johnson describes his note to Feldblum as "the memo that almost sunk the ADA." If there were no substantive changes, Bartlett would have pulled the plug on the ADA. As it was, Feldblum worked closely with Johnson now to get to yes with the least amount of movement from the disability position.

But that wasn't the only plug that was to be pulled. A far bigger issue was about to burst. The National Restaurant Association had been deeply concerned about the ADA for many reasons throughout the House considerations. Representing small and large businesses, the association was concerned that the bill was going to make the businesses pay for accommodations and barrier removal. That was bad enough from the association's point of view. But worse was that, during the height of the AIDS panic, the ADA would allow cooks and waiters who were HIV positive to handle the food served to unsuspecting patrons.

Bartlett recalls: "I ran . . . into on the street somewhere a guy named Richie Jackson from the Texas Restaurant Association. The Texas Restaurant Association is a tough lobby in Texas and was sort of take-no-prisoners. I asked him what he thought about the ADA, and he just came unglued. He said, 'Look, if I've got a guy with four employees in East Texas in a little restaurant and one of the employees gets AIDS and I have to keep him in the kitchen, then no customer in that East Texas town will ever go to my restaurant again. I'll be put out of business.' That was a compelling story. It turned out to not be true, but at the time, it was pretty compelling. I said, 'Richie, I can't do anything about it, okay? I've made my deal, and I'm not going to change it.' He said, 'What can I do?' I said, 'Well, you can get a Texas congressman to offer an amendment to exempt AIDS out of this.' That's when he went to Jim Chapman."

Jim Chapman was a representative from Texas with an uncongressional bald head, sleepy eyes, and a playful smile. He had been approached by smooth-talking, energetic Jackson, who looked more like a congressman himself than a bureaucrat. Jackson had been a lobbyist for restaurateurs, according to Chapman: "I knew Richie. He had supported me in my congressional campaign. Or the restaurateurs had. I had a relationship with him."

Given the AIDS panic at the time, Jackson was concerned that the ADA would ruin the restaurant business by permitting infected people to work as food handlers. Jackson, Chapman recalls, "convinced me that this food-handlers amendment would be important to small businesses and small restaurants. I believed that. The analogy I recall at the time was that if there was someone who had an infectious disease that was HIV positive, slicing tomatoes and making hamburgers at the local Dairy Queen in my little town of Sulphur Springs—if the community understood somebody back there was handling food that was HIV positive—Dairy Queen would close in three days." Jackson wanted nothing less than that people with HIV be carved out of key ADA protections. Since the National Restaurant Association had failed to get the bill changed in committee, it now sought to put an amendment on the House floor as a last-ditch attempt. Chapman was going to be the association's front man.

Chapman sought out the advice of Bartlett. Bartlett recalls ruefully: "To my discredit I did not dissuade Jim from offering the amendment." In 1990 there was not, Bartlett claims, widespread understanding that AIDS could not be transmitted by the casual contact that food handlers had with the products they were purveying.

Bartlett, looking back, now recognizes that "it was a six-month window during which it was not known by me anyway, but it was not
especially well known as to what were the possible transmissions of
AIDS." But in 1990, there actually was a fair amount of scientific
certainty that AIDS was only spread through sexual contact or in-
travenous contamination through blood products and unsterile nee-
dles. In fact, two years earlier, C. Everett Koop, the surgeon general
under Reagan, sent out millions of brochures to average Americans
telling them that AIDS was difficult to contract and could not be
passed casually by a kiss, saliva, or swimming in a pool. In addition, Reagan's commission on AIDS suggested that infected people
be given their full civil rights. Despite the misinformation, according
to Bartlett, "Jim made a mistake by offering the amendment. I made
a mistake by not attempting to [stop him]. Then I ended up voting
for the amendment, which I wish I hadn't."

On May 17, the full House began debating the bill. The Chapman amendment came up quickly that morning. The language of the
amendment was as follows:

> It shall not be a violation of this Act for an employer to refuse to
> assign or continue to assign any employee with an infectious or com-
> municable disease of public health significance to a job involving
> food handling, provided that the employer shall make reasonable ac-
> commodation that would offer an alternative employment opportu-
> nity for which the employee is qualified and for which the employee
> would sustain no economic damage.

In disability lore, Chapman is remembered as the person who
wanted to cut people with AIDS out of the ADA. But the amendment
seems to clearly say that people with AIDS or who are HIV positive
are not exempted from the ADA, just that they should be moved
from food handling to some other aspect of the restaurant business.
And Chapman made this point clear in proposing the amendment:
"I am not here to say that there is any evidence that AIDS can be
transferred in the process of handling food." He pointed out that
the Centers for Disease Control reported that in more than 130,000
cases of AIDS through April 1990, not one case of transmission

by food handling had been documented. So why the amendment? Chapman provided the reason, given the misinformation and AIDS panic: "The reality is that many Americans would refuse to patronize any food establishment if an employee were known to have a communicable disease."

A number of representatives spoke in opposition to Chapman. Frank McCloskey said the amendment was coming out of "feelings of irrational hysteria" and noted that the National Restaurant Association itself had said five years earlier, "Workers, including those in the food service industry, should not be restricted from work or the use of facilities and equipment solely on the basis of a diagnosis of an AIDS infection."[22] Jim McDermott, himself a doctor and opposed to the amendment, declared, "The amendment is bad medicine, bad science, bad public policy. It is indigestible. I urge my colleagues to send it back to the kitchen." John Lewis, noted African American civil rights leader, saw a parallel to those who opposed desegregation in restaurants because it would lead to white patrons refusing to eat with black people.

The White House itself had issued a letter from Louis W. Sullivan, Health and Human Services secretary, stating its opposition to the Chapman amendment, but the letter arrived at the House too late— after the Chapman debate was virtually over. The amendment was approved by the close vote of 199 to 187. Hoyer, clearly frustrated, rued, "I think [the outcome] could possibly have been different if the White House letter had come earlier."

Everyone behind the ADA was hoping for President Bush to sign the act on July 4, the symbolic day for American justice and civil rights and, conveniently, the beginning of a congressional recess. But that goal suddenly seemed unlikely given the roadblocks now in place. It had been assumed that no conference between the Senate and the House would be necessary since most of the differences between the bills were minor and that the Senate would simply vote to adopt the House bill. Now with the Chapman amendment, things looked much more dubious. Hoyer warned, "I'm sure the Senate will now ask for a conference because this amendment will not be acceptable."[23] If the Senate were going to fight the Chapman amendment, the House would fight back. Bartlett declared, "I think everybody understood it very well. My view is the Chapman amendment needs to survive conference." And then he added ominously, "If not, it will require another vote of the House."

Ultimately, the House passed the ADA, including the Chapman amendment, with the overwhelming vote of 403 to 20, approving a few minor changes and denying the Sensenbrenner–White House amendment on remedies. The action shifted to the Senate on June 6, where conservative Jesse Helms was orchestrating a parliamentary procedure that had rarely been tried before. In fact, no one could remember when the Senate had ever done this. He wanted the Senate to instruct the Senate conferees to accept the Chapman amendment passed by the House. It is not unusual for the House to instruct its conferees to vote one way or another in conference, but the Senate rarely does.

Helms repeated the notion that the current research "supposedly" showed that HIV could not be transmitted through casual means, "but you try to explain that to John Q. Public. . . . How many people would be willing to frequent a restaurant whose chef has AIDS? Like it or not, very few." Harkin snapped back that "this motion to instruct is simply this, to codify fear." Harkin said that the motion wasn't just a side bar, but "strikes at the heart and soul of the ADA." That "people with disabilities ought to be judged on the basis of their abilities . . . [not on] unfounded fear, prejudice, ignorance, or mythologies."

Kennedy and others invoked the name of Ryan White, the fourteen-year-old who had been expelled from his public school for having AIDS. He had contracted the disease after receiving infected blood products for his hemophilia. Widely regarded as a heroic victim of prejudice against people with AIDS, White had just recently died in April 1990. Kennedy said, "If Ryan White were alive and he wanted to go work in a Burger King, this amendment would say no. . . . If Ryan White happened to be a flight attendant in a plane crossing this country, this amendment would say no. If Ryan White was working in a supermarket trying to put together enough money for a college education, this amendment would say no."

Despite these impassioned objections, Helms won the day, with the Senate voting 53 to 40 to instruct the conferees to uphold the

Chapman amendment. Voting with Helms was Dole, who, when asked why he didn't vote along with disability lobbyists and Kennedy, Harkin, and others, said, "They don't own me. Just because you have a handicap doesn't mean you have to be for every screwball thing."[24] Dole's vote was not inconsequential, because after he voted, two Republicans switched their votes in favor of Helms and several Southern Democrats who hadn't yet voted cast their votes for Helms. Mo West, who briefed Dole on AIDS, recalls that he may have been exercising his tactical prerogative voting with Helms and the Republican minority knowing that he would ultimately vote on a compromise down the line.

On June 26, the conferees produced their report. The thorny issue was Chapman, but, despite the Senate vote and the House majority, the conferees agreed to drop the amendment. Kennedy recognized that the Senate had instructed the conferees to keep the amendment, but he added that such motions to instruct from the Senate were "basically meaningless." As meaningless as the motion to instruct may have been, it carried with it the weight that the full Senate and the full House had in fact voted for the Chapman amendment. The small group of conferees had gotten rid of the amendment, thus in effect wagging the dog.

The dog wasn't happy. And now there was a real problem. The next usual step was for the Senate to send the conference papers to the House. The House would then vote on them and the bill would become law. But if the Senate did that, it would essentially give up all control of the ADA to the House. Helms was still annoyed that the motion to instruct had been ignored by the conferees (indeed, only Hatch voted for the Chapman amendment). Kennedy demanded that the papers go to the House, insisting that the president would sign straight away on July 4. Hatch, clearly anguished to be at odds with Kennedy, refused to send the papers. Hoyer puts it succinctly: "[House Republicans] asked Dole to sit on the bill." Harkin put it more directly: "Those in the House who supported Chapman wanted us to sit on it because they felt during the [July 4] break they could get restaurant people to beat up" on the opponents of Chapman.[25]

To try to counter the restaurant lobbyist blitz, the disability community combined with AIDS activists and came up with a unique public relations event. Working with the gay and lesbian Human Rights Campaign Fund, which had produced talking points about AIDS and how food handlers couldn't transfer it, the combined group placed the information sheet inside brown paper bags of the kind used to carry lunches with the phrase "The National Restaurant Association Is Out to Lunch on the Chapman Amendment" and distributed them to representatives. At the press conference for this educational stunt, Wright made it clear that if the Chapman amendment remained, the disability community would drop its support for the ADA. This statement definitely upped the stakes in this new round of negotiations.[26]

Fearing that the White House might support the Chapman amendment, the disability community convened a meeting in the Roosevelt Room in the White House. Disability activists were present along with eighteen White House staffers. A moment widely recounted was when Bob Williams, a poet with severe cerebral palsy who communicated laboriously by using a pointer attached to a helmet and a board on which was printed an alphabet, told of his experiences being refused service at restaurants for his disability. He saw parallels between people with HIV/AIDS and people with cerebral palsy being booted out of restaurants. He tapped out his story on his alphabet board and then ended by saying, "It ain't civil; and it ain't right." His motto seemed to express the sentiments of the day.

Both sides lobbied heavily. The restaurant association found owners whose places of business were in the jurisdiction of senators and congresspeople and had the restaurants contact their representatives directly with a message that essentially said, "You'll never eat here again if you vote against us." Likewise, Chapman recalls that he was approached by Barney Frank, who was not out at that point but who everyone knew was gay: "I remember Barney telling me on the floor of the House one day, he said, 'Jim, I understand. I know where you're from, and I understand why you've done it.' Then he just laughed and said, 'You understand you will not be able to get service at any restaurant in Washington, DC, after you do this.'" Frank was referring to the fact that so many gay and lesbian people worked in the food trade. Chapman joked that he might have to wear disguises when he went out to eat.

The next meeting of the Senate happened on July 11, when the controversy continued. George Mitchell, the majority leader, asked that ASL interpreters be used to make this debate more accessible—the first time ever that this had occurred in the Senate. Then Mitchell ruefully announced that a select group had been trying to resolve the problems in the conference report and couldn't. "There's no prospect of success no matter how long the discussions continue," he said and then called in the full Senate to deal with the dysfunction. One issue that had come up the day before was that the civil rights bill introduced by Kennedy and Hawkins had itself come up with a mechanism for dealing with civil rights infractions that might occur in the Senate organization itself, and the suggestion was that the Senate simply adopt that one for the ADA. This version did not allow civil servants to sue in a federal court. The Senate voted to recommit the ADA to yet another conference, a very rare event in Congress, to add the new amendment from the 1964 Civil Rights Act.

But that still left the Chapman amendment. While Helms was hell-bent on keeping in the Chapman amendment, as were many Republicans, the disability people considered it a deal-breaker. As Silverstein puts it, "If we had not been able to overcome the Chapman amendment, the bill would not have gone through. You could not write a civil rights statute that had built-in discrimination." The one rule the disability folks had insisted on from the very beginning was that no single group—blind, Deaf, mobility impaired, affectively or cognitively disabled, HIV positive—would be sacrificed. No one would be thrown under the bus. Pat Wright called that principle the "all for one and one for all" idea. To emphasize this point, she held a press conference with Coretta Scott King. The press asked Wright "whether or not I would pull down the ADA if the Chapman amendment was on it. Actually, I made that statement that I would." The threat of the collapse of the ADA was real.

Silverstein sought out Hatch and "found him in a lower subbasement of the Senate, in an elevator. The two of us basically talked, and I said, 'Listen, you have a disability advisory group. You've probably heard from them that we're not going to draft a civil rights statute that includes discrimination. So all these people that you're working for, and all of that which you're working for, is not going to happen.

Reconsider. Think about it. You're a man of science. You're a supporter of NIH [the National Institutes of Health]. You have been very positive in terms of HIV issues. You really support the principle—let science decide.'"[27]

At that moment, Nancy Taylor, Hatch's advisor on health, was lying in bed in her thirty-eighth week of pregnancy with twins. She'd been told to stay in bed because of the danger of early-onset labor, given her situation. She'd been attending law school at night while working for Senator Hatch during the day and had stressed herself in this pregnancy. So she was following doctor's orders until on July 11, when the phone rang. Hatch, with a sense of great urgency, asked her to come to the Senate if she could manage it. Despite her doctor's orders, she groggily lifted herself from the horizontal and quickly got herself to the Senate cloakroom.

There Hatch and his staff were engaged in a conversation. Hatch had previously supported Chapman and Helms, but now, following his conversation with Silverstein and facing the difficulty of the possible failure of the bill he'd worked on for so long, he desperately wanted to find a way out of this quagmire. Taylor advised Hatch and Helms on the issues around AIDS, also suggesting that science should drive the decision. Taylor, Silverstein, Iskowitz, and Osolinik joined the conversation, and eventually Hatch and the others came up with a compromise. It was that the secretary of health and human services would, six months after the bill was signed, issue a list of communicable diseases and how they were spread. And then the secretary would update the list every year. If a food handler had a disease deemed communicable and was a direct threat, then the employer could relocate that employee to another non-food-handling job on the premises with no negative financial consequences. The meeting participants scribbled down their amendment with pen on paper.

As they were birthing this idea, Taylor abruptly felt the sharp pangs of a contraction, grasped her stomach, and had to hold on for support. Everyone stopped to ask her if she were okay. She felt another sharp pain and decided she had to head home. As it turned out, these were premature contractions. Subsequently her twins were born in good health. It was telling that these birth pangs were part of the final compromises that led after nine months of hearings to the completion of this long-gestating legislation.

On the floor of the Senate, the Hatch amendment was circulated in the pen and paper version since there was no time to type it up. Helms was not happy. He said the Hatch amendment would "gut" the Chapman amendment. Hatch snapped back, "It doesn't gut the amendment. It makes it better. It makes it more scientific. It makes it more medically oriented. It does away with prejudice." When the vote came down, it was 99 to 1, Helms humiliatingly being the only senator to vote against the Hatch amendment after his own amendment to support Chapman was defeated.

Immediately the following day, the House was to vote on the conference report and thus in effect vote on the ADA. Chapman, who had just discovered that his proposal was dropped from the conference report, was livid: "I learned only after the conference report was reported and filed that the [Chapman amendment] was not in the bill. I was told that Steny Hoyer [in the conference] had said that I was okay with the [Hatch] compromise. [I knew that] the position was that if we were not willing to go along with the compromise, that conference report would not have been completed. I approached Steny about that and said, 'What's that about?' I do remember Steny just looked me straight in the eye and said, 'Jim, I had to do what I had to do to pass this Bill.' He lied to the conferees, because I had never [agreed to that]."

On the House floor, Dannemeyer was one of the first on his feet objecting to the whole way that the ADA had been legislated. He complained that the Rules Committee, controlled by Democrats, essentially limited all significant debate and any ability to propose amendments, and he was particularly annoyed that he couldn't add his own amendment to exempt anyone with a communicable disease from ADA protection. "The majority makes the rules so they can do anything they want," he said.

A vote was taken on the way the legislation was proceeding, and the House overwhelmingly agreed to carry on the discussions with no ability to propose further amendments. Tom DeLay rose to protest the "closed" nature of the bill, which is a term to describe whether the Rules Committee allows an open or a closed debate, that is, one that allows amendments or one that does not. DeLay said, "This bill is probably the most closed piece of legislation that I have ever seen and ever witnessed and ever been part of in my 12 years in the legislative body. . . . There is very little media to speak of . . . and I am telling Members, the American people out there do not know this is about to become law." In saying this, DeLay was in effect protesting the very carefully controlled way that the strategists behind the ADA determined to get the law through.

Wright, Silverstein, Neas, and others had worked to keep the ADA out of the press, control the legislative process, and work in tandem to make the law come to fruition. Wright referred to the strategy as a "press blackout."[28] It was a stealth act from the first to the last. Now the strategy was paying off, although there was no reason to expect the opponents to be happy as they watched "the plot thicken," as Helms had said the day before.

And so it did thicken to an overwhelming approval of the ADA of 377 to 28. Among those voting nay were Dannemeyer, DeLay, Shuster, and Chapman. Of his vote, Chapman said, "I voted no in final passage. If I have a regret about the entire affair, having to do it again in the context of what I know this many years later, I would not have offered [the amendment]. I certainly would have voted for the bill on final passage. Quite frankly, I live with that regret. I was angry that day at Steny, and I was angry that the process had betrayed me, and had betrayed the will of the House and the will of the Congress in not including that position." Though the bill became a success, Chapman himself suffered the consequences of his actions. Three years later, on the verge of being chosen by Ann Richards, then governor of Texas, to replace the ailing Lloyd Bentsen as senator, "Chapman was hit on New Year's Eve with a barrage of charges by civil rights leaders regarding his voting record."[29] Chapman claims that one man, whom he will not name but who had direct access to the governor, called her up and told her to reject Chapman because of his vote on the ADA. It doesn't take a lot of imagination to figure out who that man might have been—a man with a lot of power and exclusive access to the Texas governor, who might have been very upset about Chapman's trying to deep-six a national bill on disability.

On July 13, the final moment of the drama of the ADA took place. Senators took turns between emotion and hyperbole. Senator Hatch, perhaps known for a certain sangfroid, could barely hold back his sentiments and his rhetoric: "I suspect every senator in this chamber will feel the floors shake as thunderous applause breaks out around America following our approval of the conference report on the Americans with Disabilities Act. I just want to say that my heart is with each disabled American in this celebration." Harkin rejoiced with cadences of oratory noting that there was "no better year than 1990" for the historic ADA to be passed: "For in 1990 history was being rewritten from Pretoria to Prague, and right here in Washington, DC," citing Nelson Mandela, the demise of apartheid, the fall of communism, and, finally, the ADA.

Then, for the first time in the history of the Senate, a member, Harkin himself, spoke entirely in sign language without verbal speech. After signing, he translated with emotion what he said: "I just wanted to say to my [Deaf] brother Frank that today was my proudest day in sixteen years of Congress; that today Congress opens the doors to all Americans with disabilities. That today we say no to fear, no to prejudice, and no to ignorance." In his sign language speech, one part he didn't translate into spoken English he said to his Deaf audience, including his brother: "The ADA is the twentieth century's Emancipation Proclamation for all Americans. Today the United States Senate will say that the days of segregation, the days of inequality, are finished. By winning your full civil rights you strengthen ours."

Senator Hatch followed with a deeply moving and emotional moment in which he cried. Hatch said he felt "very, very deeply about this bill . . . and from my heart I just want to dedicate all of the efforts that all of us have made to my brother-in-law, Ramon Hansen, for the type of life he lived, for the type of person he was."

The conference report and, by extension, the ADA were approved by a resounding 91 to 6. The act would now be law as soon as President Bush signed the legislation. Two years of waiting were over. Disability rights were now and forever civil rights.

As Harkin and Hatch exited the Senate chamber, they saw a sea of people with disabilities celebrating. Hatch recalls: "We walked out of the chamber, Harkin and I, and there was a whole roomful of persons with disabilities. They were so happy and so moved by what went on. They were pleased with the final bill as well. Both Harkin and I got very emotional, and we actually shed tears. We broke down and cried. I'm a tough old guy, but I have a real inner core of sympathy and empathy for people who, like I say, can't help themselves, but would if they could." Whether or not disability activists would agree with Hatch's characterization of them, most had to be pleased that he managed to broker the historic vote on the ADA.

FOURTEEN

ON THE WHITE HOUSE LAWN

ON JULY 26, a sunny, hot day near ninety-three degrees in Washington, DC, three thousand people with disabilities poured onto the White House South Lawn. Some were wheeling in on chairs; some were being pushed; some used canes and mobility aids. There were Deaf people, blind people, and those with cognitive, affective, invisible, and chronic disabilities. Children, young people, adults, and the elderly—every color and demographic was represented. All could sense something historic was happening. This was the largest signing ceremony ever in the Rose Garden and probably the largest in the White House itself. The signing of the 1964 Civil Rights Act, by comparison, crammed only about a hundred politicians, almost all male and white, into the East Room of the White House.

The idea for the massive event had a humble origin. Ginny Thornburgh, the wife of the attorney general, describes herself as a grassroots disability activist. She had a suggestion when it seemed that the ADA was going to become law. She said to her husband, "We need this to be a major bill signing, not just the usual kind with the inside-the-Beltway people. It needs to be massive." Ginny at first suggested the Lincoln Memorial as a possible site. "We could put a table in front of President Lincoln and have a signing right there." Thornburgh wasn't so sure. Ginny Thornburgh recalls: "Rumor came back that it was probably going to be in the East Room. And I said, 'Well, why can't it be on the White House lawn?' The worry was that if we had it outside, some people from our community would faint or have sunstroke and then that would be the news story instead of this magnificent social-justice, civil-rights event occurring for our nation." Apparently, according to her, that fear was neutralized when a disability activist responded, "We have as much right to have sunstroke as everyone else."

In fact, the occasion did take its toll on people. Lex Frieden recalls: "The day itself was a very stressful day, not by the events, but by the heat. It was a stifling, stifling day in Washington, DC. There were ambulances there, and there were people passing out. I think more than a dozen people were treated and taken to the hospital. It was just so, so hot."

Despite the sweltering heat, the energy and expectations were high. "The excitement," gushes Frieden. "Here you are on the lawn of the White House, waiting for the president of the United States, and you've got members of Congress walking up and down among these three thousand assembled souls, shaking hands, having their photos taken, smiling, patting people on the backs. You've got reporters from all over the world interviewing people."

At 10 a.m., the president appeared and mounted a platform facing the White House with the Ellipse in the background. Seated there were Justin Dart, Sandy Parrino, Barbara Bush, Vice President Dan Quayle, and the Reverend Harold Wilke. Before Bush were three thousand people with disabilities and their families. Evan Kemp began by introducing Wilke, a minister in the United Church of Christ who had been a student of Paul Tillich and Reinhold Niebuhr. Wilke was also born armless and had been involved with disability groups for his whole life. Ginny Thornburgh, who was always trying to introduce the spiritual into the area of disability, had suggested that there be a blessing at this signing ceremony, apparently the first time in US history that there was such a religious invocation at a secular event, and suggested this minister. Wilke gave an ecumenical blessing, including all the major religions of the world. Kemp then thanked the disability community and singled out Dart, Parrino, Pat Wright, and Arlene Mayerson for special mention.

The president began his well-crafted speech and spoke for more than fifteen minutes as the heat beat down on the audience. Flanked by two sign language interpreters whose hands were dancing in the mild breeze, he said, "I want to salute the members of the United States Congress, the House and the Senate, who are with us today—active participants in making this day come true." Many applauded, but Melissa Shulman, Hoyer's aide, noted the nuance. "I remember President Bush thanking the 'active participants' on the Hill. It's extraordinary in a signing ceremony that the sponsors of the legislation were not called out individually. I remember that." While she remembers feeling "joyful," she notes that "it was a very partisan signing ceremony." Her point was that the legislators weren't just "active participants," but they were the driving force that made the bill happen. The strategy in this event was, as with the press release the summer before, to make the bill seem primarily like a Bush White House endeavor. Pat Wright agrees: "To not have any Democrats anywhere near the podium was kind of an insult." Wright herself was seated far back in the fifty-fifth row. Kennedy was in the front but moved back to kibitz in solidarity with Wright and his own disabled son, Teddy Jr. In the midst of the speech, he leaned over and whispered to Wright, "I had a horrible dream last night. I dreamed that Bush read the bill, and he wouldn't sign it."

Bush continued: "I started trying to put together a list of all the people who should be mentioned today. But when the list started looking a little longer than the Senate testimony for the bill, I decided I better give up, or that we'd never get out of here before sunset . . . so . . . I will single out but a tiny handful." Those singled out were Kemp, Dart, Gray, Roper, and Parrino. One thing they all had in common was that they were Republicans. In fact, no one on the stage was a Democrat. Shulman explains: "It was Kennedy's reelection [year]. They didn't want to give them credit; they didn't want to give Harkin [also up for election] credit. It was very political." But even missing from the honor roll were Republicans Hatch and Bartlett.

Bush tried to make politics work for him in another way—by playing the human rights card. "This historic act is the world's first comprehensive declaration of equality for people with disabilities. Its passage has made the United States the international leader on this human rights issue." With the United States showing a leadership role, he also noted that other countries, including the Soviet

Union, "have announced that they hope to enact now similar legislation." Placing the legislation in line with the Constitution and the Civil Rights Act, Bush said the ADA "brings us closer to the day when no Americans will ever again be deprived of their basic guarantee of life, liberty, and the pursuit of happiness." As is typical of this type of speech, he singled out Washington State resident Lisa Carl, in the audience, who had testified in the hearings about having cerebral palsy and being denied entrance to her hometown movie theater. "Lisa, you might not have been welcome at your theater but I'll tell you—welcome to the White House. We're glad you are here." The crowd burst into applause as Carl smiled warmly. Carl was gratified then, but more gratified two years later when she won a lawsuit she brought against the Bijou Theater in Tacoma after the new law took effect.

Tellingly, then Bush addressed "our friends in the business community." He noted, "There have been concerns that the ADA may be vague or costly, or may lead endlessly to litigation," but reassured them that "my administration and the United States Senate have carefully crafted this act." He followed up with the best convincer to conservatives—cutting welfare. "It costs almost $200 billion annually to support Americans with disabilities, in effect, to keep them dependent . . . [but now] they will move proudly into the economic mainstream of American life, and that's what this legislation is all about." Freeing up the welfare rolls is an appealing notion, also combined with the idea that people with disabilities will be "a tremendous pool of people who will bring to jobs diversity, loyalty, proven low turnover rate."

Finally, he launched into the comparison between the ADA and the fall of the Berlin Wall and communism. "Last year, we celebrated a victory of international freedom. Even the strongest person couldn't scale the Berlin Wall to gain the elusive promise of independence that lay just beyond. And so together we rejoiced when the barrier fell. And now I sign legislation which takes a sledgehammer to another wall. . . . [L]et the shameful wall of exclusion finally come tumbling down." The crowd applauded wildly as Bush then moved to sign the legislation, giving pens to the people on the stage and reserving one. A memorable moment came when Bush turned to Wilke to hand over a pen. The only problem was that Wilke had no arms or hands to receive the pen. Bush hesitated for a second. But Wilke deftly slipped his shoe off and took the pen with his foot, placing it in his shoe for later retrieval. A moment like that was so emblematic of the effects of the ADA—placing front and center a disability that was hidden too long. When was the last time an armless man used his feet to take something from a US president?

As the president left the stage, he shook hands and greeted many of the politicians and the audience. As he walked by the attorney general, the president reached into his pocket and took out the last pen he had reserved from the signing, handing it to Dick Thornburgh, but saying dead seriously, "It's for Ginny. It's not for you, sir!" Clearly he was recognizing how much she had done to make the ceremony a day to remember and in influencing Thornburgh himself by her grassroots activism. Perhaps the strained relations between Sununu and the Justice Department, headed by Thornburgh, were reflected in Bush's decision to hand the pen to Ginny, speculates John Wodatch.

It was a complex day of celebration and difficulty for some. Justin Dart, who sat on the platform, had mixed emotions. "I was upset about that [being on the platform] because I was totally embarrassed that Pat Wright and Judy Heumann, and all of these other people weren't up there. I would have had thirty, forty, fifty people up on a really big stage, but they didn't listen to me." Dart added, "I thought I was going to feel euphoric but . . . I felt oppressed and depressed." Of course, Dart struggled with the disability of depression his whole life, although what most people saw as his disability was polio. He reflected, "I said, 'Justin, what the hell is the matter with you?'" What occurred to him was that the bill was signed now, but the enforcement would be difficult. "What if we did it too soon? What if we can't carry it off, and it is perceived to fail, and they will not pass another law like this for one hundred or two hundred years? Look how Prohibition failed." He went to the celebrations afterward, but he felt uneasy. "I knew at this [time] that I would never rest easy. I would be oppressed by this responsibility for the rest of my life."[1] That sense of letdown and fear of failure didn't stop Dart. He continued to work for the enforcement of the ADA till his death twelve years later, in 2002.

Perhaps after all the work, all the years of trying, all the late nights and the teamwork, the idea of a celebration was too hard. Bobby Silverstein also felt the lack of feeling something. "In some respects, [it was] somewhat anticlimactic. I recall feeling euphoria at the celebration after final passage on the Senate the first time. [But at the Rose Garden] I don't know if we were tired, or what it was. The ceremony was pretty cool, with all those people there, and what Bush had to say was pretty cool."

Likewise, Mary Lou Breslin of DREDF considered the event "the worst experience of my life." She had flown in the night before to find her wheelchair broken by the airline. Then she appeared on *Nightline* and felt she did a terrible job. The next morning was the ceremony. "There were seating issues at the signing, and it was hot, and there was this big to-do afterward—a band and a celebration and whatnot, and there were no accessible bathrooms anywhere near the place that I could use, so I spent most of the day trudging along at about half a mile an hour trying to find some office building that would be open where I could go to the bathroom."[2]

For many not involved with the gritty aspects of negotiating, the event was spectacular. Scot Bogren, director of the Community Transportation Association of America, said, "That morning the overriding emotion of the audience was one of hope."[3] John Wodatch remembers that "it was joyous, just joyous."

If you have more than three thousand people invited to an event, it can hardly be considered exclusive. And yet three significant people did not get invitations—Senator Lowell Weicker, Ralph Neas, and Chai Feldblum. Weicker had long been on the White House's blacklist, so his lack of invitation was not particularly surprising. Neas had been actively involved in the months preceding the ceremony in exhaustively fighting the White House for its judicial nominations and to get the Kennedy-Hawkins civil rights bill passed. Feldblum was working for the ACLU, also fighting those appointments and boosting that bill.

There had been a list drawn up of VIPs—perhaps fifty to a hundred people. While most of the three thousand people received mailed invitations and no RSVP was necessary, the VIPs were seated in reserved seats and feted afterward. Feldblum was told she was among this select few and to report to the White House the day before to pick up her special invitation with Liz Savage and all the other political people. When she arrived, the place was filled with dignitaries. She asked for her invitation and was told that there must have been some mix-up; the invitation would be ready for her tomorrow. When she asked later, she was told that she was not invited in the first place. Feldblum, who had nonchalantly put up with a lot of stress and hard questioning at the hearings, felt "devastated. How could I not be?"

The ACLU put out a press release saying that the White House was so intimidated by the ACLU's organization that the administration had banned the union's representative. Feldblum decided not to be deterred. "This is my party as much as anyone else's." So on the day of the signing ceremony, she put on her black-and-white polka-dot party dress and went to the signing ceremony to stand outside the corner exit and greet and be greeted.

"I had a great time that day," she remembers. "I was embarrassed at the White House when I didn't get the ticket. That was the worst time. That was the worst time. I felt humiliated and that there was something wrong with me. And then also bad when they said I couldn't go. But I decided it was my party and I'm going to dance." When Steny Hoyer emerged from the event, he hugged her warmly and, uncharacteristically, lifted her high into the air in a celebratory manner. Feldblum comments wryly that he continued to do that for years afterward every time he met her.

These snubs did not go unnoticed. The *Washington Post* ran an editorial that Sunday. Titled "Snubbing the ACLU," the editorial said, "To all outward appearances, the signing ceremony was inclusive. But legislators, staff and the disabilities interest groups that had worked for years on the bill noticed a significant absence. No one from the American Civil Liberties Union had been invited in spite of the fact that lawyers and others in its Washington and national offices had been in the forefront of those working for passage." The piece went on to mention Chai Feldblum and noted, "During the 1988 campaign, President Bush made repeated reference to the ACLU and implied that membership was somehow subversive. . . . His refusal to acknowledge the organization's contribution—when all that was required was to include a couple of people in a crowd of more than 2,000—was petty and small-minded."[4]

Justin Dart had arranged a major party afterward and made sure that all the people who were not invited to the ceremony were there. And festivities continued all day and into the night. It was a day to remember as life for people with disabilities in the United States would change in profound ways.

FIFTEEN

ENABLING THE ADA

ALL THE FIRE and smoke were over. Now, as Dart worried, came the hard work of implementing the law. In order for a law to go into effect, there have to be reams of written regulations. And one thing no one wanted was a very long period between the law being signed into law and the publication of the regulations—or "regs," as they are known in Washington. Everyone remembered the interminable wait between 504 and the regulations that took years and different presidential administrations —and which produced the HEW sit-in in San Francisco. In fact, the law specified that the regulations had to be done within a year. With that speediness in mind, the attorney general signed the ADA regulations exactly one year to the day after the White House signing ceremony, an elapsed time that Dick Thornburgh noted proudly "is a record."

The job of writing the regulations fell again to John Wodatch, who had also worked on the 504 regulations. Wodatch recalls that "it was an incredible year." Five other people along with Wodatch drafted the regulations. To do this they had to talk to the heads of many agencies at least three or four times. There were sixteen hundred pages of cross-benefit analysis charts and graphs alone, and that didn't even include the regulations themselves. These analyses calculated what the financial impact of the law would be on a cost-benefit basis for twenty thousand state and local governments and seven million public accommodations. The metrics of these calculations are fairly recondite, notes Wodatch: "You have to cost out the benefit, for an example, to a paraplegic Iraqi war veteran who takes his daughter to an accessible playground."

The regulations were done in the required year, but many things could not be covered. Indeed, regulations are an ongoing process, and these had to be revised and added to in 2004. That second round of regulations was only just finished in the Obama administration. The lengthy revision period is necessary because new situations arise all the time once a law as broad as the ADA is in place. Wodatch notes that the regulations have to be revised because of new complaints brought and new situations evolving: "There were facilities like swimming pools, miniature and regular golf courses, shooting ranges that had never been considered for regulations. We said since we had to do these rules, we had a number of things we learned from the enforcement process: things that needed either more specificity or more guidance or weren't addressed or should have been. That we were going to add those to the rules, to clean them up and [add] them to our enforcement. That took from 2004 to 2010 to get them done."

One reason for the lengthy second round was that then vice president Dick Cheney put a virtual halt to the implementation of the regulations. Cheney saw the regulations as too expensive and didn't want them going in effect until after the George W. Bush administration had left. Wodatch explains: "They didn't want one of their last acts to be creating a whole new regulation of businesses and state and local government." In addition, according to Wodatch, Cheney insisted on so many carve-outs to the regulations that these manipulations were "illegal." For example, Cheney wanted playgrounds exempted from being accessible if they were a certain size. What particularly "drove people in the White House crazy" was the expense of making witness stands in courtrooms accessible. This was one of the most costly areas of the new regulations, and in Cheney's opinion, it had the fewest measurable benefits.

Another area that Cheney wanted cut was making the stages of school auditoriums accessible. According to Wodatch, "we were adamant about it. We had witnesses who testified at our hearings about kids in high school who dropped out of the band because the band was up on the stage and they couldn't get up to the stage. Again it was another thing with a high cost, and in terms of numbers, the benefits were less than the cost. They [the White House] said under an executive order, you get rid of that." Not until the Obama administration came in were Wodatch and the Justice Department given a go-ahead to keep working on the regulations.

What did the law actually mandate, and what were the major compromises? Title I of the law prohibits discrimination by public or private employers against a person with a disability who is otherwise qualified for the job. It also requires employers to make reasonable accommodations that will not result in undue hardship, that is, significant difficulty and expense for the employer. And employers can't ask people in job interviews or applications about the nature or severity of the disability. To activate the law, discriminated employees have to file a complaint with the EEOC, which tries to settle out of court. And if that doesn't work, the EEOC decides if there are grounds for permitting a court trial. If so, the individual must then sue and, in the initial law, could only get his or her back pay and legal fees. (This limitation changed after the Civil Rights Act of 1991 took effect.) The law was phased in so that it took effect for larger employers in 1992 and for smaller ones in 1994.

Title II prohibited state and local governments from discriminating. It also said that public transportation in cities and states, including local buses, subways, trains, and other facilities, had to be accessible. Accessible vans had to be part of the transportation mix. Amtrak was required to have one accessible car per train, and all new cars manufactured had to be accessible.

Title III banned discrimination in public accommodations and commercial facilities that are privately owned, such as hotels, restaurants, theaters, food stores, and other retail outlets. There were sliding time scales for when various kinds of facilities would be covered by the law. It also dealt with private bus lines and mandated a feasibility study to see how best to make them accessible. That study determined that smaller bus lines had to be accessible in six years, larger ones in seven, although the smaller lines' buses didn't have to install accessible bathrooms.

Title IV mandated telecommunications access, including telephone relays and captioning, for Deaf and hard of hearing people.

Having the law and the regulations in place was no guarantee that the intent of the law would blanket the nation immediately. In fact, there would be a backlash against the ADA handed down in various court decisions as well as in the court of public opinion. The courts focused on the definition of disability in the ADA. The writers of the ADA simply borrowed the definition from the 504 regulations. The definition, in effect, had three prongs: (1) having a substantial impairment that limited one or more life activities; (2) having had a history of such; or (3) being regarded as such. What this practically meant was that if you were disabled to the extent that you couldn't perform certain activities, then you were protected under the law. If someone found out that you had been disabled in the past and now discriminated against you in light of your history, then you were protected. And if someone believed you to be disabled (even though you weren't) and discriminated against you, then you were protected. The overriding idea was that disability discrimination should be illegal. And that no one should be discriminated against on the grounds of disability.

But judges, probably because this three-pronged concept of disability was strange to them, spent a lot of time deciding whether plaintiffs fit into the protected class, given the definition. Part of the problem was that activists and academics were rethinking how to define disability and a new model was evolving. This new idea was called the social model and was seen as radically different from two earlier models—the charity model and the medical model. In the *charity model*, people with disabilities were seen in connection with the church as subjects of God's whim or, worse, God's judgment and were therefore pitiable and deserving of alms or charity. In the *medical model*, people with disabilities were seen as enmeshed in a relationship with medical institutions because they had an "abnormality" or a disease that was in need of remediation or cure.

Unlike the charity or medical model, the *social model* shifted the power to define disability from church and hospital to society and from individual bodies to social mechanisms. The idea was that disability was socially constructed and done so in a political way. Rather than religion or medicine having the dominant hand, government, society, and culture all worked together to "disable" people because of their impairments. Therefore, impairment—lack of mobility or sight, for example—was simply a fact about a body, but disability was produced socially by the imposition of barriers and the lack of accommodation. The disability isn't "in" the person so much as it is "in" society. And instead of prayer or cure, the social model requires accommodation and removal of barriers. Therefore, the three-pronged definition of disability in the ADA includes the idea that the impairment is only one part of being disabled—being regarded as disabled is another crucial part in the social construction of disability.

Since the ADA was a "stealth" bill, deliberately kept from the public and the media before its passage, the rather subtle and complex idea of the social model didn't infiltrate into common knowledge. Race and gender were so much more obvious as categories in which civil rights had to be protected. But this Trinitarian definition of disability was as mysterious to most people, including judges, as was the Trinity itself.

The ADA came into effect on a staggered basis as all the delays negotiated into the bill eventually timed out. Two years after the law was signed, the employment part of the ADA kicked in for larger businesses, and two years after that, for smaller businesses. Newspaper articles at that time celebrated the new era of antidiscrimination related to jobs, but also highlighted that businesses were confused about many concepts, including, of course, "reasonable accommodation" and "undue hardship," as well as "otherwise qualified."

The enforcement mechanism for the jobs portion of the bill was itself one that led to delays. A person who felt discriminated against in the workplace had to file a complaint with the EEOC. That organization gets anywhere from 15,000 to 26,000 disability complaints each year. The number has been steadily rising from an initial 15,000 to the highest number most recently. ADA complaints now make up about a quarter of all those made to the EEOC in 2013. By comparison, race tops the list at about 36 percent, with gender at 30 percent, and age-related discrimination at 22 percent. The largest category of ADA complaints concern orthopedic conditions, including spinal injury (18 percent), followed by depression (6.3 percent), cardiac conditions (4 percent), manic-depression (3.4 percent), and hearing loss (3.4 percent). But surprisingly, the category of "regarded as disabled" or "perceived disability" makes up almost 14 percent of complaints. It appears that disability discrimination itself, regardless of whether the person is actually disabled, is one of the biggest single areas of civil rights violations.

Each complaint has to be vetted, and the EEOC has to decide if the charge is valid. Then the commission has to try to settle the complaint out of court. Only then, if settlement fails, can an individual sue an employer. At that point, if the case were appealed, it might take several years for there to be significant legal rulings. In 2013, about 4,000 out of 26,000 disability cases were withdrawn because the complainant failed to follow up or withdrew the charge. About 16,000 cases were decided to be without valid cause. About 2,000 cases were withdrawn because the complainant received the benefits he or she wanted as a result of simply filing a charge. Fewer than 3,000 cases were settled through negotiations with the EEOC. About 1,000 cases went to court, and about half of those were successful.[1] The imagined litigious inferno predicted by the anti-ADA forces was clearly exaggerated.

In general, these statistics suggest that the number of complaints has gone up over the years. But the number of successful court cases has remained about the same. Meanwhile, the number of successful resolutions through court, settlement, negotiations, and the like has doubled. The EEOC seems to have been successful in weeding out unwarranted claims. The actual monetary amounts awarded are relatively low, only doubling in the years following the ADA Amendments Act (ADAAA), which provided a clearer and less ambiguous definition of disability. The avalanche of debt sustained by employers can now be seen as an exaggeration fomented in the Chicken Little scenarios at the ADA hearings. Nevertheless over $100 million was spent in monetary benefits, and this amount does not include monies derived from litigation, which breaks down to an average of $20,000 per complaint. Hardly a windfall. Legal cases can vary in what is paid, but some statistics cite $40,000 as the out-of-court settlement. Considering that lawyers will recoup $10,000 or more in fees, the settlement, again, is much less than a windfall.

It wasn't until 1998, six years after the employment sections of the bill went into effect, that the Supreme Court began to make some significant rulings. These decisions came cascading down like dangerous rocks striking the foundations of the ADA. The first of the cases that chipped away at the definition of disability was *Murphy v. United Parcel Service*. The Supreme Court ruled on a case involving Vaughn Murphy, a UPS mechanic in Kansas, who had hypertension, for which he took medication that lowered his blood pressure to normal ranges. He was fired because his unmedicated blood pressure was above the limit allowed by the Department of Transportation guidelines. Murphy sued under the ADA, claiming he was fired for having a disability. The Supreme Court ruled that because Murphy's blood pressure was in the normal range as long as he was taking his medication, he could not be defined as disabled and therefore was not covered by the ADA.

The very same day, the Supreme Court ruled on *Sutton v. United Airlines*. In this case, twin sisters and airplane pilots Karen Sutton and Kimberly Hinton, who had always wanted to fly large commercial jetliners, applied to United Airlines in 1992 and were rejected for being nearsighted. Both sisters were licensed by the Federal Aviation Agency and had flown regional jets. They were "otherwise qualified" in terms of their age and experience, and their vision was twenty-twenty when they were wearing contact lenses. The twins argued that they were covered under the ADA because they were "substantially limited" in life activities such as driving, shopping, and watching television if they were not wearing their contact lenses but were otherwise qualified with the lenses when flying. The court rejected their case, claiming that the ADA was not designed to cover cases where people like Sutton and Hinton, as well as Murphy of the UPS case, could correct their impairments through medication or corrective devices.

In another case, *Albertsons v. Kirkingburg*, the Supreme Court ruled on mitigating circumstances that weren't even about medication or devices. In this case, a person legally blind in one eye was deemed nondisabled because he merely saw differently than others and therefore was not "substantially limited" enough to qualify as disabled. Plaintiffs and the courts were being tangled up in the three-pronged definition and were missing the point of the ADA—not how to define disability but how to stop discrimination resulting from ableist prejudice.

An earlier case that focused more on the definition of disability rather than discrimination was *Bragdon v. Abbott*, decided by the Supreme Court the year before. Sidney Abbott was an HIV-positive woman who lived in Bangor, Maine. She went to her local dentist, Randon Bragdon, and in the course of filling out routine forms, she disclosed her HIV status. Bragdon refused to treat her in his office, saying that he would only do so in a hospital setting and that Abbott would have to pay the costs of the hospital services. She brought suit under the ADA. The dentist claimed that Abbott was a "direct threat" to his health. She claimed that she was disabled by being HIV positive. The hitch in this was the pesky definition of disability as having a substantial impairment that limits one or more life activities. Which life activity could Abbot not perform? She did not have full-blown AIDS and was not symptomatic. Her answer was that the life activity was reproduction, since she could not have sex with someone without the threat of infecting the partner and that there was a reasonable chance of passing HIV to the child in the process of childbirth.

The problematic nature of the definition of disability led to the rather convoluted argument on Abbott's part that was in effect: "You have to fill my cavities because I can't have sex so I can have a baby." The court ruled that Abbott was correct and that, further, she did not pose a direct threat according to the guidelines of the American Dental Association and other official bodies in the field of dentistry. Again, definition trumped discrimination.

In *Toyota v. Williams*, a worker with chronic tendonitis and carpal tunnel syndrome claimed she could not do certain specific jobs at the Toyota plant. The Supreme Court ruled that she was not disabled because she didn't have substantial limitations in performing a range of life activities like brushing her teeth, shopping, or tidying the house. If there were a specific job she could not perform at work because of tendonitis and carpal tunnel syndrome, that fact alone would not determine that she was disabled. The bar had to be higher.

And in one particularly absurd case settled in the district court, *Hirsch v. National Mall and Service, Inc.*, a man with cancer, who died before the case came to trial, was retroactively judged not disabled enough to claim the title of disabled—even though his non-

Hodgkin's lymphoma killed him. A fatal disease would seem insufficient, under this high bar, to qualify as a disability.

As the judges proceeded with their cases, they ended up being like rabbinical scholars parsing the text of the Talmud and in the process getting caught up in the ambiguities of the ADA rather than the main intent—preventing discrimination. Under the new rulings, if you were fired for having a disability that was correctable, you could not sue because although you were fired for that very disability, you actually weren't disabled. And if you were HIV positive and were refused service, you had to argue tortuously that you were disabled because you couldn't have unprotected sex. If you couldn't perform a task at work and were fired because of an impairment, you weren't disabled unless you couldn't perform significant "life activities" at home. With all these odd interpretations coming down from the courts, something had to be done.

Not all of the court rulings were about definitions, but they were still about parsing the ambiguities of the law. One decision actually opened up the law in profound ways. In *Olmstead v. LC*, Lois Curtis and Elaine Wilson were two women with affective and cognitive disabilities who were confined to an institution. Both were deemed competent to live in a community-based setting, but because of the state's reluctance to pay for their housing and care, they languished in the institution. They contacted the Atlanta Legal Aid Society, where they met Susan Jamieson, a lawyer there. She sued under the ADA to have the two women live in a group home or some other freer setting. While a lower court ruled that the women should be freed, the state of Georgia, under the director of social services, Tommy Olmstead, appealed to the Supreme Court, saying that such arrangements would be too costly. The Supreme Court ruled in an important decision that people who are deemed competent should be placed in the least restrictive setting that would match their competence and that not doing so violated their civil rights. Wilson went on to live in a home with a caregiver and friend, although Wilson died a few years later.

Curtis went on to a much more productive life. An African American woman who is now an artist, she describes herself as "a person with a vision and a spirit."[2] During her time in the institution, she was unproductive, a behavior problem kept numbed out on heavy drugs. But people recalled that she used to draw incessantly. On her release, she was encouraged to keep drawing, and now her art is sold and collected. President Obama gave her an award at the White House, and she has received the Tubman African American Museum Act of Courage Award for "standing up and taking action during challenging circumstances to make a difference for yourself and the lives of others." Upon receiving the award, she said, "I want to tell everybody, so people can get out."[3]

The legacy of *Olmstead* has been mixed as the courts have wrestled with its legal implications. An expert analysis of the effect of *Olmstead* concludes, "The decision established a broad legal standard for measuring the adequacy of publicly funded health program design for persons with disabilities. At the same time, it is evident that its lofty goals, which parallel those of the ADA itself, can be reached only through a national commitment to reforms that extend far beyond the power of courts to devise."[4]

Another positive decision, *Tennessee v. Lane*, involved George Lane, of Benton, Tennessee, who suffered a crushed hip and pelvis during a car accident. After recovering, he was charged with two misdemeanors, including driving with a revoked license. Lane arrived at the Polk County Courthouse with both legs in casts and using a wheelchair. He discovered that the trial was on the second floor of a building without an elevator. To make his court date, Lane dragged himself up the stairs to get to the courtroom. By his own admission, the pain in doing this was excruciating: "On a pain scale of 1 to 10, it was way past 10," he noted and pointed out that the judge and courthouse employees "stood at the top of the stairs and laughed at me."[5]

Lane's case was arraigned, and another date was set. On that second occasion, he refused to drag himself up the steps or to be carried upstairs by police officers. Remarkably, he was arrested and jailed for failing to appear at his trial. At subsequent proceedings, he remained downstairs and his lawyer shuttled up and down stairs to communicate with him and the court. Eventually, he pleaded guilty to the count of driving with a revoked license. He decided in return to bring a lawsuit against Tennessee under the ADA for having inaccessible courthouses. He was joined in his suit by Beverly Jones, also a wheelchair-using paraplegic. She was a court reporter whose job often ran up against inaccessible courtrooms and buildings. Jones identified forty-four such locations and asked for modifications on some of them. Her requests were denied. She joined Lane's suit.

The Supreme Court ultimately decided the case. The main defense by the state was that the ADA abrogated states' rights, particularly their right to "sovereign immunity" guaranteed under the Eleventh Amendment to the Constitution. The legal details are quite complex, but a series of preceding court cases had actually bolstered states' rights to a point where it seemed possible for the state to say that a federal law could not apply. The one area, though, that the courts had upheld was the right of the federal government to step in when a class of people's civil rights were being violated by the state. The court so ruled in this case, and the upshot was that all state and local courthouses had to be accessible. Lane eventually lost one leg and now walks with a prosthetic one. The Polk County Courthouse installed an elevator two years after the ruling.

In a well-known case, Casey Martin, a top-notch golfer, had a circulatory problem that made walking difficult. He had Klippel-Trenaunay-Weber syndrome, a painful, degenerative circulatory disorder that obstructed blood flow from his right leg back to his heart. Further dangers include hemorrhaging, clotting, and fracturing the tibia. Martin wanted to use a golf cart to play in the PGA Tour, but the PGA Tour denied him the right to use the cart. Martin won in the lower court, but the PGA Tour appealed to the Supreme Court. The court ruled in 2001 that Martin could use the cart because he had a disability, the PGA was a place of public accommodation, the cart was a reasonable accommodation, and walking was not an essential activity of golfing. The only two justices dissenting were Scalia and Thomas.

Scalia's withering dissenting opinion contested what he called the "Kafkaesque" role of government in determining the rules of sporting events. But his ending epigraph, retooled from the opening line of Kurt Vonnegut's cautionary, dystopic short story "Harrison Bergeron," tells more about Scalia's overall frame of mind about leveling the playing field for people with disabilities. He wrote, with sarcasm dripping, "The year was 2001, and 'everybody was finally equal.'" (Vonnegut's opening line begins "It was 2081, and everyone was finally equal.") For Scalia, the dystopic future had come eighty years early with this court ruling.

Just as the courts were narrowing the law in the case of defining disability and expanding the reach of the law in other ways, business interests along with some conservatives continued to attack the law now that it was in effect. A significant attack was launched by the well-known and respected actor Clint Eastwood, who made his Dirty Harry anti-disability-rights salvo in 2000. Eastwood is the owner of the Mission Ranch Inn in Carmel, California. A patron with disabilities had sued his hotel under the ADA, claiming that the restrooms and the registration cabin were inaccessible and the only accessible guest room was more than double the price of others in the hotel. Eastwood went on a public relations campaign in advance of his approaching lawsuit to criticize the ADA. He said the law was subject to misuse in frivolous lawsuits by serial drive-by lawyers seeking to rack up legal fees. The jury ultimately decided that the plaintiff's claim was not valid, because she never actually went to the hotel, but that the hotel was in violation of the act itself.

Representative Mark Foley, egged on by Eastwood and the hotel and restaurant lobbying groups, proposed the ADA Notification Act in 2000. That act provided a ninety-day period during which a firm accused of discriminating against the disabled could fix that problem without being sued or penalized. Disability groups opposing the Notification Act said it would take the teeth out of the ADA by encouraging companies simply to do nothing and just wait until receiving notice of intent to sue before they complied with the law. Eastwood went to Washington to testify at the hearings for the Notification Act in a subcommittee of the Judiciary Committee. Playing the role of the aw-shucks American guy, he said, "I am here just to help." He complained about the use of the ADA by lawyers who he said are "perverting the law." Admitting he was "naive" about the politics, Eastwood, under questioning, also admitted that his case would not actually be affected by a federal law since he was being sued under California's own law. The ADA Notification Act never made it to the House floor at that time. It has subsequently been proposed several more times, as recently as 2013, without any success. But its intent reflects a growing backlash against the ADA.

Eastwood managed to make himself an enemy of disability activists not just through his double-barreled attack on the ADA but also because of his film *Million Dollar Baby*, which ends with a prizefighter becoming disabled and ultimately preferring death to life using a wheelchair and other assistive devices.

A preponderance of the cases being brought under the ADA was being lost. Like the old joke about the operation that was a success, but the patient died, the ADA was a success, but its application was failing. The only answer was to make a new act that would fix the problems of the old act. The first steps toward that end was a 2004 report titled *Righting the ADA* by the National Council on Disability, the very group that had created the first version of the ADA and that directly reported to the president. In the current era, the organization was headed by Lex Frieden. Bob Burgdorf, who wrote the earliest version of the ADA, was the staff lawyer who now put together this report.

The report proposed an ADA Amendments Act because despite congressional and executive branch approval, "the judiciary all too often has given the Act [the original ADA] the cold shoulder."[6] The cold shoulder made it harder for people to qualify as disabled. Indeed any diseases that can be mitigated with drugs and the like were not to be treated as disabilities. The report specifies that according to the rash of legal decisions, the following diseases were not considered disabilities: alcoholism, drug addiction, heart disease, seizures, diabetes, cancer, hemophilia, Tourette's syndrome, asthma, Ménière's disease, hepatitis C, and ADHD. It also allowed various other considerations like job seniority to take priority over the intent of the law. The courts further made it harder to bring a lawsuit in the first place—which is the main way that the ADA can be enforced. The courts banned punitive damages in private suits and made it harder for the prevailing party to get legal fees paid. Also, the idea that reasonable accommodations should be made for an employee unless it put an undue hardship on the employer "opened up a troublesome can of worms. It invites employers to interject their own possibly eccentric and prejudiced views about what is reasonable" instead of having the standard be undue hardship, which is provable by the more concrete measure of financial ability.[7]

The Amendments Act sought to rid the ADA of the problematic phrase that disability was an impairment that "substantially limits one or more life activity" and to simply say flat out that disability was a "physical or mental impairment." Such impairments were further defined as (1) any physiological disorder or condition, cosmetic disfigurement, or anatomical loss affecting one or more of the following body systems: neurological; musculoskeletal; special sense organs; respiratory, including speech organs; cardiovascular; reproductive; digestive; genito-urinary; hemic and lymphatic; skin; and endocrine; or (2) any mental or psychological disorder, such as mental retardation, organic brain syndrome, emotional or mental illness, and specific learning disabilities.

Thus, there would be no room for legal parsing. A disability was a disability. Period.

Perhaps the most interesting and even moving language in the report proposing the Amendments Act is a concise and clear paragraph that states the "social model" of disability:

> Although variations in people's abilities and disabilities across a broad spectrum are a normal part of the human condition, some individuals have been singled out and subjected to discrimination because they have conditions considered disabilities by others; other individuals have been excluded or disadvantaged because their physical or mental impairments have been ignored in the planning and construction of facilities, vehicles, and services; and all Americans run the risk of being discriminated against because they are perceived as having conditions they actually may not have or because of misperceptions about the limitations resulting from conditions they do have.[8]

This statement is, after all, the heart and soul of the ADA—that discrimination against disability is not about particular people as much as it is about a social, cultural, and political environment that stigmatizes various aspects of human physical and mental diversity. This discrimination can be built into the environment so that it appears invisible, but invisible or not, it is still discrimination. And the statement points out that disability isn't about "them"—it is about "us" since disability is the equal-opportunity identity category that allows anyone to be part of it given the serendipity of birth, trauma, or disease.

On July 31, 2008, Harkin and Sensenbrenner introduced the ADA Amendments Act to the Senate and the House, respectively. The committee markup and report came out speedily the following day. About a month later, on September 11, the bill went to the Senate floor. Hatch, Harkin, and Kennedy spoke for it. Unlike the tortuous path of the ADA, this new bill passed with unanimous consent the same day. There was no dissent or much discussion other than to praise the bill and condemn the court decisions. The House also passed the bill by voice vote with no individual record on September 17. George W. Bush signed the bill the following week. The bill under Bush Sr. had taken two years to come to fruition; the Amendments Act was voted on within two months of its introduction. Sometimes, history ends with a whimper rather than a bang.

The original proposal was modified slightly in committee. The two major changes were that an exception to the mitigating measures would be glasses and contact lenses (thus, *Sutton v. United Airlines* would remain unchanged), and that a "perceived disability" would not be grounds for an accommodation.

But the overall effects of both the ADA and the ADAAA were palpable. In 2013 the National Council on Disability issued a report called *A Promising Start* to President Obama stating that the ADAAA seemed to be having a positive effect, although it might be too early to say for sure. The report states: "The central message from the review of the case law is that, in the decisions rendered so far, the ADAAA has made a significant positive difference for plaintiffs in ADA lawsuits. In six of the seven Circuit Court decisions in which the provisions of the ADAAA were applied, the plaintiff prevailed on the issue of establishing a disability; and in the district court decisions analyzed in cases under the ADAAA, plaintiffs prevailed on the showing of disability in more than three out of four decisions—a substantial improvement over pre-ADAAA decisions in achieving the broad scope of ADA coverage that Congress intended."[9]

In the twenty-five years since the ADA was passed, the landscape of the United States has changed. Many of these changes no doubt came about with previous legislation, like the Architectural Barriers Act, but the ADA supercharged the effect of much of this legislation. In addition, it provided a national template rather than the mixed tessellation of laws throughout the states. Now the streets and buildings look different. We no longer are surprised to see ramps and electronic doors. Curb cuts and accessible bathrooms are the rule rather than the exception. It is not strange to see ASL interpreters for a variety of public events and functions. Wheelchair lifts on buses raise many passengers but few eyebrows. Trains and city subways are accessible in many locations.

Bob Kafka, the curly-haired hippy activist from ADAPT, sees the world differently now. Living in Texas, he can visit his in-laws in Washington with ease. "I call up SuperShuttle, an accessible SuperShuttle van comes up. I am able to transfer onto kind of an acceptable air transport, fly; a motorized wheelchair gets put into an accessible plane. Off the plane, I go onto an accessible transit metro in Washington, DC, and then I'm able to roll down accessible sidewalks to my in-laws' house." In the past he would not have had the civil rights that would allow him to do what any able-bodied person does without a second thought. Kafka comments, "We now take freedom of movement for granted in terms of how the ADA [works. Also] I'm able to interact with people. If my friends want to go out to eat and just go to a restaurant, the vast majority now are accessible for me to go. I don't have the embarrassment of either having a staircase that's inaccessible or deciding not to go because you didn't want to take the chance."

Lisa Cape, a blond-haired, blue-eyed All-American model who uses a wheelchair, noticed a change. When Cape first sought modeling jobs, she found that casting directors couldn't see past her wheelchair. After the ADA, she received many more calls. "I think it has to do with the general shift in attitude over the last few years. There is more effort to see people with disabilities as another population that should be represented." Cape also worked as public relations manager of the Shepherd Center for spinal cord and brain injury in Atlanta. Being able to get to work and around town was much improved. "It is getting so that I don't think twice about where I can go." But not all public accommodations are accessible, and now with the ADA, the threat of a lawsuit empowers wheelchair users like Cape. She also can use the power of the disabled purse: "I will not patronize a place that is blatantly discriminatory. Most of the time, I will tell the manager that I would be eating at this restaurant or shopping at this store if it could accommodate me."[10]

While some business owners like Eastwood were fighting back against the ADA, others were taking advantage of it to hire qualified people. United Parcel Service, which later did fight the act, in this case hired James Holland, twenty-eight, as a programming instructor. Holland was blind since the age of twelve. He uses a text-to-voice program on his computer and other assistive devices. Holland says, "[UPS's] attitude is, 'Except for adaptive equipment, we're going to treat you like anyone else.' I've always been thankful for that. I'm a firm believer that people's abilities come from within. You have limitations. Everyone has. You have to overcome your limitations and work with your abilities." Fred Fernandez, who ran the UPS equal employment opportunity program that hired Holland notes, "For us, the Disabilities Act does not present itself as some horrific new regulatory problem. We're looking at it as an opportunity."[11]

Laura Clowers, then thirty-one, noticed changes by the fifth year of the ADA. "When I go out with friends now, I don't really have to worry as much about will I be able to get into someplace or what happens if I have to go to the bathroom. You know you are still disabled and in a wheelchair, but you don't feel like an outcast." Clowers noticed that the plastic-bag dispensers in the supermarket were now at a level she could reach. So was an ATM located near her home. Also the changing rooms in a department store she frequented were now accessible. Yet, buying food for her parrot is still a challenge since her pet store is not accessible, and a local thrift shop has aisles too narrow for her to negotiate. "There seems to be more awareness now," Clowers mused.[12]

Carrie S. Smoot, also thirty-one, a freelance writer with cerebral palsy who uses a wheelchair, feels more capable of getting around Washington, DC. At first, after the ADA, there were few buses with wheelchair lifts, and she had to wait a long time. At the Metro stations, an employee had to be summoned to open a special gate. But more recently, she has had to wait much less time because, in 1995, about 60 percent of buses in the DC area were made accessible. And she can now easily open the gate with a special card. "It is still not perfect," said Smoot, who is concerned about the frequent malfunction of the elevator in the station. "But I can generally count on there being a working chair lift. I feel much more relaxed about the trip."[13]

Aside from the personal triumphs and the legal imperatives, the majority of employers and store owners simply had to be educated about the provisions of the act. There was widespread ignorance and even wider spread prejudice. John Hockenberry, journalist and wheelchair user, tells the story of a local bicycle store owner in Brooklyn where Hockenberry used to buy tires for his chair. After the ADA was passed, the proprietor said to him, "I see there where your president signed that law for you guys." Hockenberry replied, "You mean the Americans with Disabilities Act?" The owner responded, "Yeah! Things are going to be great for you guys!" Taking advantage of the moment, Hockenberry pointed out, slightly kidding, "Well, it probably means you're going to have to ramp that front step of yours." Without a pause the owner deflected, "Oh, no. No, no, no. See, it's for new stuff. Not me. Just for new stuff."[14]

The bike shop owner might or might not win in a court case. As a public accommodation, his shop is required to be accessible, even though it has already been built. On the other hand, the owner could claim undue hardship, although it is hard to imagine that a ramp would break his business. Hockenberry's point is that rather than understand his obligation to make his place accessible, the owner focused on the technicalities that might get him off. The shopkeeper also confused the employment titles of the bill with the public accommodations section of the bill. The problem here is also that a law is only as effective as the educational component of it.

A Harris poll conducted four years after the act documents an improvement in life for people with disabilities. Seventy-five percent of respondents said access to public facilities has improved. Sixty-three percent saw improved attitudes toward people with disabilities, and 60 percent said access to public transportation was better.[15]

Incrementally, life was improving. By 2013, the number of municipal transit buses accessible by either lift or ramp was 99 percent, whereas trolley buses were 100 percent.[16] The requirement that each Amtrak railroad train have an accessible car had been enforced, and all cars made were now accessible. However, one big area of noncompliance is in the stations themselves. In 2010 only 20 percent of Amtrak stations were accessible. Many will not be accessible even after 2040, the cutoff date extended by the Department of Transportation. Rural areas are often without any bus service, and as a result, people with disabilities in those regions are particularly affected by a lack of transportation. A recent report from the American Association of People with Disabilities concluded, "In the past two decades since passage of the ADA, some progress has been made; however transportation options for people with disabilities remain unacceptably limited."[17]

Employment is the biggest area in which the ADA has not succeeded. In 2013, 82.4 percent of people with disabilities were unemployed and were a little less than twice as likely to work in part-time jobs as those without disabilities.[18] In 2012, people with disabilities had a median monthly family income of $2,856, about 60 percent of the median monthly family income for people without disabilities ($4,771). Approximately 29 percent of people aged fifteen to sixty-four with severe disabilities lived in poverty, while 18 percent of people with nonsevere disabilities and 14 percent of people with no disability lived in poverty. The one somewhat bright area is that the number of people with disabilities working for federal, state, and local government has risen, because of the ADA.[19]

All of this unemployment malaise is not necessarily a result of the ADA itself, which, after all was an antidiscrimination bill, not an employment bill. Although the argument was made to the business and conservative sector that the bill would create jobs and take people with disabilities off government benefits, that clearly was an argument that has not yet been borne out. Perhaps people even knew that to be the case at the time. As Thornburgh says looking back, "It [the argument about getting the disabled off government benefits] was a good line, to be sure, but nobody had any gift of prophecy that saw this actually working in the employment area.

Nobody would have given you a guarantee. They would give you a guarantee of maximum effort and trying to enlist—and they are wonderful stories, individual stories, that have been told in the wake of the act about how people have, in truth, found accommodations for people with disabilities, but in the aggregate, it has not been a success story."

One reason, perhaps, for the lack of success in the private sector despite some success in the government sector is that the ADA had no quotas. In the governmental area, there are mandated goals and directives to have a certain percentage of the workforce composed of disabled people. But that was never the case in the private sector. In the George H. W. Bush administration, quotas were anathema, as they are today in general. In fact, at that time Bush opposed the Kennedy-Hawkins civil rights bill, calling it a quota bill. Yet, two-thirds of the European Union states have some form of quota system, as does Japan. In France, all companies with more than twenty workers are required to have 6 percent of the employees be people with disabilities. The average rate of unemployment for EU workers with disabilities is about 5 percent of those who want to work and are not "inactive." Compare that with the 80 percent unemployment rate in the United States. Quotas are not the only answer in the European Union. There are far more programs that seek to put disabled people to work in the private sector.[20] But the goals hoped for by the passage of the ADA are clearly desires in progress. The ADA is the beginning, not the end.

There is some valid criticism of the ADA as being the perfect bill for left and right to agree on because, in some sense, while providing increased access and barrier removal, it stresses the mutually admired concept of independent living. On the left, independent living would mean that people with disabilities were increasingly autonomous and able to determine their own fate and freedom. On the right, being independent and autonomous meant that people would become part of the workforce and the consumer society, relieving the government of providing benefits and powering the engine of the economy. The Left didn't have the power to make this a funded mandate with its own enforcement agency, because the Right would never have allowed more government money to be poured into a social welfare program. Thus, where left and right could meet, the ADA would by definition have to be a compromise bill.

In terms of neoliberalism, the goal of the ADA was simply to bring the disabled citizen and consumer up to par with other citizens and consumers in the multinational, global economy. There was no attempt to use the bill to structurally transform the society in general. Disabled citizens under the ADA would have the same rights, or lack of rights, of any citizen-worker in the United States. Since so many Republicans were strongly supporting the bill, it had to have a kind of pull-yourself-up-by-your-own-bootstraps approach in the typical American ideal. While other countries saw disability as a problem of social transformation and government mandate, the United States had its own tough-guy, tough-love approach. Even on the liberal side, there was not unanimous support for the act. Labor unions were not especially in favor of some of the provisions of the ADA and were particularly upset when seniority might be trumped by a disability accommodation.

But the ADA offers us what no other legislation had done before. It highlights the rights of people with disabilities as civil rights, not the rights of a patient to treatment or an unfortunate to charity. A whole cohort of people, sometimes called "the ADA generation," has come of age in the past twenty-five years. Like the women who came after the feminist movement, and LGBT people coming after many of the struggles in the queer community, this generation can often be a bit blasé about the rights achieved. Andraéa LaVant, a beautiful, stylish African American woman with muscular dystrophy who uses a wheelchair and is an inclusion specialist at the Girl Scouts Council of America, wrote, "As part of the so-called 'ADA Generation,' for much of my life I have felt entitled to the rights that I knew I had as a person with a disability. Although I couldn't necessarily pinpoint the specific legislation that afforded me those rights, I vividly recall instances where I'd roll up to the entrance of an inaccessible building or to some form of inaccessible public transportation and confidently (and possibly arrogantly) appraise the situation: 'Hey! There's a law against this! I could sue!'"[21]

The empowerment inherent in those last two sentences is now built into the social and cultural kit of people with disabilities. The ADA incorporates not only the stick of the ADA but the carrot as well. LaVant was able to go on supplemental security income (SSI) when she was eighteen, which allowed her to afford college and to pay for her motorized wheelchair. "What I do know is that I wouldn't be where I am physical, mentally, spiritually, emotionally if it weren't for" her having her current job, which was made possible by the ADA.[22]

Like LaVant, Emalie Fogg was also part of the ADA generation. She was five years old when the ADA was passed. A redhead sporting wire-frame glasses, she had cerebral palsy and was blind in one eye, enduring eight major surgeries from age four to seventeen. She used a power wheelchair to get around. "I never really knew the time before ADA," she said. "I grew up expecting, and most often seeing, the impact of ADA in my life. . . . Although I use a wheel chair, I was able to physically access almost every place I wanted to go growing up. . . . I did have to avoid certain movie theaters or shops in the small towns I frequented because they were too old to be covered under the accessible design standards of the ADA." Also like LaVant, Fogg knew that behind her was a strong force: "The legacy of ADA for me has been that it has taught me to expect and sometimes demand equal treatment. When I run up against an obstacle to full access, I know I have a leg to stand on when making a complaint. Believe me, I'm not shy about voicing my opinions and demanding that they be heard! In these ways I grew up a child of ADA."[23]

Fogg attended Keene State College in her native New Hampshire. In college, she was further empowered by discovering a course taught by Graham Warder on disability history. The class taught her what she never actually knew. "I am ashamed to say that for a long time I took the ADA's existence for granted." Her education led to a new determination on her part to help disseminate the history of disability. As she eloquently put it, "Learning about disability history in general, and the Disability Rights Movement in particular, has taught me that while the ADA has always been a presence in my life, it was not created out of thin air. It was born out of the commitment, struggle, and sacrifice of a group of activists with and without disabilities working to create a society where people with disabilities are seen not as burdens to be pitied but as fully participating members of their communities."

Fogg went on to work at the Smithsonian Museum with the curator Katherine Ott, developing an online museum about disability history, using disability artifacts at the museum.[24] Unfortunately, Fogg did not go on fighting for disability rights. She developed a very serious gastric disorder that led to her premature death in 2013 at the age of twenty-seven, just two years before she could celebrate the twenty-fifth anniversary of the act.

One of the difficulties of the ADA is that to get it to work, you have to go litigious. Curtis Richards, a visually impaired man who works in disability advocacy, doesn't drive, because of his disability. In 1993, he decided to buy his wife, who has normal vision, a car as a surprise present. Richards took a sighted friend along to drive him to the dealership and then try out the new vehicle. When Richards and his friend returned from the test drive, Richards was ready to buy the car. He added that his friend, who had a valid license, would drive the vehicle home. But when it was time to sign the papers, "to my amazement, [they] . . . inform[ed] me that they could not sell me the car because I did not have a valid driver's license and was a liability to the car dealership." Richards felt he was the victim of discrimination under the ADA, and told the people at the dealership so. He made a scene, and the staff left to discuss the issue. Upon their return, he said, "they suddenly changed their story. Suddenly it was a 'matter of corporate policy' that they could not sell a car to an unlicensed driver. Now, I was not just mad, but full-fledged angry." But what do you do when you are angry? The first thing Richards did was to go to another dealership that allowed him to purchase the vehicle he wanted.

Having bought the car, Richards still felt upset. "So, now I found myself faced with a big dilemma. I'm not a litigious person. What should I do now?" Many victims of discrimination face this same problem. Do you become a troublemaker in response to a questionable practice? "I began to question whether this was really discrimination or just another sleazy way this car dealer practices its trade. I did, after all, achieve my end goals. We had the car; she was surprised." But Richards found himself haunted by the discrimination and fearing that the "corporate policy" would harm other disabled people coming after him. "I couldn't shake the emotions of how much pain and grief the whole experience had on me. I talked with peers and lawyers, and finally decided that I had to act. . . . So, I filed a formal complaint" with the Department of Justice and the California Department of Employment and Fair Housing. Eventually the complaint was settled amicably and out of court, with the dealership agreeing to have their employees go through an ADA training session; the corporate policy altered; and a small financial remedy applied.[25]

The complexities of going litigious are illustrated by Sara Lane, a post-polio newspaper reporter who uses a wheelchair and who worked at various papers before the ADA. She had many of her access needs met by simple politeness and the care of her employers. But the ADA's passage changed the playing field so that now, she did not have to depend on the kindness of strangers. At the *Midwest Tribune*, where she ended up, it took four years to get the newspaper to give her an accessible bathroom on the floor where she worked. She found the process "degrading beyond belief. It was infuriating." "Someone actually said to me [after the ADA was passed], 'We treated you terribly. And we'll now try to make up and try to do something.' Yeah, it really took that law to get them to realize it."[26]

But even under those promising conditions, someone like Lane is reluctant to use the ADA directly. She wants more-flexible hours and the ability to work at home but feels safer working with the union than with ADA lawyers. "I think that [the union] is less threatening to them [the publisher]. As much as [the publisher] respects me and does for me what he says he can, you have to play the game; you have to be careful. And there is a point in my career when I don't want my disability to be out there that much. You know, so going by the guild it's the more proper way to do it."

It is not just a question of guts to make the ADA work; it's also a question of strategy. How do you want to be perceived by your employer and colleagues? "You are perceived as a whiner," Lane said. "And you are perceived as someone [who makes employers think], oh well, we didn't realize you'd be so much trouble when we hired you."

And she's not just concerned about herself: "You're always thinking what if someone [who is disabled] comes after me. You don't want to spoil it for them. . . . The next generation of disabled employees are going to be screwed because they [the publisher] didn't like you."

When you listen to these stories, you realize that a written law is like a sheet of music. Both are written by someone who had an idea how things are supposed to sound or be. But each player, each orchestra, each person has to bring those signs on the page into reality. With the ADA, people like Bobby Silverstein, Chai Feldblum, and John Wodatch wrote the words; politicians argued about the phrasing and content; and judges added their parsing and timing. But each day, a person has to wake up, go to work, apply for a job, go to a store, try to get services, find housing, take the bus or train. And each of these people has to think, "How am I going to interpret the words on the page of the law? What will it mean for me to take this passage and play it in a way that works for me?" A law sits above us all like a Platonic concept, but each person actualizes it by doing what the law says or by protesting when someone doesn't do what the law says. So like a symphony, the law only exists when someone translates the signs on the page into living reality.

A bill that highlights and defines rights does not necessarily change other factors in society. Cultural and social attitudes toward disability are not automatically affected by a law. Just as racism, sexism, and homophobia continue long after the laws and legal decisions that gave rights to those various identity groups, the ADA doesn't automatically change attitudes toward people with disabilities. Ableism, the equivalent to those other discriminatory *isms*, continues to hold sway even twenty-five years after the passage of the ADA. Ableism operates not only in the eye of the discriminator but also in the eyes of the person discriminated against.

Feelings of shame, inferiority, and unworthiness can often result from living in an ableist world. For that reason, people with disabilities might not want to call attention to themselves by bringing complaints. Further, discrimination operates on levels that can't be touched by a law. One of the most powerful forms of discrimination is relational. People with disabilities are often not seen as worthy partners for dating, sex, and marriage. The way the media portrays people with disabilities can aid or hinder the acceptability of a person with a disability as someone a "normal" person would choose as a partner or a friend.

I often ask my nondisabled students if they are ableist. The answer, of course, is a resounding no! But when I ask them how many of them have dated people with disabilities, the response is usually that almost none of them have. When I point out that this is because they are actively, although perhaps unconsciously, practicing and enforcing ableism, they seem guiltily aware of that truth. Discrimination is not something that unkind people do; it's something that is carried out by good people under the influence of much bigger social and cultural norms. Choosing a partner brings into play the values of a society, and many of us are quite sensitive to violating those values.

On July 26, 2015, the ADA will have been a law for a quarter of a century. On the morning of that day, many people will get up and do things they would not have been able to do in 1990. Carol will wake up and, with the help of a personal assistant, will bathe, dress, and get into her power wheelchair. She'll leave her ramped house, get into her hand-controlled car, and head off to her job as a computer programmer in downtown Chicago. Fred will have some coffee and look at ASL vlogs (video blogs) on his computer. He has to give a lecture at a local community center, where his signed talk will be voiced for the hearing audience by a team of ASL interpreters. Sharon will be staying home with her two young boys. She'll use a screen reader to voice the morning paper. As a telecommuter, she will also print out braille texts of an article she's writing for a new journal. Jonah will be talking on the phone via a relay service with a business connection in California. His hard-to-understand speech will be made easily understood as he types his responses into his computer and his message is relayed via an operator. Sarah has a busy day. She's meeting up with some friends to go to the movies, do some clothes shopping, and eat out in a restaurant—using leg braces and crutches to get around, she'll be taking the bus and the subway. Later she's going to her local Y to take a class in movement conducted in the pool. Sam is going for his job interview at a local bank. As someone with depression and anxiety, he expects he'll have as much a chance of landing the job as anyone else. And he knows he has the ADA behind him. In fact, all of these people do. It's a long way from the time when my parents were essentially alone in the world. Their disability was, in effect, their own problem. Nothing out there in the world gave them faith that if they complained, they would be heard. No wind at their back, no stick, no carrot. With the ADA, for people with disabilities the ordinary now has become possible.

The ADA may not be perfect. It may not have solved all problems. But it is powerful support of people and a clarion call for justice and fairness. We are so much better off that the ADA is there than if it were not. And for that, we have to thank the dedication of a small band of outsiders, a small band of insiders, and activists everywhere for creating, what is after all, a most enabling act.

ACKNOWLEDGMENTS

JOANNA GREEN, my editor at Beacon, provided the best of editorial help and direction. I also thank her for buying me lunch at the MLA and suggesting I write this book. My agent, Anne Edelstein, provided skills and advice that I sorely lacked. My research assistant, Alex Luft, was amazingly helpful. Also, special thanks go to the Kessler Foundation for generously providing support to fund the research and development of this book.

CAST OF CHARACTERS

INSIDERS: STAFF, LOBBYISTS, AIDES

- Janine Bertram, activist and wife of Evan Kemp
- Mary Lou Breslin, Disability Rights Education and Defense Fund (DREDF)
- Bob Burgdorf, lawyer for the National Council on Disability
- David Capozzi, disability lobbyist for transportation
- Tim Cook, Michael Dukakis's disability advisor
- Justin Dart, cochair of the National Council on Disability
- Yoshiko Dart, activist and wife of Justin Dart
- Mark Disler, legal aide to Sen. Orrin Hatch
- Rochelle Donat, senior aide to Rep. Tony Coelho
- Chai Feldblum, lawyer for the American Civil Liberties Union; currently professor of law at Georgetown University and commissioner of the Equal Employment Opportunity Commission (EEOC)
- Lex Frieden, director of the National Council on Disability
- Bob Funk, DREDF
- Marilyn Golden, DREDF
- Michael Iskowitz, aide to Sen. Ted Kennedy on HIV/AIDS issues
- Randel "Randy" Johnson, lawyer for the US House of Representatives; currently at the US Chamber of Commerce
- Evan Kemp, director of the Disability Rights Center; commissioner of EEOC
- Arlene Mayerson, lawyer for DREDF
- Pat Morrissey, aide to Rep. Steve Bartlett
- Ralph Neas, director of the Leadership Conference for Civil Rights
- Carolyn Osolinik, aide to Sen. Ted Kennedy
- Liz Savage, activist and organizer of lobbying efforts
- Melissa Shulman, aide to Sen. Steny Hoyer

- Bobby Silverstein, aide to Sen. Tom Harkin; wrote the first draft version of the Kennedy-Harkin Americans with Disabilities Act (ADA)
- Karen Peltz Strauss, lawyer for Deaf issues
- Nancy Taylor, health expert for Sen. Orrin Hatch
- James Weisman, lawyer for Eastern Paralyzed Veterans of America; worked on the transportation side of the ADA
- Mo West, aide to Sen. Bob Dole
- Patrisha Wright, DREDF

POLITICIANS

- Rep. Steve Bartlett (R-Texas), Republican point person on the ADA
- Rep. Jack Brooks (D-Texas), chair of the House Judiciary Committee
- Rep. Tony Coelho (D-California), majority whip and early sponsor of the ADA
- Rep. William Dannemeyer (R-California), member of the Energy and Commerce Committee; member of the Judiciary Committee
- Rep. John Dingell (D-Michigan), chair of the House Energy and Commerce Committee
- Sen. Bob Dole (R-Kansas), sponsor of the ADA
- Sen. David Durenberger (R-Minnesota), sponsor of the ADA
- Rep. Newt Gingrich (R-Georgia), minority whip
- Sen. Tom Harkin (D-Iowa), sponsor of the ADA
- Sen. Orrin Hatch (R-Utah), sponsor of the ADA
- Sen. Jesse Helms (R-North Carolina), opponent of the ADA
- Sen. Ted Kennedy (D-Massachusetts), strong supporter of the ADA
- Rep. Buz Luken (R-Ohio), chair of the Subcommittee on Transportation of the Energy and Commerce Committee
- Rep. Bob Michel (R-Illinois), minority leader
- Rep. Norm Mineta (D-California), chair of the Subcommittee on Surface Transportation of the House Committee on Transportation and Public Works
- Rep. Major Owens (D-New York), chair of the House Committee on Education and Labor

- Rep. James Sensenbrenner (R-Wisconsin), member of the House Judiciary Committee
- Rep. Bud Shuster (R-Pennsylvania), member of the Subcommittee on Surface Transportation of the House Committee on Transportation and Public Works

ACTIVISTS

- Wade Blank, leader of Americans Disabled for Accessible Public Transport (ADAPT)
- Marca Bristo, president of the National Council on Independent Living
- Curt Decker, National Disability Rights Network
- Fred Fay, cofounder of the Boston Center for Independent Living; cofounder and president of the American Coalition of Citizens with Disabilities
- Eunice Fiorito, director of the New York City Mayor's Office for the Handicapped; cofounder and president of the American Coalition of Citizens with Disabilities
- Judy Heumann, leader of Disabled in Action; deputy director of the Center for Independent Living, Berkeley, California; cofounder of the World Institute on Disability
- Bob Kafka, ADAPT leader
- Mary Johnson, editor of *The Disability Rag*
- Cynthia Jones, editor of *Mainstream* magazine
- Paul Marchand, director of Arc; head of the Disability Coordinating Committee
- Ed Roberts, cofounder of the Center for Independent Living, Berkeley

WHITE HOUSE

- David Bates, secretary of the Office of Cabinet Affairs
- William Bennett, "drug czar"
- President George H. W. Bush
- Dick Darman, director of the Office of Management and Budget
- C. Boyden Gray, White House counsel
- Janet Hale, Dick Darman's assistant
- Daniel Heimbach, associate director for Domestic Policy

- Hans Kuttner, associate director of Health and Social Services Policy
- Lee Liberman, associate White House counsel
- Grace Mastalli, deputy assistant attorney general, Justice Department
- Marianne McGettigan, associate director of Legal Policy
- Roger B. Porter, director of the Office of Economic and Domestic Policy
- William L. Roper, director of the Office of Policy Development
- Sam Skinner, secretary of transportation
- David Sloan, special assistant for Legislative Affairs (Senate)
- John Sununu, chief of staff
- Dick Thornburgh, attorney general
- John Wodatch, Civil Rights Division, Justice Department
- Ken Yale, executive secretary of the Domestic Policy Council

BIBLIOGRAPHICAL NOTE

IN WRITING THIS BOOK, I have tried to present as much as I could a true, historical record. For this reason, I haven't let my own political viewpoint dominate the results, as much as that is possible. I also haven't whitewashed what perhaps has been overlooked in the past. Obviously, the truth is a slippery creature, and I've done my best to double-check informants' claims and to rely on contemporary accounts in print as much as possible. Where informants disagree, I point that out. I interviewed over fifty people who were on the scene, and behind the scenes, in the legislative process, and I interviewed some of these people several times. Additionally, I interviewed activists and lobbyists. While some people have amazing memories, others have more-creative memories, and some people's memories are vague or even absent. Where possible, I've quoted people directly; some interviewees have asked to be off the record or otherwise anonymous, and I have honored those requests. Chai Feldblum, Bobby Silverstein, and Hans Kuttner provided me with diaries and calendar entries. Ralph Neas was incredibly helpful in so many ways. My biggest regret is not having been able to interview those no longer with us: Teddy Kennedy was a personality who everyone acknowledges was larger than life and whose influence on the legislative process was enormous. Justin Dart would have been fascinating to talk with. Not being able to interview Evan Kemp, who died in 1997, is also a big regret of mine. Major Owens died during the writing of this book and after I'd made initial contact with him.

I have tried to embody a combination of journalist, historian, and storyteller. I am trained only as the latter, although being a professor of literature and disability, my expertise bleeds a bit into the former two. In talking about and analyzing the law, I clearly am no lawyer. Elizabeth Emens, professor of law at Columbia University, graciously vetted portions of the manuscript at the eleventh hour, but I am sure there will be areas in which my insight may be wanting. All mistakes are mine alone. In addition, I could add politician, legislator, political scientist, and lobbyist to the list of things I am not. So, as Plato said, perhaps writers should be yanked out of the republic because they write about things they do not know. In writing this book, my learning curve has been immense, but I know there will be errors that others will pick up, and for these errors, I apologize in advance.

Anyone writing about the ADA must acknowledge several sources that are iconic and justifiably so. Jonathan Young's *Equality of Opportunity: The Making of the Americans with Disabilities Act* is the account that almost everyone I interviewed referred me to. This painstaking work of journalism and scholarship should remain the gold standard for historical accounts of the ADA, despite its never having been commercially published. Joseph Shapiro's *No Pity: People with Disabilities Forging a New Civil Rights Movement* is by far the best journalistic account of the disability movement that includes a section on the ADA. In addition, Fred Pelka did an amazing job of gathering first-person accounts by the major players in his book *What We Have Done: An Oral History of the Disability Rights Movement*. I have relied heavily on both books, as my endnotes will show. Ruth Colker's *The Disability Pendulum: The First Decade of the Americans with Disabilities Act* has a couple of valuable chapters on the ADA. Other works that I have relied on include Doris Zames Fleischer and Frieda Zames's *The Disability Rights Movement: From Charity to Confrontation*, Ruth O'Brien's *Crippled Justice: The History of Modern Disability Policy in the Workplace*, and Kim E. Nielsen's *A Disability History of the United States*. The disability oral history archives at the Bancroft Library at the University of California, Berkeley, were also tremendously useful.

For reasons of efficiency, I've chosen not to add an endnote to any speech or testimony that is available through the *Congressional Record*. In terms of other citations, wherever I have not included an endnote, the quotations should be regarded as drawing from the hours of interviews I conducted on my own. Most of the following

interviews were by telephone, except where otherwise indicated. The
interviews generally lasted one hour.

Steve Bartlett: March 29 and August 5, 2013
Janine Bertram: July 16, 2013
Mary Lou Breslin: April 14, 2014
President George H. W. Bush: May 23, 2013 (written answers)
David Capozzi: July 10, 2014
James Chapman: October 21, 2013
Tony Coelho: April 24 and May 1, 2013
Yoshiko Dart: September 14, 2013
Curt Decker: July 9, 2014
Sen. Bob Dole: February 7, 2013 (in person)
Sen. David Durenberger: June 18, 2013
Chai Feldblum: February 7, 2013 (in person); December 2,
    2013; October 27 and 31, 2014
William Fisher: August 13, 2013
Lex Frieden: July 30 and 31, 2013; August 4, 2013; May 20,
    2014
Bob Funk: July 18, 2013
Marilyn Golden: August 13, 2013
Tammy Gravenhorst (Berberi): August 22, 2014
C. Boyden Gray: June 18, 2013
Sen. Tom Harkin: April 25, 2013 (in person)
Sen. Orrin Hatch: October 28, 2014 (written answers); Octo-
    ber 30, 2014
Rep. Steny Hoyer: July 10, 2013
Michael Iskowitz: December 16, 2013
Mark Johnson: June 21, 2013; October 24, 2014
Mary Johnson: November 1, 2013
Randel "Randy" Johnson: February 7, 2013 (in person)
Bob Kafka: September 17, 2013
Hans Kuttner: June 18, 2013
John Lancaster: August 30, 2013
Paul Marchand: August 26, 2013
Grace Mastalli: July 17, 2013; September 14 and 17, 2013; and
    by e-mail

Arlene Mayerson: August 14, 2013
Marianne McGettigan: August 30, 2013
Pat Morrissey: August 1, 2013
Katy Neas: August 30, 2013
Ralph Neas: September 16 and October 3, 2013; July 15, 2014
Carolyn Osolinik: August 8, 2013
Roger Porter: August 15, 2013
William Roper: July 10, 2013
Bobby Silverstein: August 5 and 12, 2014
Samuel Skinner: July 19, 2013
Nancy Taylor: August 1, 2013
Ginny Thornburgh: July 22, 2013
Dick Thornburgh: June 18, 2013
Lisa Walker: August 21 and September 7, 2014
James Weisman: July 14, 2014
Jane West: July 25, 2014
Mo West: July 15, 2014
John Wodatch: June 20, 2013; November 4, 2014
Pat Wright: June 19 and November 11, 2013
Ken Yale: July 17, 2013

NOTES

AUTHOR'S NOTE

1. In this book, I'll be using the by-now standard distinction between *Deaf* and *deaf*. The former describes a person who is socially and culturally deaf—who uses sign language and is part of the Deaf community. I'll be using the lowercased *deaf* simply to describe an impairment of hearing or a person who happens to have lost hearing but otherwise has no connection with Deaf culture.

2. "Disability Stats and Facts," *Disability Funders Network*, accessed June 17, 2014, www.disabilityfunders.org.

3. Robert Mauro, "Disability Statistics," *Cornucopia of Disability Information*, accessed October 6, 2014, http://codi.tamucc.edu.

PROLOGUE: JULY 28, 1989

1. Fred Pelka, *What We Have Done: An Oral History of the Disability Rights Movement* (Amherst: University of Massachusetts Press, 2012), 537.

2. I've assembled the incident as told to me by many of the participants and from Edward M. Kennedy, *True Compass: A Memoir* (New York: Twelve, 2009). Obviously, each person will have his or her specific recollections.

3. Church of Jesus Christ of Latter-Day Saints, "First Presidency Statement on Disabilities," *Church News*, April 29, 1989, 7, www.lds.org/topics/disability /basics/first-presidency-statement?lang=eng.

CHAPTER 1: FORTY-FOUR WORDS THAT CHANGED HISTORY

1. *Legislative History of Public Law 101-336: The Americans with Disabilities Act*, in three volumes, prepared for the Committee on Education and Labor, US House of Representatives, 101st Congress, second session, 1325 (Washington, DC: House Committee on Education and Labor, December 1990), http://babel.hathitrust.org.

2. George Will, "The Inclusion of the Handicapped," *Nashua (NH) Telegraph*, June 24, 1983, http://news.google.com/newspapers?nid=2209 &dat=19830624&id=64lKAAAAIBAJ&sjid=EJQMAAAAIBAJ&pg =5357,5589666.

3. *Congressional Record*, January 20, 1972, 525.

4. Richard Scotch, *From Good Will to Civil Rights: Transforming Federal Disability Policy* (Philadelphia: Temple University Press, 2009), gives the best and most detailed account of the regulation-writing process.

5. Jack Anderson and Les Whitten, "Handicapped Plan 10-City Sit-In," *Washington Post*, March 26, 1977.

6. Ibid.

7. Brian T. McMahon and Linda Shaw, *Enabling Lives: Biographies of Six Prominent Americans with Disabilities* (Boca Raton, FL: CRC Press, 2000), 116.

8. Martin Luther King Jr., "The Hammer of Civil Rights," *Nation*, March 9, 1964, www.thenation.com/article/157742/hammer-civil-rights.

CHAPTER 2: DC OUTSIDERS TURN WASHINGTON INSIDERS

1. Fred Pelka, *What We Have Done: An Oral History of the Disability Rights Movement* (Amherst: University of Massachusetts Press, 2012), 415.

2. "Polio Strikes Negroes 1st in Louisiana," *Washington Post*, August 21, 1951.

3. "The Press: Pearson v. McCarthy," *Time*, March 12, 1951.

4. Jon Weiner, "The End of the Jerry Lewis Telethon: It's About Time," *Nation* (blog), September 2, 2011, www.thenation.com/blog/163119/end-jerry -lewis-telethon-its-about-time.

5. Mary Thornton, "Reagan, Aide Differ on Hiring Policy," *Washington Post*, December 18, 1981.

6. Pelka, *What We Have Done*, 449.

7. Ronald Reagan, "White House Report on the Program for Economic Recovery," American Presidency Project, accessed April 24, 2014, www .presidency.ucsb.edu.

8. Pelka, *What We Have Done*, 504.

9. Arlene B. Mayerson, Disability Rights and Independent Living Movement Oral History Project (Berkeley: University of California, 2012), http:// digitalassets.lib.berkeley.edu.

10. Cited in Jonathan M. Young, *Equality of Opportunity: The Making of the Americans with Disabilities Act* (Washington, DC: National Council on Disability, 1997), 26.

11. Ibid., 27.

12. Ralph Neas, interview, and "Professional Life Vocation and Commitment," in *Work and Faith in Society: Catholic Perspectives* (South Bend, IN: Bishops' Committee on the Laity, 1983), 17–18.

CHAPTER 3: THE TEXAS CONNECTION

1. Brian T. McMahon and Linda Shaw, *Enabling Lives: Biographies of Six Prominent Americans with Disabilities* (Boca Raton, FL: CRC Press, 2000), 66.

2. Ibid., 67.

3. Ibid., 70.
4. Ibid., 74.
5. Ibid., 76.
6. "Justin Dart Remembered," *Ability*, accessed May 30, 2014, www .abilitymagazine.com.
7. At this time, there were a number of disability groups with unusual and provocative names like SO FED UP (Students Organization for Every Disability United) and WARPATH (World Association to Remove Prejudice Against the Handicapped).
8. Hunt Hamill, letter to the editor, *Life*, May 27, 1970, 20A, wrote, "How many Kent State tragedies do the liberals in our magnificent free press need to awaken them to the fact that with freedom must inevitably go responsibility?"
9. Fred Pelka, *What We Have Done: An Oral History of the Disability Rights Movement* (Amherst: University of Massachusetts Press, 2012), 423.

CHAPTER 4: LET RIGHT BE DONE
1. Lloyd v. Illinois Regional Transportation Authority, United States District Court, N. D. Illinois, E. D., September 30, 1982.
2. Robert A. Katzmann, *Institutional Disability: The Saga of Transportation Policy for the Disabled* (Washington, DC: Brookings Institution, 1986), 176.
3. Mary Johnson and Barrett Shaw, *To Ride the Public's Buses: The Fight That Built a Movement* (Louisville, KY: Avocado Press, 2001), 9.
4. The opinion of Judge Mannsmann was reported in Doris Zames Fleischer and Frieda Zames, *The Disability Rights Movement: From Charity to Confrontation* (Philadelphia: Temple University Press, 2011), 67.
5. It was second only to Hillsdale College, which also pursued a similar strategy to that of Grove City by refusing all federal funds to avoid having to comply with government regulations and laws. "Top 10 Most Politically Conservative Colleges," *Princeton Review*, December 1, 2012, www .huffingtonpost.com/2012/10/01/the-most-conservative-col_n_1930291 .html.
6. Martin Morse Wooster, "Too Good to Be True," *Wall Street Journal*, April 1, 2005, www.wsj.com/articles/SB111232604205595288.
7. Katzmann, *Institutional Disability*, 48.
8. Mart L. LaVor, "Commentary: Section 504; Past, Present, and Future," *Archives of Physical Medicine and Rehabilitation* 61 (June 1980): 283.
9. Fred Pelka, *The ABC-CLIO Companion to the Disability Rights Movement* (Santa Barbara, CA: ABC-CLIO, 1997), 67.
10. Arlene B. Mayerson, Disability Rights and Independent Living Movement Oral History Project (Berkeley: University of California, 2012), http:// digitalassets.lib.berkeley.edu.
11. Ibid.

12. Ibid., 105.
13. Ibid., 106.
14. Ibid.

CHAPTER 5: BANGING THE DRUM LOUDLY

1. Fred Pelka, *What We Have Done: An Oral History of the Disability Rights Movement* (Amherst: University of Massachusetts Press, 2012), 435.
2. Ibid., 430.
3. Jonathan M. Young, *Equality of Opportunity: The Making of the Americans with Disabilities Act* (Washington, DC: National Council on Disability, 1997), 46.
4. Pelka, *What We Have Done*, 431.
5. Ibid., 432–33.
6. Last part of the quote from ibid., 426.
7. Ibid., 432.
8. Ibid., 436.
9. Ibid., 434.
10. Ibid.; interview with Frieden.

CHAPTER 6: FLAT EARTH, DEAF WORLD

1. Richard Scotch, *From Good Will to Civil Rights: Transforming Federal Disability Policy* (Philadelphia: Temple University Press, 1984) (and Kindle edition, loc. 1635, 1642).
2. Ruth Colker, *The Disability Pendulum: The First Decade of the Americans with Disabilities Act* (New York: New York University Press, 2005), loc. 614 (Kindle edition).
3. Fred Pelka, *What We Have Done: An Oral History of the Disability Rights Movement* (Amherst: University of Massachusetts Press, 2012), 450–51.
4. Obviously, any relationship has two sides. Wright has been, according to Feldblum, very secretive about the relationship, so we are only able to get one side's point of view.
5. Doris Zames Fleischer and Frieda Zames, *The Disability Rights Movement: From Charity to Confrontation* (Philadelphia: Temple University Press, 2011), 90.
6. Arlene B. Mayerson, Disability Rights and Independent Living Movement Oral History Project (Berkeley: University of California, 2012), 12, http://digitalassets.lib.berkeley.edu.
7. Pelka, *What We Have Done*, 427.
8. Ibid., 465–66.
9. Cynthia Jones, in Pelka, *What We Have Done*, 485; and Cynthia Jones, interview with Mary Lou Breslin, March 14, 1999, Oral History, Disability Rights and Independent Living Movement Archives, Bancroft Library, University of California, Berkeley, http://tinyurl.com/poyernk.

10. Pelka, *What We Have Done*, 453.

11. Ibid., 454.

12. "In Their Own Words," Deaf President Now, Gallaudet University, accessed July 12, 2014, www.gallaudet.edu/dpn_home/profiles_and_viewpoints/in _their_own_words.html.

13. Jonathan M. Young, *Equality of Opportunity: The Making of the Americans with Disabilities Act* (Washington, DC: National Council on Disability, 1997), 58.

14. *Congressional Record*, September 27, 1988, 36.

15. Young, *Equality of Opportunity*, 58.

16. Doris Zames Fleischer and Frieda Zames, *The Disability Rights Movement: From Charity to Confrontation* (Philadelphia: Temple University Press, 2011), 90.

17. "Americans with Disabilities Act," *Presidential Timeline*, accessed July 14, 2014, http://presidentialtimeline.org.

18. Andrew Rosenthal, "Dukakis Releases Medical Details to Stop Rumors on Mental Health," *New York Times*, August 4, 1988, www.nytimes.com /1988/08/04/us/dukakis-releases-medical-details-to-stop-rumors-on-mental -health.html.

19. 134 *Congressional Record* (1988) at 21425, cited in Colker, *The Disability Pendulum*, loc. 737 of 5218 (Kindle edition).

20. Young, *Equality of Opportunity*, 69.

21. Pelka, *What We Have Done*, 485.

22. George Bush, "The Second Bush–Dukakis Presidential Debate," October 13, 1988, transcript, Commission on Presidential Debates, www.debates.org /index.php?page=october-13-1988-debate-transcript.

23. Young, *Equality of Opportunity*, 68.

24. Joseph Shapiro, *No Pity: People with Disabilities Forging a New Civil Rights Movement* (New York: Crown, 1993), 125.

25. George H. W. Bush, written responses to my written questions, May 23, 2013.

CHAPTER 7: A NEW BAND OF REFORMERS

1. Jonathan M. Young, *Equality of Opportunity: The Making of the Americans with Disabilities Act* (Washington, DC: National Council on Disability, 1997), 67.

2. This, of course, excludes the incredibly unproductive 112th Congress. Josh Tauberer, "Kill Bill: How Many Bills Are There? How Many Are Enacted?," *Govtrack* (blog), August 4, 2011, www.govtrack.us/blog/2011 /08/04/kill-bill-how-many-bills-are-there-how-many-are-enacted/.

3. Liz Savage, Disability Rights and Independent Living Movement Oral History Project (Berkeley: University of California, 2012), http://digitalassets .lib.berkeley.edu.

4. Arlene B. Mayerson, Disability Rights and Independent Living Movement Oral History Project (Berkeley: University of California, 2012).

5. Fred Pelka, *What We Have Done: An Oral History of the Disability Rights Movement* (Amherst: University of Massachusetts Press, 2012), 467.

6. Ibid., 495–97.

CHAPTER 8: A NEW DAY, A NEW ADA

1. Although Silverstein was working for Tom Harkin, and although others worked on this draft of the bill, I will be referring to this draft as "Silverstein's" for convenience.

2. Center for Media and Democracy, "C. Boyden Gray," *Sourcewatch*, last modified April 9, 2013, outlined the many hats that Gray wore: "In a lengthy profile of Gray in 1997, the *New Republic* magazine wrote 'So many different money trails lead to, by and through Gray it is bewildering.' There is Gray the lobbyist, Gray the lawyer, Gray the former White House Counsel, Gray the chairman of Citizens for a Sound Economy (CSE), Gray the head of the Alliance for Reasonable Regulation, Gray the co-chair of the Air Quality Standards Coalition, Gray the board member of Federalist Society for Law and Public Policy Studies, Gray the major *soft money* contributor to the Republican Party, Gray the friend of judges and justices (many of whom owe their jobs to him), to name but a few."

3. Charles Kolb, *White House Daze: The Unmaking of Domestic Policy in the Bush Years* (New York: Free Press, 1994), xvi.

4. Ibid., xvii.

5. Ibid., 63.

6. Karen Hosler, "Bad Cop Sununu Haunted by Reputation as Bully," *Baltimore Sun*, June 27, 1991, http://articles.baltimoresun.com/1991-06-27/news/1991178046_1_sununu-new-hampshire-jolly-elf.

7. Ibid.

CHAPTER 9: WHITE HOUSE BATTLES SENATE

1. Neal Devins, "Reagan Redux, Civil Rights Under Bush," *Notre Dame Law Review* 68 (1993): 955–57.

2. Ruth Marcus, "What Does Bush Really Believe? Civil Rights Record Illustrates Shifts," *Washington Post*, August 18, 1992.

3. Ibid.

4. Ibid.

5. Jonathan M. Young, *Equality of Opportunity: The Making of the Americans with Disabilities Act* (Washington, DC: National Council on Disability, 1997), 92–93.

6. US National Archives and Records Administration, "The Americans with Disabilities Act, 1964–1990," *Presidential Timeline*, accessed August 7, 2014, www.presidentialtimeline.org/#/exhibit/41/06.

7. Ibid.

8. Fred Pelka, *What We Have Done: An Oral History of the Disability Rights Movement* (Amherst: University of Massachusetts Press, 2012), 468.

9. Thornburgh, via his wife Ginny, says that he "has no recollection of any such problem with the White House relative to his testimony." Ginny Thornburgh, e-mail to the author, August 12, 2014.

10. Pelka, *What We Have Done*, 509.

11. Kathleen Teltsch, "As the Labor Pool Dwindles, Doors Open for the Disabled," *New York Times*, June 22, 1989, www.nytimes.com/1989/06/22 /us/as-the-labor-pool-dwindles-doors-open-for-the-disabled.html.

CHAPTER 10: SECRET MEETINGS AND BAGEL BREAKFASTS

1. Fred Pelka, *What We Have Done: An Oral History of the Disability Rights Movement* (Amherst: University of Massachusetts Press, 2012), 497.

2. Ted Kennedy to John Sununu, March 30, 1990, *Presidential Timeline* (US National Archives and Records Administration), www.presidentialtimeline .org/#/exhibit/41/06.

3. All quotes from the Kemp memo are from author's interview with Bobby Silverstein and from US National Archives and Records Administration, "The Americans with Disabilities Act, 1964–1990," *Presidential Timeline*, accessed August 7, 2014, www.presidentialtimeline.org/#/exhibit/41/06.

4. Jonathan M. Young, *Equality of Opportunity: The Making of the Americans with Disabilities Act* (Washington, DC: National Council on Disability, 1997), 96.

5. Charles Kolb, *White House Daze: The Unmaking of Domestic Policy in the Bush Years* (New York: Free Press, 1994), xvii.

6. Ibid., xvi.

7. Paul Blustein, "Congress Puzzles over the 'New' Dick Darman: Budget Chief's Softer Style May Be Part of Plan to Cut Deficit," *Los Angeles Times*, July 5, 1989, http://articles.latimes.com/1989-07-05/business/fi-3209_1 _dick-darman.

8. Maureen Dowd, "'Three Stooges' Flop on the Hill," *New York Times*, October 6, 1990, http://alb.merlinone.net.

9. John Podhoretz, *Hell of a Ride: Backstage at the White House Follies, 1989–1993* (New York: Simon and Schuster, 1993), 57.

10. US National Archives and Records Administration, "The Americans with Disabilities Act, 1964–1990."

11. Paula Yost, "Accord Set on Disabled-Worker Bill: White House, Senators Endorse Anti-Discrimination Legislation," *Washington Post*, August 3, 1989.

CHAPTER 11: "THIS MEANS WAR!"

1. US National Archives and Records Administration, "The Americans with Disabilities Act, 1964–1990," *Presidential Timeline*, accessed August 7, 2014, www.presidentialtimeline.org/#/exhibit/41/06.

2. Susan F. Rasky, "Bill Barring Bias Against Disabled Holds Wide Impact," *New York Times*, August 14, 1989, www.nytimes.com/1989/08/14/us/bill -barring-bias-against-disabled-holds-wide-impact.html.

3. Susan F. Rasky, "How the Disabled Sold Congress on a New Bill of Rights," *New York Times*, September 17, 1989, www.nytimes.com/1989/09 /17/weekinreview/the-nation-how-the-disabled-sold-congress-on-a-new-bill -of-rights.html.

4. Fred Pelka, *What We Have Done: An Oral History of the Disability Rights Movement* (Amherst: University of Massachusetts Press, 2012), 475.

5. "Blank Check for the Disabled," *New York Times*, September 6, 1989.

6. Pelka, *What We Have Done*, 485.

7. Ruth Colker, *The Disability Pendulum: The First Decade of the Americans with Disabilities Act* (New York: New York University Press, 2005) (Kindle edition).

CHAPTER 12: BUILDING THE ACCESSIBLE RAMP TO THE HOUSE OF REPRESENTATIVES

1. Fred Pelka, *What We Have Done: An Oral History of the Disability Rights Movement* (Amherst: University of Massachusetts Press, 2012), 502.

2. National Disability Rights Network, *All Aboard (Except People with Disabilities): Amtrak's 23 Years of ADA Compliance Failure* (Washington, DC: National Disability Rights Network, October 2013), http://dadsupport .ndrn.org/pub/NDRN_Amtrak_Report.pdf.

CHAPTER 13: THE CAPITOL CRAWL

1. Joseph Shapiro, *No Pity: People with Disabilities Forging a New Civil Rights Movement* (New York: Crown, 1993), 131.

2. Michael Winter, "I Was There . . . Michael Winter, Washington DC, 1990," *ADAPT History Project*, accessed October 13, 2014, www.adapt.org /freeourpeople/adapt25/narratives/15adapt.htm.

3. Jennifer Keelan, "Climbing the Capitol Steps for ADA," YouTube video, 4:25, posted July 21, 2010, http://www.youtube.com.

4. While our attention is fixed on the ADA, the committee at that session was marking up not just that bill but also H.R. 3386, Safe Transportation of Food Act (101st Congress [1989–1990], http://thomas.loc.gov/cgi-bin /query/z?c101:H.R.+3386:); H.R. 4167, to provide for a short-term extension of the strategic petroleum reserve (101st Congress [1989–1990], http:// thomas.loc.gov/cgi-bin/query/z?c101:H.R.+4167:); H.R. 3656, Coordinated Clearance and Settlement Act of 1989 (101st Congress [1989–1990], http:// thomas.loc.gov/cgi-bin/query/z?c101:H.R.+3656:); H.R. 3657, Securities Markets Stabilization Act of 1989 (101st Congress [1989–1990], http:// thomas.loc.gov/cgi-bin/query/z?c101:H.R.+3657:); H.R. 3155, Fish and Fish Products Safety Act of 1989 (101st Congress [1989–1990], http://

thomas.loc.gov/cgi-bin/query/z?c101:H.R.+3155:); H.R. 3520, Hazardous
Materials Transportation Act Uniform Safety Amendments of 1989 (101st
Congress [1989–1990], http://thomas.loc.gov/cgi-bin/query/z?c101:H.R.
+3520:); H.R. 1457, Waste Reduction Act (101st Congress [1989–1990],
http://thomas.loc.gov/cgi-bin/query/z?c101:H.R.+1457:); H.R. 2921,
Telephone Advertising Regulation Act (101st Congress [1989–1990], http://
thomas.loc.gov/cgi-bin/query/z?c101:H.R.+2921:); and H.R. 3030, Clean
Air Act Amendments of 1989 (101st Congress [1989–1990], http://thomas
.loc.gov/cgi-bin/query/z?c101:H.R.+3030:).

5. Steven A. Holmes, "Disabled Protest and Are Arrested," *New York Times*,
    March 14, 1990, www.nytimes.com/1990/03/14/us/disabled-protest-and
    -are-arrested.html.

6. Mary Johnson, "The Crawl-In," *Disability Rag*, May–June 1990, 21.

7. William M. Welch, "Police Arrest Wheelchair-Bound Demonstrators in
    Capitol Protest," Associated Press, March 13, 1990, www.apnewsarchive
    .com/1990/Police-Arrest-Wheelchair-Bound-Demonstrators-in-Capitol
    -Protest/id-ebb69bb27bfa8d72e757887c877c15e8.

8. Shapiro, *No Pity*, 134.

9. Welch, "Police Arrest Wheelchair-Bound Demonstrators."

10. Ibid.

11. Shapiro, *No Pity*, 135.

12. Mary Johnson, "Opportunity Lost," *Disability Rag*, May–June 1990, 31.

13. Jess Zimmerman, "'Capitol Crawl': Americans with Disabilities Act of
    1990," *History by Zim*, September 9, 2013, www.historybyzim.com/?s
    =capitol+crawl.

14. Steven A. Holmes, "Measure Barring Discrimination Against Disabled
    Runs into Snag," *New York Times*, March 13, 1990, www.nytimes.com
    /1990/03/13/us/measure-barring-discrimination-against-disabled-runs-into
    -snag.html.

15. US National Archives and Records Administration, "The Americans with
    Disabilities Act, 1964–1990," *Presidential Timeline*, accessed July 14,
    2014, www.presidentialtimeline.org/#/exhibit/41/06.

16. Julie Rovner, "Bush Seeking Modifications in Disability-Rights Bill," *Con-
    gressional Quarterly Weekly Report*, March 17, 1990, 837.

17. Julie Rovner, "With Bush's Blessing, ADA Bill Sails Through Senate Panel,"
    Congressional Quarterly Weekly Report, August 5, 1989, 2044.

18. US National Archives and Records Administration, "The Americans with
    Disabilities Act, 1964–1990."

19. Julie Rovner, "Law/Judiciary: Third House Committee OKs Disability
    Rights Measure," *Congressional Quarterly Weekly Report*, April 7, 1990,
    1082.

20. US National Archives and Records Administration, "The Americans with
    Disabilities Act, 1964–1990."

21. Randy Johnson, copy of letter provided to author.

22. Chapman rebutted this statement saying that the quote was indeed published in a National Restaurant Association publication but was within an article quoting a CDC statement.

23. Julie Rovner, "House Is Nearing Passage of Disability-Rights Bill," *Congressional Quarterly Weekly Report*, May 19, 1990, 1559.

24. Julie Rovner, "Law/Judiciary: Senate Instructs Conferees on Disability-Rights Bill," *Congressional Record Weekly Report*, June 9, 1990, 1793.

25. Julie Rovner, "Law/Judiciary: Last-Minute Snag Means Delay for Disabled Rights Measure," *Congressional Record Weekly Report*, June 30, 1990, 2071.

26. Jonathan M. Young, *Equality of Opportunity: The Making of the Americans with Disabilities Act* (Washington, DC: National Council on Disability, 1997), 139.

27. Coelho disputes this story with a rather colorful objection: "Oh that's a bunch of bullshit. That's somebody embellishing. . . . Oh, that's a bullshit story."

28. Young, *Equality of Opportunity*, 154.

29. Gebe Martinez and J. Michael Kennedy, "Texas Gov. Richards to Appoint Krueger to Replace Sen. Bentsen," *Los Angeles Times*, January 5, 1993, http://articles.latimes.com/1993-01-05/news/mn-1071_1_texas-gov-richards.

CHAPTER 14: ON THE WHITE HOUSE LAWN

1. Fred Pelka, *What We Have Done: An Oral History of the Disability Rights Movement* (Amherst: University of Massachusetts Press, 2012), 546–47.

2. Mary Lou Breslin, interview with Susan O'Hara, December 11, 1997, Disability Rights and Independent Living Movement Archives, University of California, Berkeley, Bancroft Library, http://tinyurl.com/l445vbq.

3. Scott Bogren, "The ADA's 20-Year Anniversary: Commentary," Community Transportation Association, http://web1.ctaa.org/.

4. "Snubbing the ACLU," editorial, *Washington Post*, July 29, 1990.

CHAPTER 15: ENABLING THE ADA

1. Equal Employment Opportunity Commission, accessed November 14, 2014, www.eeoc.gov/eeoc/statistics/enforcement/index.cfm.

2. IHDDmedia, "Lois Curtis Art Exhibit Captioned," YouTube video, 2:15, uploaded June 21, 2012, www.youtube.com/watch?v=sKTq8Pwt7Vo.

3. "*Olmstead v. LC and EW*: Landmark Case," Atlanta Legal Aid Society, accessed November 14, 2014, www.atlantalegalaid.org/impact.htm.

4. Sarah Rosenbaum and Joel Teitelbaum, *Olmstead at Five: Assessing the Impact*, Kaiser Foundation report issued by Department of Health Policy, George Washington University Medical Center (Washington, DC: George Washington University Medical Center, June 2004), 26, http://

kaiserfamilyfoundation.files.wordpress.com/2013/01/olmstead-at-five
-assessing-the-impact.pdf.

5. Adam Cohen, "Can Disabled People Be Forced to Crawl Up the Courthouse
Steps?," *New York Times*, January 11, 2004, www.nytimes.com/2004/01/11
/opinion/11SUN3.html?gwh=5FF7A57055FB65AC41A03E80C4CBE391
&gwt=pay&assetType=opinion.

6. National Council on Disability, *Righting the ADA* (Washington, DC: National Council on Disability, 2004), 39, www.ncd.gov.

7. Ibid., 85.

8. Ibid., 107.

9. National Council on Disability, *A Promising Start: Preliminary Analysis
of Court Decisions Under the ADA Amendments Act* (Washington, DC:
National Council on Disability, July 23, 2013), www.ncd.gov.

10. Maureen Downey, "A New Focus: Disability Handicapped Take
High-Profile Path in Their Campaign for Greater Access," *Atlanta Journal
and Constitution*, May 21, 1992.

11. Peter T. Kilborn, "Major Shift Likely as Law Bans Bias Toward Disabled,"
New York Times, July 19, 1992.

12. Eric Lipton, "Disabled Winning an Uphill Battle; Slow and Steady Progress
Is Seen Five Years After Passage of Access Law," *Washington Post*, September 3, 1995.

13. Ibid.

14. Mary Johnson, "The Prime of John Hockenberry: At Last He's Mad as
Hell," *Village Voice*, August 12, 1992, reprinted in *Ragged Edge Online*,
www.raggededgemagazine.com/departments/news/000469.html.

15. Anita Manning, "Disabled Say Legislation Only a Start to Better Life,"
USA Today, July 21, 1994.

16. "20th Anniversary of Americans with Disabilities Act: July 26," US Census,
accessed November 9, 2014, www.census.gov/newsroom/releases/archives
/facts_for_features_special_editions/cb10-ff13.html; American Public
Transportation Association, *2013 Public Transportation Fact Book*, 64th
ed. (Washington, DC: American Public Transportation Association, 2013),
www.apta.com/resources/statistics/Documents/FactBook/2013-APTA-Fact
-Book.pdf.

17. "Equity in Transportation for People with Disabilities," Leadership Conference Education Fund, accessed November 9, 2014, www.civilrightsdocs
.info/pdf/transportation/final-transportation-equity-disability.pdf.

18. Bureau of Labor Statistics, US Department of Labor, "Persons with a Disability: Labor Force Characteristics—2013," press release USDL-14-1076,
June 11, 2014, www.bls.gov/news.release/pdf/disabl.pdf.

19. Matthew W. Brault, "Americans with Disabilities: 2010," US Census
Bureau, accessed November 9, 2014, www.census.gov/people/disability
/publications/sipp2010.html.

20. Bent Greve, *The Labour Market Situation of Disabled People in European Countries and Implementation of Employment Policies: A Summary of Evidence from Country Reports and Research Studies*, report for the Academic Network of European Disability Experts, University of Leeds, April 2009, http://www.disability-europe.net.

21. Andraéa LaVant, "The Americans with Disabilities Act (ADA): An 'ADA Generation' Perspective," *National Collaborative on Workforce and Disability for Youth* (blog), July 25, 2011, www.ncwd-youth.info/blog/?p=201.

22. Choose Work, "Andraéa LaVant's Story: Helping Young People with Disabilities Find Their Passion," YouTube video, 9:51, April 15, 2014, www.youtube.com/watch?v=AHqVhNGXh2U.

23. Emalie Fogg, "The Disability Rights Movement & 21 Years of the Americans with Disabilities Act," *National Collaborative on Workforce and Disability for Youth* (blog), July 27, 2011, www.ncwd-youth.info/blog/?p=208.

24. The project Fogg developed is the website *Everybody: An Artifact History of Disability in America*, http://everybody.si.edu.

25. Curtis Richards, "Navigating ADA in the Private Sector: A Driver's Lesson (Reflections on the Anniversary of ADA: Part 2)," *National Collaborative on Workforce and Disability for Youth* (blog), July 29, 2011, www.ncwd-youth.info/blog/?p=211.

26. David M. Engel and Frank W. Munger, *Rights of Inclusion: Law and Identity in the Life Stories of Americans with Disabilities* (Chicago: University of Chicago Press, 2010), 26–27.

INDEX